Assessing Vocabulary

THE CAMBRIDGE LANGUAGE ASSESSMENT SERIES

Series editors: J. Charles Alderson and Lyle F. Bachman

In this series:

Assessing Languages for Specific Purposes *by Dan Douglas*
Assessing Reading *by J. Charles Alderson*

Assessing Vocabulary

John Read

CAMBRIDGE
UNIVERSITY PRESS

PUBLISHED BY THE PRESS SYNDICATE OF THE UNIVERSITY OF CAMBRIDGE
The Pitt Building, Trumpington Street, Cambridge, United Kingdom

CAMBRIDGE UNIVERSITY PRESS
The Edinburgh Building, Cambridge CB2 2RU, UK   http://www.cup.cam.ac.uk
40 West 20th Street, New York, NY 10011–4211, USA   http://www.cup.org
10 Stamford Road, Oakleigh, Melbourne 3166, Australia
Ruiz de Alarcón 13, 28014 Madrid, Spain

First published 2000

Printed in the United Kingdom at the University Press, Cambridge

Typeface Utopia (*The Enschedé Font Foundry*) 9.5/13 pt.   *System* 3B2 [CE]

A catalogue record for this book is available from the British Library

Library of Congress Cataloguing in Publication data applied for

ISBN 0 521 62182 8 hardback
ISBN 0 521 62741 9 paperback

For my mother, Joyce Read

Contents

Series editors' preface

This book in the Cambridge Language Assessment Series is both timely and authoritative. It is timely because, after many years of neglect, the study of vocabulary in applied linguistics is now flourishing. Research on vocabulary has made a significant contribution to this development and will assume greater importance as researchers and practitioners recognise the need for a stronger theoretical foundation for their work and for more sophisticated ways of measuring vocabulary knowledge and use.

It is also authoritative because it is written by a scholar who has devoted many years to the study of vocabulary in the context of second and foreign language learning, teaching and assessment. John Read is at the forefront of recent work in the area, and in this book provides us with an in-depth consideration of how the results of empirical research and thoughtful scholarship can be applied to assessment. The book is unique in bringing together the most important empirical research in this area for reference by test developers and classroom teachers. This reflects the fact that Read is not only a researcher on vocabulary assessment but also a language teacher familiar with the challenges faced by students acquiring vocabulary in a second language as well as by their teachers in assessing what the learners have acquired.

Having established what is known about vocabulary knowledge and use, and how this might be measured, Read then deals at length with the implications for vocabulary assessment.

He presents a framework that expands the traditional concept of a vocabulary test to cover a range of procedures for assessing the vocabulary knowledge of second language learners. These procedures can be useful for addressing practical assessment needs as well as providing tools for conducting research into the lexical dimension of language.

Finally, Read looks forward, taking us beyond current research and concerns, and speculates on new directions in vocabulary assessment, in particular the contribution of computerised corpus analysis. Just as Read's research has already influenced the field of vocabulary studies, it is likely that this final chapter on future directions will itself, in the years to come, influence the work of language testers, practitioners and researchers alike.

Like other volumes in the series, it is practical in focus, addressing those issues which concern teachers, researchers and test developers. At the same time, it also takes account of what is known about relevant aspects of language, from the point of view of both language teaching, and research in language education and applied linguistics.

It skilfully incorporates practical advice to teachers and item writers, clear and constructive criticism of existing tests and words of caution to those who believe that it is a simple matter to devise tasks that require learners to 'write a sentence that shows you know the meaning of the word'. Read's book epitomises what we as series editors are trying to achieve: integrate theory and research in applied linguistics into language assessment, for the benefit of the test developer and the classroom teacher.

J. Charles Alderson
Lyle F. Bachman

Acknowledgements

I wish to acknowledge first of all the contribution of the series editors, Charles Alderson and Lyle Bachman. Charles originally asked me to write this volume at a time when I doubt that he had much reliable evidence of my capacity to deliver. I have appreciated his good-humoured encouragement along the way and done my best to ensure that his initial confidence in me was not misplaced. Lyle has been a demanding reader of my work and has spurred me on at various points to achieve more than I thought I was capable of.

It was Paul Nation who first interested me in vocabulary tests and in his gentle way acted as a mentor in the early years. Like any successful pupil I think I can teach him a thing or two about vocabulary assessment these days but I am very grateful for all the help he has generously given me up to the present time.

Paul Meara gave a much-needed sense of direction to my research on vocabulary testing in 1990 when I spent three months working with him at Birkbeck College, London. Since then he has continued to stimulate me, like so many others, with his original ideas and his deep distrust of conventional truths. He too has always been ready to provide assistance and support when I needed it.

I am particularly indebted to Carol Chapelle. We were delighted to discover our mutual interest in vocabulary testing in 1995 and she has subsequently had a great influence on my thinking about the subject. She helped me to see the connections between language testing and second language vocabulary research which I had been struggling to make for some years before that. She has also challenged me to break new ground with this book and deserves much of the credit if I have succeeded in doing so.

Norbert Schmitt has emerged as a productive scholar in second language vocabulary research in recent years while still retaining his youthful enthusiasm for the subject. I have used him as a sounding board in the latter stages of the writing and benefited greatly from his wide knowledge of the field.

All of these people have read the book in manuscript form. While I was naturally flattered by their very positive evaluations of my work, their close reading of the text has obliged me to clarify a number of the main ideas, take a more sceptical view of certain matters and correct errors in the detail. Any remaining problems with the book are not for want of effort on their part and I thank them all for their dedication to the task.

Part of the book was written during a period of leave I spent at the Centre for Advanced Research in English at the University of Birmingham in 1996. I am grateful to Malcolm Coulthard, Dave Willis and all the staff of English Language Research who provided me with such good facilities and congenial company during that time.

My family – Siew Hean, Melanie and Martin – have been tolerant of my silent preoccupation with the project and my long hours on the home computer at times. I suppose I might have completed the work sooner without having them around, but my life would have been much the poorer for it.

The publishers and I are grateful to the authors, publishers and others who have given permission for the use of copyright material identified in the text. It has not been possible to identify, or trace, sources of all the materials used and in such cases the publishers would welcome information from copyright owners.

Bachman, L.F. and A.S. Palmer. 1996. *Language Testing in Practice*. Oxford University Press; Pawley, A. and F.H. Syder. 1983. Two puzzles for linguistic theory: nativelike selection and nativelike fluency. In J.C. Richards and R.W. Schmidt (eds.). *Language and Communication*. Longman 1983, Reprinted by permission of Pearson Education Limited; Richards, J.C. 1976. The Role of Vocabulary Teaching. *TESOL Quarterly*, 10 (1). Page 83; Nation, I.S.P. 1990. *Teaching and Learning Vocabulary*. Heinle and Heinle; Nagy, W., P.A. Herman and R.C. Anderson. 1985. Learning words form context. *Reading Research Quarterly*, 20 (2) by permission of International Reading Association: Newark, USA; Sternberg, R.J. and J.S. Powell. 1983. Comprehending Verbal Comprehension. American Psychologist, 38 by permission of APA; Mondria, J.A. and M. Wit-De Boer. 1991. The effects of contextual richness on the guessability and the retention of words in a foreign language. *Applied Linguistics*, 12 (3) Oxford University Press; Tarone, E. 1978. Conscious communication strategies in inter-language: a progress report. In H.D. Brown, C.A. Yorio and R. Crymes (eds.). *On TESOL '77. Teaching and Learning English as a Second Language*. Washington, DC: TESOL; *ACTFL Proficiency Guidelines*. 1986. Level descriptors from American Council on the Teaching of Foreign Languages. ACTFL: Yonkers NY; Wesche, M. and T.S. Pari-bakht. 1996. Assessing second language vocabulary knowledge: depth versus breadth. Canadian Modern Language Review, 53 (1) page 17, UTP Journals: Toronto; J. McQueen. 1996. Rasch scaling: how valid is it as the basis for content-referenced descriptors of test performance? In G. Wigglesworth and C. Elder (eds.), The Language Testing Cycle: From Inception to Washback. *Australian Review of Applied Linguistics*, Series S, No 13, page 152; Dolch, E.W. and D. Leeds. 1953. Vocabulary tests and depth of meaning. Journal of Educational Research 47 (3); Verhallen, M. and R. Schoonen. 1993. Lexical knowledge of monolingual and bilingual children. *Applied Linguistics*, 14 (4) Oxford University Press; Stalnaker and W. Kurath. 1935. A comparison of two types of foreign language vocabulary test. Journal of Educational Psychology 26 (6) by permission of APA; Hale, G.A., C.W. Rock, M.M. Hicks, F.A. Butler and J.W. Oller, Jr. 1989. The relation of multiple-choice cloze items to the Test of English as a Foreign Language. *Language Testing*, 6 (1), by permission of Arnold; Laufer, B. and P. Nation. 1995. Vocabulary size and use: Lexical richness in L2 written production. *Applied Linguistics*, 16 (3) Oxford University Press; Paribakht, T.S. and M. Wesche. 1997. Vocabulary enhancement activities and reading for meaning. In *Second Language Vocabulary Acquisition*. Coady and Huckin (eds.). Cambridge University Press; Oller, J.W. Jr. and B. Spolsky. 1979. The Test of English as a Foreign Language (TOEFL). In *Some Major Tests. Advances in Language Testing Series*, 1. B. Spolsky (ed.), Arlington, VA: Center for Applied Linguistics; Pike, L.W. 1979. An Evaluation of Alternative Item formats for Testing English as a Foreign Language. *TOEFL Research Reports*, No 2. Educational Testing Service. Page 19; Hale, Stansfield, Rock, Hicks, Butler and Oller 1988. Multiple Choice Cloze Items and the Test of English as a Foreign Language. *TOEFL Research Reports*, No 26. Educational Testing Service. Page 67; Henning, G. 1991. A Study of the Effects of Contextualization and Familiarization on Responses to the TOEFL Vocabulary Test Items. *TOEFL Research Reports*, No 35. Educational Testing Service. Page 4–5; *TOEFL Sample Test*. 5th

Edition. 1995. Educational Testing Service. Page 34; *TOEFL Sampler.* [CD-ROM]. 1998. Educational Testing Service; TSE Rating Scale from the *TSE Score User's Manual.* Educational Testing Service. Page 21; Hughes. 1989. *Testing for Language Teachers.* Cambridge University Press; Clarke, M. and S. Silberstein. 1977. Toward a realization of the psycholinguistic principles in the ESL reading classroom. *Language Learning,* 27. Blackwell: Oxford; Goulden R., P. Nation and J. Read. 1990. How large can receptive vocabulary be? *Applied Linguistics,* 11. Oxford University Press; Nation, P. 1993. Measuring readiness for simplified material: A test of the first 1000 words of English. In M.L. Tickoo (ed.), *Simplification: Theory and Application.* Singapore: SEAMEO Regional Language Centre; Engber, C.A. 1995. The relationship of Lexical proficiency to the quality of ESL compositions. *Journal of Second Language Writing,* 4 (2); O'Loughlin, K. 1995. Lexical density in candidate output on direct and semi-direct versions of an oral proficiency test. *Language Testing,* 12 (2), by permission of Arnold; Jacobs, H.L., S.A. Zigraf, D.R. Wormuth, V.F. Hartfiel and J.B. Hughey. 1981. Testing ESL Composition: A Practical Approach. Rowley, MA: Newbury House; Brown, J.D. and K. Bailey. 1984. A categorical instrument for scoring second language writing skills. *Language Learning,* 34 (4). Blackwell: Oxford; Weir, C.J. 1990. *Communicative Language Testing.* Prentice Hall 1990, Reprinted by permission of Pearson Education Limited; McCarthy, M. 1990. *Vocabulary.* Oxford University Press;

....

CHAPTER ONE

The place of vocabulary in language assessment

Introduction

At first glance, it may seem that assessing the vocabulary knowledge of second language learners is both necessary and reasonably straightforward. It is necessary in the sense that words are the basic building blocks of language, the units of meaning from which larger structures such as sentences, paragraphs and whole texts are formed. For native speakers, although the most rapid growth occurs in childhood, vocabulary knowledge continues to develop naturally in adult life in response to new experiences, inventions, concepts, social trends and opportunities for learning. For learners, on the other hand, acquisition of vocabulary is typically a more conscious and demanding process. Even at an advanced level, learners are aware of limitations in their knowledge of second language (or L2) words. They experience lexical gaps, that is words they read which they simply do not understand, or concepts that they cannot express as adequately as they could in their first language (or L1). Many learners see second language acquisition as essentially a matter of learning vocabulary, so they devote a great deal of time to memorising lists of L2 words and rely on their bilingual dictionary as a basic communicative resource. Moreover, after a lengthy period of being preoccupied with the development of grammatical competence, language teachers and applied linguistic researchers now generally recognise the importance of vocabulary learning and are exploring ways of promoting it more effectively. Thus, from various points of view, vocabulary can be seen as a priority area in language teaching, requiring tests to monitor the

1

learners' progress in vocabulary learning and to assess how adequate their vocabulary knowledge is to meet their communication needs.

Vocabulary assessment seems straightforward in the sense that word lists are readily available to provide a basis for selecting a set of words to be tested. In addition, there is a range of well-known item types that are convenient to use for vocabulary testing. Here are some examples:

Multiple-choice   (*Choose the correct answer*)

The principal was <u>irate</u> when she heard what the students had done.

a. surprised
b. interested
c. proud
d. angry

Completion   (*Write in the missing word*)
At last the climbers reached the s_____ of the mountain.

Translation   (*Give the L1 equivalent of the underlined word*)
They worked at the <u>mill</u>.

Matching   (*Match each word with its meaning*)

1	accurate	____	a.	not changing
2	transparent	____	b.	not friendly
3	constant	____	c.	related to seeing things
4	visual	____	d.	greater in size
5	hostile	____	e.	careful and exact
			f.	allowing light to go through
			g.	in the city

These test items are easy to write and to score, and they make efficient use of testing time. Multiple-choice items in particular have been commonly used in standardised tests. A professionally produced multiple-choice vocabulary test is highly reliable and distinguishes learners effectively according to their level of vocabulary knowledge. Furthermore, it will usually be strongly related to measures of the learners' reading comprehension ability. Handbooks on language testing published in the 1960s and 1970s (for example Lado, 1961; Harris, 1969; Heaton, 1975) devote a considerable amount of space to vocabulary testing, with a lot of advice on how to write good items and avoid various pitfalls.

Tests containing items such as those illustrated above continue to be written and used by language teachers to assess students' progress in vocabulary learning and to diagnose areas of weakness in their knowledge of **target-language** words, i.e. the language which they are learning. Similarly, scholars with a specialist interest in the learning and teaching of vocabulary (see, for example, McKeown and Curtis, 1987; Nation, 1990; Coady and Huckin, 1997; Schmitt and McCarthy, 1997) generally take it for granted that it is meaningful to treat words as independent units and to devise tests that measure whether – and how well – learners know the meanings of particular words.

Recent trends in language testing

However, scholars in the field of language testing have a rather different perspective on vocabulary-test items of the conventional kind. Such items fit neatly into what language testers call **the discrete-point approach** to testing. This involves designing tests to assess whether learners have knowledge of particular structural elements of the language: word meanings, word forms, sentence patterns, sound contrasts and so on. In the last thirty years of the twentieth century, language testers progressively moved away from this approach, to the extent that such tests are now quite out of step with current thinking about how to design language tests, especially for proficiency assessment.

A number of criticisms can be made of discrete-point vocabulary tests.

- It is difficult to make any general statement about a learner's vocabulary on the basis of scores in such a test. If someone gets 20 items correct out of 30, what does that say about the adequacy of the learner's vocabulary knowledge?
- Being proficient in a second language is not just a matter of knowing a lot of words – or grammar rules, for that matter – but being able to exploit that knowledge effectively for various communicative purposes. Learners can build up an impressive knowledge of vocabulary (as reflected in high test scores) and yet be incapable of understanding a radio news broadcast or asking for assistance at an enquiry counter.
- Learners need to show that they can use words appropriately in

their own speech and writing, rather than just demonstrating that they understand what a word can mean. To put it another way, the standard discrete-point items test receptive but not productive competence.

- In normal language use, words do not occur by themselves or in isolated sentences but as integrated elements of whole texts and discourse. They belong in specific conversations, jokes, stories, letters, textbooks, legal proceedings, newspaper advertisements and so on. And the way that we interpret a word is significantly influenced by the context in which it occurs.

- In communication situations, it is quite possible to compensate for lack of knowledge of particular words. We all know learners who are remarkably adept at getting their message across by making the best use of limited lexical resources. Readers do not have to understand every word in order to extract meaning from a text satisfactorily. Some words can be ignored, while the meaning of others can be guessed by using contextual clues, background knowledge of the subject matter and so on. Listeners can use similar strategies, as well as seeking clarification, asking for a repetition and checking that they have interpreted the message correctly.

The widespread acceptance of the validity of these criticisms has led to the adoption – particularly in the major English-speaking countries – of **the communicative approach** to language testing. Today's language proficiency tests do not set out to determine whether learners know the meaning of *magazine* or *put on* or *approximate*; whether they can get the sequence of tenses right in conditional sentences; or whether they can distinguish *ship* and *sheep*. Instead, the tests are based on **tasks** simulating communication activities that the learners are likely to be engaged in outside of the classroom. Learners may be asked to write a letter of complaint to a hotel manager, to show that they understand the main ideas of a university lecture or to discuss in an interview how they hope to achieve their career ambitions. Presumably good vocabulary knowledge and skills will help test-takers to perform these tasks better than if they lack such competence, but neither vocabulary nor any other structural component of the language is the primary focus of the assessment. The test-takers are judged on how adequately they meet the overall language demands of the task.

Recent books on language testing by leading scholars such as

Bachman and Palmer (1996) and McNamara (1996) demonstrate how the task has become the basic element in contemporary test design. This is consistent with broader trends in Western education systems away from formal standardised tests made up of multiple items to measure students' knowledge of a content area, towards what is variously known as alternative, performance-based or standards-based assessment (see, for example, Baker, O'Neil and Linn, 1993; Taylor, 1994; O'Malley and Valdez Pierce, 1996), which includes judging students' ability to perform more open-ended, holistic and 'real-world' tasks within their normal learning environment.

Is there a place, then, for vocabulary assessment within task-based language testing? To look for an answer to this question, we can turn to Bachman and Palmer's (1996) book *Language Testing in Practice*, which is a comprehensive and influential volume on language-test design and development. Following Bachman's (1990) earlier work, the authors see the purpose of language testing as being to allow us to make inferences about learners' language ability, which consists of two components. One is **language knowledge** and the other is **strategic competence**. That is to say, learners need to know a lot about the vocabulary, grammar, sound system and spelling of the target language, but they also need to be able to draw on that knowledge effectively for communicative purposes under normal time constraints. As I noted above, one of the main criticisms of discrete-point vocabulary items is that they focus entirely on the knowledge component of language ability.

Within the Bachman and Palmer framework, language knowledge is classified into numerous areas, as presented in Table 1.1. The table shows that language knowledge covers more areas than I indicated in the previous paragraph, but at the same time knowledge of vocabulary appears to be just a minor component of the overall system, a sub-sub-category of organisational knowledge. It is classified as part of Grammatical knowledge, which suggests a very narrow view of vocabulary as a stock of meaningful word forms that fit into slots in sentence frames. I will have a great deal more to say about the nature of vocabulary in Chapter 2, but for now let me point out that vocabulary knowledge is a significant element in several other categories of the table. The most obvious area is Sociolinguistic knowledge, which includes 'natural or idiomatic expressions', 'cultural references' and 'figures of speech'. Most people would regard these as belonging to the vocabulary of the language. In addition, the sociolinguistic

Table 1.1 *Areas of language knowledge (Bachman and Palmer, 1996: 68)*

Organisational knowledge
(how utterances or sentences and texts are organised)

Grammatical knowledge
(how individual utterances or sentences are organised)

Knowledge of vocabulary
Knowledge of syntax
Knowledge of phonology/graphology

Textual knowledge
(how utterances or sentences are organised to form texts)

Knowledge of cohesion
Knowledge of rhetorical or conversational organisation

Pragmatic knowledge
(how utterances or sentences and texts are related to the communicative goals of the language user and to the features of the language use setting)

Functional knowledge
(how utterances or sentences and texts are related to the communicative goals of language users)

Knowledge of ideational functions
Knowledge of manipulative functions
Knowledge of heuristic functions
Knowledge of imaginative functions

Sociolinguistic knowledge
(how utterances or sentences and texts are related to features of the language use setting)

Knowledge of dialects/varieties
Knowledge of registers
Knowledge of natural or idiomatic expressions
Knowledge of cultural references and figures of speech

---

category includes knowledge of registers, which are varieties of language associated with particular users, uses and contexts. One of the primary features of a register is the distinctive words and phrases used in it (McCarthy, 1990: 61–64). Thus, in these and other ways, Table 1.1 understates the contribution of vocabulary to language knowledge.

Bachman and Palmer (1996: 67) acknowledge that many language tests focus on just one of the areas of language knowledge, such as vocabulary. They give as an example a test for primary school children learning English as a foreign language in an Asian country. In the context of a teaching unit on 'Going to the zoo', the students are tested on their knowledge of the names of zoo animals (Bachman and Palmer, 1996: 354–365). The authors argue that, even at this elementary level of language learning, vocabulary testing should relate to some meaningful use of language outside the classroom.

However, their main concern is with the development of test tasks that not only draw on various areas of language knowledge but also require learners to show that they can activate that knowledge effectively in communication. An illustration of the latter kind of task is found in an academic writing test for non-native speakers of English entering a writing programme in an English-medium university (Bachman and Palmer, 1996: 253–284). The test-takers are required to write a proposal for improving the institution's admissions procedures. Rather than the single global scale that is often employed to rate performance on such a task, Bachman and Palmer advocate the use of several analytic scales, which provide separate ratings for different components of the language ability to be tested. In the case of the academic writing test, they developed five scales, for knowledge of syntax, vocabulary, rhetorical organisation, cohesion and register. Thus, vocabulary is certainly being assessed here, but not separately; it is part of a larger procedure for measuring the students' academic-writing ability.

Three dimensions of vocabulary assessment

Up to this point, I have outlined two contrasting perspectives on the role of vocabulary in language assessment. One point of view is that it is perfectly sensible to write tests that measure whether learners know the meaning and usage of a set of words, taken as independent semantic units. The other view is that vocabulary must always be assessed in the context of a language-use task, where it interacts in a natural way with other components of language knowledge. To some extent, the two views are complementary in that they relate to different purposes of assessment. Conventional vocabulary tests are most likely to be used by classroom teachers for assessing progress in vocabulary learning and diagnosing areas of weakness. Other users of these tests are researchers in second language acquisition with a special interest in how learners develop their knowledge of, and ability to use, target-language words. On the other hand, researchers in language testing and those who undertake large testing projects tend to be more concerned with the design of tests that assess learners' achievement or proficiency on a broader scale. For such purposes, vocabulary knowledge has a lower profile, except to the extent that it contributes to, or detracts from, the performance of communicative tasks.

As with most dichotomies, the distinction I have made between the two perspectives on vocabulary assessment oversimplifies the matter. There is a whole range of reasons for assessing vocabulary knowledge and use, with a corresponding variety of testing procedures. In order to map out the scope of the subject, I propose three dimensions, as presented in Figure 1.1.

The dimensions represent ways in which we can expand our conventional ideas about what a vocabulary test is in order to include a wider range of lexical assessment procedures. I introduce the dimensions here, then illustrate and discuss them at various points in the following chapters. Let us look at each one in turn.

Discrete – embedded

The first dimension focuses on the construct which underlies the assessment instrument. In language testing, the term construct refers to the mental attribute or ability that a test is designed to measure. In the case of a traditional vocabulary test, the construct can usually be labelled as 'vocabulary knowledge' of some kind. The practical significance of defining the construct is that it allows us to clarify the meaning of the test results. Normally we want to interpret the scores on a vocabulary test as a measure of some aspect of the learners' vocabulary knowledge, such as their progress in learning words from the last several units in the course book, their ability to supply derived forms of base words (like *scientist* and *scientific*, from *science*), or their skill at inferring the meaning of unknown words in a reading passage. Thus, a **discrete** test takes vocabulary knowledge as a distinct construct, separated from other components of language competence. Whether it is valid to do so is a matter for debate and an issue that I

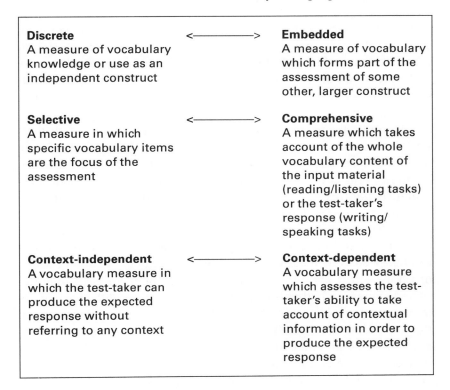

Figure 1.1 Dimensions of Vocabulary Assessment

return to in Chapter 4. However, most existing vocabulary tests are designed on the assumption that it is meaningful to treat them as an independent construct for assessment purposes and can thus be classified as discrete measures in the sense that I am defining it here.

In contrast, an **embedded** vocabulary measure is one that contributes to the assessment of a larger construct. I have already given an example of such a measure, when I referred to Bachman and Palmer's task of writing a proposal for the improvement of university admissions procedures. In this case, the construct can be labelled 'academic writing ability', and the vocabulary scale is one of five ratings which form a composite measure of the construct. Another example of an embedded measure is found in reading tasks consisting of a written text followed by a set of comprehension questions. It is common practice to include in such tests a number of items assessing the learners' understanding of particular words or phrases in the text. Usually the vocabulary item scores are not separately counted; they simply form part of the measure of the learners' 'reading-comprehension ability'. In that sense, vocabulary assessment is more embedded here than in the academic-writing test, where the vocabulary rating may well be included in a profile report of each learner's writing ability.

It is important to understand that the discrete–embedded distinction does not refer primarily to the way that vocabulary is presented to the test-takers. Many discrete vocabulary tests do require the learners to respond to words which are presented in isolation or in a short sentence, but this is not what makes the test discrete. Rather, it is the fact that the test is focusing purely on the construct of vocabulary knowledge. A test can present words in quite a large amount of context and still be a discrete measure in my sense. For instance, I can take a suitable reading passage, select a number of content words or phrases in it and write a multiple-choice item for each one, designed to assess whether learners can understand what the vocabulary item means as it is used in the text. This may appear to be very much the same kind of test as the one I described in the last paragraph to illustrate what an embedded measure is, but the crucial difference is that in this case all the items are based on vocabulary in the passage and I interpret the test score as measuring how well the learners can understand what those words and phrases mean. I do not see it as assessing their reading comprehension ability or any other broader construct. Thus, to determine whether a particular vocabulary measure is discrete or embedded, you need to consider its purpose and the way the results are to be interpreted.

Selective – comprehensive

The second dimension concerns the range of vocabulary to be included in the assessment. A conventional vocabulary test is based on a set of target words selected by the test-writer, and the test-takers are assessed according to how well they demonstrate their knowledge of the meaning or use of those words. This is what I call a **selective** vocabulary measure. The target words may either be selected as individual words and then incorporated into separate test items, or alternatively the test-writer first chooses a suitable text and then uses certain words from it as the basis for the vocabulary assessment.

On the other hand, a **comprehensive** measure takes account of all the vocabulary content of a spoken or written text. For example, let us take a speaking test in which the learners are rated on various criteria, including their range of expression. In this case, the raters are not listening for particular words or expressions but in principle are forming a judgement of the quality of the test-takers' overall vocabulary use. Similarly, as we shall see in Chapter 7, some researchers have investigated productive vocabulary use by setting learners a written composition task and then counting the number of different words or the number of 'sophisticated', low-frequency words used.

Comprehensive measures can also be applied to the input material for reading or listening tests. It is common practice for test-writers to use a readability measure as one way of judging the suitability of a text for the assessment of a particular group of test-takers. Readability formulas almost always include a vocabulary component, typically in the form of a calculation of the percentage of 'long' words in the text. It is well established in English that there is an inverse relationship between the length of a word and its frequency of occurrence in the language, which means that a text with a high proportion of long words is likely to challenge the learners both linguistically and conceptually. Although of course other factors influence readability and listenability as well, the use of a readability formula in this way illustrates a vocabulary-assessment measure that is both comprehensive and embedded.

Context-independent – context-dependent

The role of context, which is an old issue in vocabulary testing, is the basis for the third dimension. Traditionally contextualisation has meant that a word is presented to test-takers in a sentence rather than as an isolated element. From a contemporary perspective, it is necessary to broaden the notion of context to include whole texts and, more generally, discourse. In addition, we need to recognise that contextualisation is more than just a matter of the way in which vocabulary is presented. The key question is to what extent the test-takers are being assessed on the basis of their ability to *engage with* the context provided in the test. In other words, do they have to make use of contextual information in order to give the appropriate response to the test task, or can they just respond as if the words were in isolation?

We can illustrate the distinction by looking at a vocabulary item embedded in a reading-comprehension test.

> Humans have an innate ability to recognise the taste of salt because it provides us with sodium, an element which is essential to life. Although too much salt in our diet may be unhealthy, we must <u>consume</u> a certain amount of it to maintain our wellbeing.

> What is the meaning of <u>consume</u> *in this text*?
>
> a   use up completely
> b   eat or drink
> c   spend wastefully
> d   destroy

The point about this test item is that all four options are possible meanings of the word *consume*. Thus, the test-takers need some understanding of the context in order to be confident that they have chosen the correct option, rather than simply relying on the fact that they have learned 'eat and drink' as the meaning of *consume*. To that extent, the item is context dependent. I will explore this matter further in discussing the vocabulary items in the Test of English as a Foreign Language (TOEFL) in Chapter 5.

The issue of context dependence also arises with cloze tests, in which words are systematically deleted from a text and the test-takers' task is to write a suitable word in each blank space. As we shall see in Chapter 4, language testing researchers have debated whether cloze-test items can mostly be answered correctly just by looking at the immediate context of the blank (the phrase or clause in which it occurs), or whether it is necessary to draw on information from the wider context of the passage in many cases. Some researchers have made detailed analyses of the contextual information required to respond to individual cloze items, while others have sought to show more globally that cloze-test items are or are not context dependent in a broad sense. Thus, the degree of context dependence can be approached either as a characteristic of individual test items or as a property of the test as a whole.

Generally speaking, vocabulary measures embedded in writing and speaking tasks are context dependent in that the learners are assessed on the appropriateness of their vocabulary use in relation to the task.

Judgements about appropriateness take us beyond the text to consider the wider social context. For instance, take a proficiency test in which the test-takers are doctors and the test task is a role play simulating a consultation with a patient. If vocabulary use is one of the criteria used in rating the doctors' performance, they need to demonstrate an ability to meet the lexical requirements of the situation; for example: understanding the colloquial expressions that patients use for common symptoms and ailments, explaining medical concepts in lay terms, avoiding medical jargon, offering reassurance to someone who is upset or anxious, giving advice in a suitable tone and so on. Vocabulary use in the task is thus influenced by the doctor's status as a highly educated professional, the expected role relationship in a consultation and the affective dimension of the situation. This is a much broader view of context than we are used to thinking of in relation to vocabulary testing, but a necessary one nonetheless if we are to assess vocabulary in contemporary performance tests.

An overview of the book

The three dimensions are not intended to form a comprehensive model of vocabulary assessment. Rather, they provide a basis for locating the variety of assessment procedures currently in use within a common framework and, in particular, they offer points of contact between tests which treat words as discrete units and ones that assess vocabulary more integratively in a task-based testing context. At various points through the book I refer to the dimensions and exemplify them. Since a large proportion of work on vocabulary assessment to date has involved instruments which are relatively discrete, selective and context independent in nature, this approach may seem to be predominant in several of the following chapters. However, my aim is to present a balanced view of the subject, and I discuss measures that are more embedded, comprehensive and context dependent wherever the opportunity arises, and especially in the last two chapters of the book.

Chapter 2 takes up the question of what we mean by vocabulary. We tend to think of it as consisting of individual words, as in the headwords of a dictionary; however, even the definition of a 'word' is by no means straightforward. It is also necessary to consider lexical units that are larger than single words, such as compound nouns, phrasal verbs, idioms and fixed expressions of various kinds. For assessment purposes, vocabulary is not just a set of linguistic units but also an attribute of individual language learners, in the form of vocabulary knowledge and the ability to access that knowledge for communicative purposes.

To explore further the nature of vocabulary ability, in Chapter 3 I review the main lines of enquiry by researchers on second language vocabulary acquisition. Apart from the extensive work on methods of conscious vocabulary learning, researchers are investigating how acquisition of word knowledge occurs in a more incidental fashion through reading and listening activities. Other areas of interest are the ability of learners to guess the meaning of unknown words which they encounter in their reading, and the strategies they use to overcome gaps in their vocabulary knowledge when engaged in speaking and writing tasks.

In Chapter 4 I consider research in language testing that either has involved the investigation of vocabulary tests or has a bearing on vocabulary assessment. One issue in this area is whether the notion of a 'pure' vocabulary test is at all tenable. I trace the move away from discrete-point vocabulary tests and look in some detail at the extent to which the cloze procedure and its variants can be regarded as measures of vocabulary. Much recent work on vocabulary testing has focused on estimating how many words learners know (or their vocabulary size). A complementary perspective is provided by other studies that seek to assess the quality (or 'depth') of their vocabulary knowledge.

Chapter 5 presents case studies of four vocabulary tests:

- Nation's Vocabulary Levels Test;
- Meara and Jones's Eurocentres Vocabulary Size Test;
- Paribakht and Wesche's Vocabulary Knowledge Scale; and
- the vocabulary items in the Test of English as a Foreign Language (TOEFL).

In addition to being influential instruments in their own right, these tests exemplify several of the main currents in vocabulary testing discussed in the previous chapter.

Practical issues in the design of vocabulary tests are discussed in Chapter 6, which focuses on relatively discrete and selective tests. The chapter includes discussion of two specific examples of test design from my own experience. One looks at some typical items for classroom progress tests, and the other is an account of my efforts to develop a workable test to measure depth of vocabulary knowledge.

Chapter 7 focuses on comprehensive measures of vocabulary which can be used in task-based language testing, particularly for embedded assessment. The largest section of the chapter covers procedures that have been applied to the assessment of learners' writing. These include 'objective' counts of the relative proportions of different types of word in a composition, as well as 'subjective' rating scales. I also consider the application of comprehensive measures, such as readability formulas, to the analysis of input material for tests involving reading and listening tasks.

Finally, in Chapter 8, I look at current and future directions in work on vocabulary assessment. This includes discussion of ways in which computer-based corpus research can contribute to the development of vocabulary measures. A second major theme is the need to broaden our view of the nature of vocabulary. More consideration should be given to the role of multi-word lexical items in language use. Another priority is to gain a better understanding of the vocabulary of speech, as distinct from written language. There should also be more focus on the social dimension of vocabulary use.

....

CHAPTER TWO

The nature of vocabulary

Introduction

Before we start to consider how to test vocabulary, it is necessary first to explore the nature of what we want to assess. Our everyday concept of vocabulary is dominated by the dictionary. We tend to think of it as an inventory of individual words, with their associated meanings. This view is shared by many second language learners, who see the task of vocabulary learning as a matter of memorising long lists of L2 words, and their immediate reaction when they encounter an unknown word is to reach for a bilingual dictionary. From this perspective, vocabulary knowledge involves knowing the meanings of words and therefore the purpose of a vocabulary test is to find out whether the learners can match each word with a synonym, a dictionary-type definition or an equivalent word in their own language.

However, when we look more closely at vocabulary in the light of current developments in language teaching and applied linguistics, we find that we have to address a number of questions that have the effect of progressively broadening the scope of what we need to assess.

The first question is: What is a word? This is an issue that is of considerable interest to linguists on a theoretical level, but for testing purposes we have more practical reasons for asking it. For example, it becomes relevant if we want to make an estimate of the size of a learner's vocabulary. Researchers who have attempted to measure how many words native speakers of English know have produced wildly varying figures, at least partly because of their different ways of defining what a word is.

Next, we need to ask: Does vocabulary consist only of single words, or should we be thinking in terms of larger lexical items as well? It is a well-established practice to classify idioms as a special category within vocabulary, but there is currently a trend among both theoretical and applied linguists towards analysing many other types of common phrases and sentences as lexical rather than grammatical units. It seems that there are a lot more fixed expressions in language than we normally realise and they play a major role in both comprehension and production.

If we can settle on a satisfactory working definition of a lexical item, the third question is: What does it mean to know such an item? At a beginner's level of learning a second language, it may be sufficient for the learners to show that they understand L2 words by being able to match them with an equivalent word in their own language or with an L2 synonym. Certainly many conventional vocabulary-test items are designed on this basis. However, as their L2 proficiency develops, learners need to know more about the words and other lexical items they are acquiring, especially if they are to use them in their own speech and writing.

A fourth, broader issue is: What is the nature of the construct that we set out to measure with a vocabulary test? As I noted in Chapter 1, Bachman and Palmer (1996) propose that the general construct underlying language tests, which they call language ability, is made up not only of multiple areas of knowledge but also strategic competence. If we apply this concept to vocabulary, we realise that vocabulary ability involves more than just knowing a lot of lexical items; learners must have ready access to that knowledge and be able to draw on it effectively in performing language-use tasks. In addition, they need to have strategies for dealing with situations where their vocabulary knowledge is insufficient to meet their communication needs.

What is a word?

A basic assumption in vocabulary testing is that we are assessing knowledge of *words*. But the word is not an easy concept to define, either in theoretical terms or for various applied purposes.

There are some basic points that we need to spell out from the start. One is the distinction between **tokens** and **types**, which applies to any count of the words in a text. The number of tokens is the same as the total number of word forms, which means that individual words occurring more than once in the text are counted each time they are used. On the other hand, the number of types is the total number of the *different* word forms, so that a word which is repeated many times is counted only once. When I set my students the task of writing a composition of 500 words, they and I understand that this refers to the number of tokens (or running words, if you like), many of which – especially words like *the*, *a*, *to*, *and*, *in* and *that* – are multiple occurrences of the same type. However, the number of types is substantially less than 500. The relative proportions of types and tokens (known as the **type–token ratio**) is a widely used measure of the language development of both language learners and native speakers (see Chapter 7).

Mention of words like *the*, *a*, *to*, *and*, *in* and *that* leads to the question of whether they are to be regarded as vocabulary items. Words of this kind – articles, prepositions, pronouns, conjunctions, auxiliaries, etc. – are often referred to as **function words** and are seen as belonging more to the grammar of the language than to its vocabulary. Unlike **content words** – nouns, 'full' verbs, adjectives and adverbs – they have little if any meaning in isolation and serve more to provide links within sentences, modify the meaning of content words and so on. Generally speaking, when we set out to test vocabulary, it is knowledge of content words that we focus on.

Even when we restrict our attention to content words, another problem is that these words come in a variety of forms. For example, we have the word *wait*, but then there are also *waits*, *waited* and *waiting*; similarly, there are *society*, *societies*, *society's* and *societies'*. In both cases, we would normally regard these as different forms of the same word. Grammatically speaking, what is involved is adding inflectional endings to a base form, without changing the meaning or the word class of the base. In vocabulary studies, the base and inflected forms of a word are collectively known as a **lemma**. When researchers undertake a study that involves counting the number of words (in the sense of types) in a written or spoken text, one of the first steps is normally to lemmatise the tokens, so that inflected forms are counted as instances of the same lemma as the base form.

However, base words not only take inflectional endings but also have a variety of derived forms, which often change the word class and add a new element of meaning. An example is the word *leak*, with

the inflected forms *leaks, leaking* and *leaked* as well as these derivatives: *leaky, leakiness, leakage* and *leaker*. Even though there is a
distinction between the literal 'loss of a fluid' and the more metaphorical 'loss of secret information', all these words are closely related in
form and meaning. Such a set of word forms, sharing a common
meaning, is known as a **word family**.

The situation is more complex with a word like *society* and the
numerous other words that resemble it to varying degrees in form and
meaning: *social, socially, sociable, unsociable, sociability, socialise,
socialisation, socialism, socialist, socialite, sociology, sociologist, sociological, societal* and so on. These words all share the same *soci-* form
and seem to have a common underlying meaning, which might be
expressed as 'relating to humans or animals in a group or organisation of some kind'. However, since collectively the words express
quite a range of meanings, we would not want to say that they are
members of the same word family. That might be true of certain
subsets – say *sociable, unsociable, sociably* and *sociability*; or *socialism, socialist, socialistic* and *socialistically* – but not the words as a
whole. The problem is how to separate them into their word families.

Distinguishing word forms and word families is particularly important in relation to measures of vocabulary size, which I discuss further
in Chapter 4. One reason for the widely varying estimates of how
many words a native speaker knows is that some researchers are
counting word forms while others focus on word families. If a
vocabulary-size test is based on a sample of, say, 200 items taken
from a list which includes a lot of related word forms, it will lead to a
larger estimate of vocabulary size than a 200-item sample taken from
a list of word families. Goulden, Nation and Read (1990) give a
detailed description of how they sampled words from *Webster's Third
New International Dictionary* (1961) and then pruned the sample
systematically to produce a fairly conservative listing of base words
(each one representing a word family). In the process, we deleted
derived forms, proper names, compound nouns, abbreviations, affixes
and various other non-base items.

Even if a test is not intended as a measure of vocabulary size, we
can ask what can be inferred from learner performance on particular
test items. Let us say that an item is designed to assess knowledge of
the word *critical* and the learners answer it correctly. Do we credit
them just with knowing *critical*, or is it reasonable to assume that
they also know *critically, crisis* and *criticism*? To put it another way, is

it the individual word form that is being assessed or the whole word family to which that word form belongs?

One further complication in defining what words are is the existence of **homographs**. These are single word forms that have at least two meanings that are so different that they obviously belong to different word families. One commonly cited example is the noun *bank*, which has two major meanings: an institution which provides financial services, and the sloping ground beside a river. It also refers to a row of dials or switches, and to the tilting of an aircraft's wings as it turns. There is no underlying meaning that can usefully link all four of these definitions, so in a real sense we have several distinct word families here. In dictionaries, they are generally recognised as such by being given separate entries (rather than separate senses under a single entry). In the testing context, we cannot assume, just because learners demonstrate knowledge of one meaning, that they have acquired any of the others.

Thus, the term word can refer to a variety of lexical units. Normally, in vocabulary assessment it applies to content rather than function words, but in other respects its specific reference may be quite unclear. Certain assessment procedures require a clear definition of what the relevant unit is and explicit criteria for distinguishing one unit from another. For instance, those who compile word lists for teaching or testing have to define what they mean by a word, especially if the list is based on a frequency count of words in a long text or a **corpus** (a large collection of texts stored on computer). As I mentioned earlier, using a test to estimate the size of a learner's vocabulary is another situation in which the definition of a word plays a crucial role. I discuss this further in Chapter 4. A third case is where learners' written or spoken production is evaluated by means of what I called in Chapter 1 comprehensive measures, which involve calculating the relative proportions of various types of words that the learners have produced: types vs. tokens, content words vs. function words, low-frequency words vs. high-frequency words and so on. These measures are considered in more detail in Chapter 7.

What about larger lexical items?

The second major point about vocabulary is that it consists of more than just single words. For a start, there are the phrasal verbs (*get across, move out, put up with*) and compound nouns (*fire fighter, love letters, practical joke, personal computer, applied social science, milk of magnesia*), which are generally recognised as lexical units consisting of more than one word form. Then there are idioms like *a piece of cake, the Good Book, to go the whole hog, let the cat out of the bag.* These are phrases and sentences that cause great difficulty for second language learners because the whole unit has a meaning that cannot be worked out just from knowing what the individual words mean.

Such multi-word items have long been accepted as part of the vocabulary learning task that students face and as such are often included in vocabulary tests. However, more recently scholars have pointed out that fluent speakers and writers have a large amount of other kinds of 'prefabricated language' at their disposal. Pawley and Syder (1983) argued that the ability to speak fluently is based on knowledge of thousands of memorised sentence stems and whole sentences that are 'lexicalised' to varying degrees. As they put it, 'memorised sentences and phrases are the normal building blocks of fluent spoken discourse, and at the same time, . . . they provide models for the creation of many (partly) new sequences that are memorable and in their turn enter the stock of familiar usages' (p. 208). This challenged the influential view of the linguist Noam Chomsky that linguistic competence primarily involves knowing a system of grammatical rules which allow the language user to produce and understand a potentially infinite set of possible sentences.

Sinclair (1991: 109–115), who has conducted extensive research on written texts stored in computerised corpora, brings together these two perspectives by proposing that two principles are required to give an adequate explanation of how texts are constructed. One is **the open-choice principle**, which is essentially the Chomskian view that sentences are produced creatively on the basis of an underlying system of rules. The sentences contain slots that can be filled by a wide range of possible words, depending on the language user's choice. However, corpus research has revealed that in practice lexical choices are much more limited than you would expect if only the open-choice principle were operating. Words commonly come together in combinations, or **collocations**, of two, three, four or more that seem to form relatively fixed expressions. Thus, according to Sinclair, the open-choice principle needs to be complemented by **the idiom principle**, which he defines this way: 'a language user has available to him or her a large number of semi-preconstructed phrases that constitute single choices, even though they might appear to be analysable into segments' (p. 110). This helps to explain why very frequent 'content' words like *take, make* and *get* seem to contribute very little specific meaning of their own but have to be understood in relation to the whole phrases in which they occur. Sinclair believes that, while linguists have traditionally taken the open-choice principle as the basis for their work, the principle of idiom is at least as important in the construction and interpretation of texts.

Working from a similar point of view, Nattinger and DeCarrico (1992) have developed the concept of a **lexical phrase**, which is a group of words that looks like a grammatical structure but operates as a unit, with a particular function in spoken or written discourse. They identify four categories of lexical phrases:

1 Polywords: short fixed phrases that perform a variety of functions, such as *for the most part* (which they call a qualifier), *at any rate* and *so to speak* (fluency devices), and *hold your horses* (disagreement marker).
2 Institutionalised expressions: longer utterances that are fixed in form and include proverbs, aphorisms and formulas for social interaction. Examples are: *a watched pot never boils, how do you do?, long time no see,* and *once upon a time . . . and they lived happily ever after.*
3 Phrasal constraints: short- to medium-length phrases consisting of a basic frame with one or two slots that can be filled with various words or phrases. These include *a [day / year / long time] ago, yours [sincerely / truly], as far as I [know / can tell / am aware],* and *the [sooner] the [better].*
4 Sentence builders: phrases that provide the framework for a complete sentence, with one or more slots in which a whole idea can be expressed. Examples are: *I think that X; not only X, but also Y* and *that reminds me of X.*

(Nattinger and DeCarrico, 1992: 38–47)

Pawley and Syder (1983: 206–208) offer a lengthy list of longer utterances of a similar kind. Here are some of their items:

> It's on the tip of my tongue.
> I'll be home all weekend.
> Have you heard the news?

I'll believe it when I see it.
There's nothing you can do about it now.
I thought you'd never ask.
Call me as soon as you get home.
She never has a bad word to say about anyone.

We do not normally think of expressions such as these – especially the longer, more sentence-like ones – as being part of the vocabulary of the language. But they do not fully belong to the grammar either. What is it, then, that makes longer sequences of words lexical rather than grammatical in nature? Writers on this topic (see, for example, Moon, 1997: 44) emphasise that there is no sharp distinction. However, lexical sequences have certain characteristics. First, they are relatively fixed in form, although there may be some variation in the actual words used. Second, it may be difficult, if not impossible, to work out what they mean from just knowing the meanings of the individual words that make them up. Third, we recognise them as familiar expressions because we use them regularly for various purposes in everyday communication. They typically have a pragmatic function that may be more significant than the semantic meaning. For example, I know that *Nice to meet you* is an appropriate and conventional way to say goodbye to someone I have just been introduced to. If someone says to me, *I'm afraid I have some bad news for you*, I immediately expect that I am about to be told about something really serious, such as the death of a relative or the loss of my job. And so on.

In vocabulary assessment, multi-word items have received much less attention than individual words. This is particularly true of the lexical phrases which Nattinger and DeCarrico have identified and classified. One reason is that conventional vocabulary tests have been of the discrete, selective kind, taking single words and short phrases (phrasal verbs, compound nouns) as their target items. These items have the advantage of being easy to distinguish and count, whether manually or by computer, and there are good resources for test-writers to draw on, in the form of word-frequency lists and dictionaries. By contrast, lexical phrases are not nearly so well documented. It is only through recent work in fields like discourse analysis and corpus linguistics that their significance has been widely recognised. Second, no matter how carefully they are defined, they represent an open-ended set of items, and the fact that they can vary in form does not help in locating them. As Moon (1997) points out, the latest computer corpora allow linguists and lexicographers to identify multi-word items more systematically and to estimate how frequently they occur in the language. Research by Moon and others shows that longer fixed phrases such as idioms, proverbs and similes are not very frequent in English; very few occur more than once in a million running words of text. Thus, if frequency in the language is an important criterion for choosing lexical items for a selective vocabulary test, only a small number of multi-word items may qualify on that basis.

On the other hand, multi-word items are likely to play more of a role in embedded, comprehensive and context-dependent vocabulary measures. One consideration here is the pragmatic dimension to the meaning of lexical phrases, as I pointed out previously. If the use of these phrases has to be judged in terms of their suitability for the social context, it makes little sense to assess them in the isolated, context-independent fashion in which individual words have traditionally been tested. Another point worth remembering is that Pawley and Syder (1983) saw lexical phrases as the key to understanding two attributes of native speakers of a language. One is their ability to 'say the right thing': to select the appropriate form of expression from a range of grammatically acceptable alternatives, for example, *I want to marry you*, rather than *I wish to be wedded to you* or *My becoming your spouse is what I want*. The other attribute is their ability to produce fluent stretches of speech or writing without apparent planning or effort. Conversely, when learners are performing production tasks in their second language, their limited command of lexical phrases means that their performance is non-nativelike in both of the senses that Pawley and Syder identified. They may confine themselves to a limited range of familiar vocabulary, or else produce expressions that sound odd, unidiomatic or unintentionally amusing; and they are likely to be hesitant, to speak more slowly and write less than native speakers do.

More research is needed to investigate how learners' use of multi-word lexical items influences the way that they are assessed in speaking and writing tasks. This would provide a better basis for defining rating scales to be used as embedded, comprehensive measures of vocabulary. It might also give insight into the way that vocabulary use in a broad sense influences raters' overall judgements of test-takers' speaking or writing ability. I explore these possibilities further in Chapters 7 and 8.

What does it mean to know a lexical item?

Let us now leave aside the question of what units vocabulary is composed of and take up the issue of what it means to know lexical items of various kinds. To put it another way, how do we go about describing the nature of vocabulary knowledge?

One approach is to try to spell out all that the learners should know about a word if they are to fully acquire it. An influential statement along these lines was produced by Richards (1976). In his article he outlined a series of assumptions about lexical competence, growing out of developments in linguistic theory in the 1960s and 1970s. The first assumption is that the vocabulary knowledge of native speakers continues to expand in adult life, in contrast to the relative stability of their grammatical competence. The other seven assumptions cover various aspects of what is meant by knowing a word:

2 Knowing a word means knowing the degree of probability of encountering that word in speech or print. For many words we also know the sort of words most likely to be found associated with the word.
3 Knowing a word implies knowing the limitations on the use of the word according to variations of function and situation.
4 Knowing a word means knowing the syntactic behaviour associated with the word.
5 Knowing a word entails knowledge of the underlying form of a word and the derivations that can be made from it.
6 Knowing a word entails knowledge of the network of associations between that word and other words in the language.
7 Knowing a word means knowing the semantic value of a word.
8 Knowing a word means knowing many of the different meanings associated with a word.

(Richards, 1976: 83)

This set of assumptions has frequently been taken as a general framework of vocabulary knowledge, although – as Meara (1996b) points out – Richards did not intend it as such and it is not as comprehensive as it might seem at first glance. Nevertheless, it highlights the complex nature of vocabulary learning, which involves a great deal more than just memorising the meaning of a word.

Nation (1990) took this approach a step further by incorporating Richards' assumptions and several other components into an

Table 2.1 *Components of word knowledge (Nation, 1990: 31)*

Form		
Spoken form	R	What does the word sound like?
	P	How is the word pronounced?
Written form	R	What does the word look like?
	P	How is the word written and spelled?
Position:		
Grammatical patterns	R	In what patterns does the word occur?
	P	In what patterns must we use the word?
Collocations	R	What words or types of words can be expected before or after the word?
	P	What words or types of words must we use with this word?
Function:		
Frequency	R	How common is the word?
	P	How often should the word be used?
Appropriateness	R	Where would we expect to meet this word?
	P	Where can this word be used?
Meaning:		
Concept	R	What does the word mean?
	P	What word should be used to express this meaning?
Associations	R	What other words does this word make us think of?
	P	What other words could we use instead of this one?

Key: R = receptive; P = productive

analytical table (Table 2.1) to specify the scope of the learner's task. Nation has built into the table a distinction that is not explicitly included in Richards' assumptions: receptive vs. productive knowledge. It is the difference that we are all familiar with between being able to recognise a word when you hear or see it and being able to use it in your own speech or writing. According to Nation's classification system, the ability to use a word requires extended knowledge beyond what you need just to understand it. In that sense, then, production involves a higher level of knowledge than reception does. I have more to say about this distinction in Chapter 6.

One useful observation Nation makes is that 'knowing a word as it is described [in Table 2.1] applies completely to only a small proportion of the total vocabulary of a native speaker' (1990: 32). Thus, this kind of full specification of word knowledge is an idealised account, rather than a realistic description of what native speakers know about most of the words in their repertoire.

When we look at Nation's table from an assessment perspective, it appears rather daunting. As Meara (1996a: 46) notes, 'it might be possible in theory to construct measures of each of these types of knowledge of particular words; in practice, it would be very difficult to do this for more than a handful of items.' In Chapter 6, I report on my own efforts to develop a test of various components of word knowledge. Another scholar who has worked in this area is Schmitt (Schmitt and Meara, 1997; Schmitt, 1998c). Both his work and mine tend to confirm Meara's judgement concerning the practical difficulties involved both in developing suitable measures (see Schmitt, 1998a; 1998b) and in eliciting evidence of learners' knowledge.

An alternative approach to describing vocabulary knowledge is a more developmental one. Several L1 vocabulary researchers have produced scales to represent the varying degrees of partial knowledge that people can have of the meaning of words they know. For example, Dale (1965: 898) defined four basic stages in knowing a word:

Stage 1: 'I never saw it before.'
Stage 2: 'I've heard of it, but I don't know what it means.'
Stage 3: 'I recognize it in context – it has something to do with . . .'
Stage 4: 'I know it.'

He also discusses what is in effect a fifth stage: being able to distinguish the word from others that are closely related to it in meaning and/or form.

A few scales of this kind have been developed for use with second language learners. For instance, Paribakht and Wesche (1993) produced what they call the Vocabulary Knowledge Scale for a research study to find out how much knowledge students acquired of a set of target words during a one-semester university ESL (English as a second language) programme. The learners reported their knowledge of each word in response to the following series of statements:

1 I have never seen this word.
2 I have seen this word before, but I don't know what it means.

3 I have seen this word before, and I *think* it means ____. (synonym or translation)
4 I know this word. It means ____.(synonym or translation)
5 I can use this word in a sentence.

I will look at this measure in some detail in Chapter 5, as a case study of a vocabulary test which assesses depth of vocabulary knowledge.

One assumption I have made so far in discussing the nature of vocabulary knowledge is that it is necessary to assess how well individual lexical items are known by learners. This may be necessary for some purposes, such as research on certain aspects of second language vocabulary acquisition. However, Meara (1996a: 46) makes a useful distinction between testing how well individual words are known and making an overall assessment of the state of a learner's vocabulary. The distinction has much in common with the one I made in Chapter 1 between selective and comprehensive measures of vocabulary. For general proficiency purposes, Meara favours the second approach and proposes two key measures: an estimate of vocabulary size and a measure of how well organised the learner's vocabulary knowledge is. I will have more to say about these measures later in the book, but for the present Meara's proposal highlights the point that we should not define the construct of vocabulary knowledge simply in terms of knowing individual lexical items.

What is vocabulary ability?

Mention of the term construct brings me back to the main theme I developed in Chapter 1, which was that scholars with a specialist interest in vocabulary teaching and learning have a rather different perspective from language testers on the question of how – and even whether – to assess vocabulary. My three dimensions of vocabulary assessment represent one attempt to incorporate the two perspectives within a single framework. However, a more ambitious effort has been undertaken by Chapelle (1994), who proposed a definition of vocabulary ability based on Bachman's (1990; see also Bachman and Palmer, 1996) general construct of language ability. Like Bachman's construct, the definition includes 'both knowledge of language and the ability to put language to use in context' (Chapelle, 1994: 163). Thus, its three components are as follows:

1 The context of vocabulary use;
2 Vocabulary knowledge and fundamental processes;
3 Metacognitive strategies for vocabulary use.

Chapelle's definition is a comprehensive one and it is worth exploring at some length. I look at each component in turn, while taking the opportunity to elaborate on some of the key ideas.

The context of vocabulary use

Traditionally in vocabulary testing, the term *context* has referred to the sentence or utterance in which the target word occurs. For instance, in a multiple-choice vocabulary item, it is normally recommended that the stem should consist of a sentence containing the word to be tested, as in the following example:

> The committee <u>endorsed</u> the proposal.
>
> A. discussed
> B. supported
> C. knew about
> D. prepared

Under the influence of integrative test formats, such as the cloze procedure, our notion of context has expanded somewhat beyond the sentence level. Advocates of the cloze test, especially Oller (1979), pointed out that many of the blanks could be filled successfully only by picking up on contextual clues in other sentences or paragraphs of the text. Thus, in this sense the whole text forms the context that we draw on to interpret the individual lexical items within it.

However, from a communicative point of view, context is more than just a *linguistic* phenomenon. Vocabulary ability also draws on the various types of pragmatic knowledge specified by Bachman and Palmer (see Table 1.1 in Chapter 1). In other words, the social and cultural situation in which lexical items are used significantly influence their meaning. I mentioned this earlier as a significant feature of lexical phrases, but the same applies to single words as well.

Let me give some examples to illustrate the point. These examples do not involve second language learners, but they nicely highlight some of the effects of context on word meaning and by implication show what learners are up against in developing a high level of lexical ability in their second language.

When I was in secondary school, one of my classmates returned home one day and told his mother that the movie he had just seen was 'deadly'. She was surprised that this seemed to be a term of approval for him because to her it meant that the movie had been terribly boring. However, in our teenage slang of the time, *deadly* was applied to anything that we considered really good. In telling us this anecdote later, my classmate was intrigued by the fact that a word that had such a positive association for our generation when used in this way apparently had just the opposite connotation for our parents.

Another interesting example is reported by Holmes (1995). As a professor at a New Zealand university, she had recently served on several appointment panels and in that capacity had been reading referees' reports written on behalf of applicants. As a linguist she was interested to note an ambiguity involving the word *quite* in references written by scholars in the US, who made statements such as 'X's basic scientific training is quite strong' and 'I was quite impressed with X'. Holmes's New Zealand colleagues interpreted the word as having a qualifying function here (meaning 'fairly' or 'to a certain extent'), whereas the American writers were using it as an intensifier (meaning 'very' or 'to the fullest extent'). Obviously this was a significant mis-interpretation because it meant that the readers were interpreting the reference as giving less support to the applicant than the writer in-tended. This could even have affected the applicant's chances of being offered the job.

A third illustration comes from a pioneering article on vocabulary testing by Cronbach (1942), who wanted to find out how well under-graduate students in an introductory psychology course knew the meanings of technical terms in psychology. At the beginning of the course, the students were given a checklist of terms and asked to indicate which ones they knew. Then at the next class they were required to explain in their own words the meaning of a selection of the terms. Cronbach found that the checklist was not a good indicator of the students' knowledge of the terms, especially in the case of ones like *reflex, perspective, probable error* and *maturation*, which had other meanings that the students were familiar with. This meant that they could claim to 'know' the words without being able to explain their specific use in psychology.

Thus, we have here various ways in which context can affect lexical meaning:

- Differences across generations (teenagers vs. adults) and between colloquial and more formal uses of words.
- Differences in interpretation across language varieties (New Zealand vs. American English).
- Differences between everyday usage and specialised terminology in particular fields of study (e.g. in psychology).

I am sure that you can think of many other examples of contextual effects. Clearly, then, the influence of context needs to be incorporated into a definition of vocabulary ability. I have already signalled its importance with the context-independent – context-dependent dimension of my assessment framework and we will frequently return to the role of context in later chapters of the book.

Chapelle (1994: 164) proposes the theory of context developed by Halliday and Hasan (1989) as a suitable framework for looking at context from a social perspective rather than a purely linguistic one. The theory consists of three complex elements, termed **field, tenor** and **mode**, which can be used to analyse how the features of spoken or written language relate to aspects of the social situation in which the language is being used. Field includes the type of activity that the language users are engaged in and the subject matter involved. Tenor refers to the relative social status of the language users and their role relationship. Mode covers the channel of communication, and in particular the features that distinguish speech from writing. Thus, to use Chapelle's examples, the kind of vocabulary ability that learners need for reading a newspaper at home is quite different from that required for listening to a chemistry lecture in a classroom. I discuss this social dimension of vocabulary use in more depth in Chapter 8.

Vocabulary knowledge and fundamental processes

The second component in Chapelle's (1994) framework of vocabulary ability is the one that has received the most attention from applied linguists and second language teachers. Chapelle outlines four dimensions of this component:

- Vocabulary size: This refers to the number of words that a person knows. In work with native speakers scholars have attempted to measure the total size of their vocabulary by taking a sample of words from a large unabridged dictionary. In the case of second language learners the goal is normally more modest: it is to estimate how many of the more common words they know based on a test of their knowledge of a sample of items from a word-frequency list. I discuss this further in Chapter 4 and in Chapter 5 we look at two vocabulary-size tests. As Chapelle (1994: 165) points out, though, if we follow the logic of a communicative approach to vocabulary ability, we should not just seek to measure vocabulary size in an absolute sense, but rather in relation to particular contexts of use. For example, how adequate is the learner's vocabulary for reading an international news magazine, as distinct from discussing a tennis match with friends or completing a lab report for a university engineering course?

- Knowledge of word characteristics: I discussed the frameworks developed by Richards (1976) and Nation (1990) earlier in the chapter, and this is where they fit into Chapelle's definition. Just as native speakers do, second language learners know more about some words than others. Their understanding of particular lexical items may range from vague to more precise (Cronbach, 1942). As Laufer (1990) points out, learners are likely to be confused about some of the words that they have learned, because the words share certain common features, e.g. *affect, effect; quite, quiet; simulate, stimulate; embrace, embarrass*. And again, as with vocabulary size, the extent to which a learner knows a word varies according to the context in which it is used.

  The other two dimensions of this component are potentially significant areas of second language acquisition research on vocabulary, with less direct application to practical assessment activities at this stage. The role of vocabulary tests here is more as research tools than as assessment instruments, until the researchers have established a sounder basis for interpreting test-taker performance in ways that are relevant to language teaching and learning.

- Lexicon organization: This concerns the way in which words and other lexical items are stored in the brain. Aitchison's book *Words in the Mind* (1994) provides a comprehensive and very readable account of psycholinguistic research on the mental lexicon of proficient language users. There is a research role here for vocabulary tests to explore the developing lexicon of second language learners and the ways in which their lexical storage differs from that of native speakers. Meara (1984; 1992b) has worked in this area using word-association and lexical-network tasks.

• Fundamental vocabulary processes: Language users apply these processes to gain access to their knowledge of vocabulary, both for understanding and for their own speaking and writing. Psycholinguists have identified a substantial number of processes of this kind. Obviously they operate faster and more automatically for native speakers than for less proficient learners, who have gaps in their knowledge of L2 words as well as, perhaps, a mental lexicon that is less efficiently organised. Meara (personal communication) has sought to measure automaticity by testing people's ability to recognise hidden English words quickly, and preliminary research results indicated that even non-native speakers with large vocabularies perform the task much more slowly than native speakers do.

Metacognitive strategies for vocabulary use

This is the third component of Chapelle's definition of vocabulary ability, and is what Bachman (1990) refers to as 'strategic competence'. The strategies are employed by all language users to manage the ways that they use their vocabulary knowledge in communication. Most of the time, we operate these strategies without being aware of it. It is only when we have to undertake unfamiliar or cognitively demanding communication tasks that the strategies become more conscious. For example, I am carefully choosing my words as I write this chapter, trying (or should that be *attempting* or *striving*, perhaps?) both to express the ideas clearly and to get/achieve the level of (in)formality that the editors seem to be looking for. Here are some other situations in which native speakers may need to apply more conscious strategies: deciphering illegible handwriting in a personal letter, reading aloud a scripted speech, breaking the news of a relative's death to a young child, or conversing with a foreigner. As language teachers we become skilled at modifying the vocabulary that we use so that our learners can readily understand us. By contrast you have probably observed inexperienced native speakers failing to communicate with foreigners because they use slang expressions, they do not articulate key words clearly, they are unable to rephrase an utterance that the other person has obviously not understood and so on. Of course, more is involved in all these cases than just vocabulary, but the point is that lexical strategies play a significant role.

Learners have a particular need for metacognitive strategies in communication situations because they have to overcome their lack of vocabulary knowledge in order to function effectively. Blum-Kulka and Levenston (1983) see these strategies in terms of general processes of simplification. The basic approach when learners are attempting to express themselves in speech or writing is avoidance. Learners may avoid using a specific lexical item either because they simply do not know it or because they are not confident about producing it with its correct pronunciation, spelling or grammatical form. Some particular strategies discussed by Blum-Kulka and Levenston and other researchers in this field (e.g. Tarone, Cohen and Dumas, 1983) are the following:

- Paraphrase: using *a dog's house* for *a kennel*; or *a thing you dry your hands on* for *a towel*.
- Language switch: when the learner uses an L1 word to substitute for an unknown L2 one, as when a French speaker says *We get this HOSTIE from LE PRÊTRE.*
- Use of superordinate terms: when the learner uses a more general term in place of a specific one, as in *tool* for *hammer*.
- Appeal to authority: asking *How do you say 'staple' in French?*

I discuss the research on communication strategies in more detail in Chapter 3.

In language testing, we are most likely to observe the effects of these metacognitive strategies in speaking tests. Recently several researchers (e.g. Ross and Berwick, 1992; Young and Milanovic, 1992; Young, 1995) have been looking at oral proficiency interviews and using techniques from discourse analysis in order to find out to what extent the interviews are like real-life conversations. Ross and Berwick (1992) discuss how interviewers may 'accommodate', or adjust, their way of speaking if they perceive early on that the interviewee is operating at a fairly low level of proficiency. This may lead an interviewer in the end to give the test-taker a lower rating than is justified because the interviewer has 'overaccommodated' and is not able to elicit the best performance that the learner is capable of producing. Ross and Berwick identify lexical simplification as one of the accommodation strategies that interviewers use, and it would also be interesting to investigate to what extent the test-takers' lexical strategies in an interview affect the way that their performance is assessed. Something similar could be done for writing tests too, to see how raters are influenced by the lexical features of the learner's text in judging the overall quality of the writing.

On the receptive side, the obvious situation in which learners need to apply metacognitive strategies is when they encounter in their reading words that they have never seen before. They have various options:

- read on without trying to understand the word;
- look it up in a dictionary or a glossary;
- ask the teacher or some other proficient person what it means; or
- try to guess the meaning using contextual clues.

This last strategy is one that is often recommended to be explicitly taught to learners. For example, Clarke and Nation (1980; see also Nation, 1990: 160–166) devised a five-step strategy that learners can use to guess unknown words. As with other aspects of reading or listening performance, though, it is not so obvious in a test situation whether a test-taker is applying such strategies and, if so, how successfully, unless test items are carefully designed for this specific purpose.

Overall, Chapelle's definition outlines the range of concepts, research areas and assessment activities that need to be incorporated into a comprehensive framework of vocabulary ability. While not seeking to isolate it from other language abilities, Chapelle has highlighted the broad role that vocabulary plays in language competence and performance. In terms of my dimensions of vocabulary assessment, she has defined vocabulary as a discrete construct, in contrast to the embedded way in which it is defined in Bachman and Palmer's (1996) formulation of language ability. Thus, her construct definition allows us to identify more carefully what particular vocabulary tests are designed to measure and to see how one kind of test is related to another.

Conclusion

My intention in this chapter has been to draw attention to the complexity of the subject matter in any assessment of vocabulary. At the simplest level vocabulary consists of words, but even the concept of a word is challenging to define and classify. For a number of assessment purposes, it is important to clarify what is meant by a 'word' if the correct conclusions are to be drawn from the test results.

The strong association in our minds between vocabulary and single words tends to restrict our view of the topic. For this reason, during the writing of the book I considered the possibility of dispensing with both the terms **vocabulary** and **word** as much as possible in favour of terms like **lexicon**, **lexis** and **lexical item**, in order to signal that I was adopting a much broader conception than the traditional ideas about vocabulary. In the end, I have retained 'vocabulary' as the term for the subject matter and I have also used 'word' much more than 'lexical item' to refer to the individual unit, unless multi-word items are specifically included. This reflects the reality that a large proportion of current research and practice in vocabulary assessment still focuses on knowledge and use of individual words. Nevertheless, it is necessary to keep the broader view in mind, especially in the light of current and likely future developments in the field.

One implication of the broader view is that vocabulary assessment needs to take account of multi-word lexical items. Admittedly, further basic research is required to identify these items more definitively and understand their functions in normal language use. To the extent that language teachers decide it is worthwhile for their students to spend time formally learning the meaning and use of multi-word items, there is a role for discrete, selective tests to assess how successful the learners have been in acquiring them. However, I suspect that longer lexical items have a significant contribution to make in the development of embedded and comprehensive measures of learner performance in task-based language tests. If a learner is able to handle these items both productively and receptively in communication, this seems to indicate a high level of proficiency in the language. Therefore, it would be useful to explore ways in which that ability can be assessed: through the design of specific item types, through the way in which rating scales are defined, or through the use of various frequency counts as comprehensive measures.

The other issue I have discussed in this chapter is how to define vocabulary as a construct. Construct definition plays a central part in the validation of language tests because, unless we are clear about what it is we are setting out to assess, there is a real danger of making a faulty interpretation of the test results. Most attention up until now has focused on the concept of vocabulary knowledge. As I have indicated, there have been numerous efforts to specify the components of vocabulary knowledge and to propose what the key variables are. Although there is still work to be done to clarify the knowledge construct, Chapelle's work points the way towards a definition of vocabulary ability that covers a wider range of assessment purposes and at the same time is consistent with Bachman and Palmer's general construct of language ability. Whereas a construct of vocabulary knowledge may be satisfactory as the basis for the design of discrete, selective and context-independent tests, Chapelle's definition provides a better theoretical foundation for a construct that can incorporate embedded, comprehensive and context-dependent vocabulary measures as well.

CHAPTER THREE

....

Research on vocabulary acquisition and use

Introduction

The focus of this chapter is on research in second language vocabulary acquisition and use. There are three reasons for reviewing this research in a book on vocabulary assessment. The first is that the researchers are significant users of vocabulary tests as instruments in their studies. In other words, the purpose of vocabulary assessment is not only to make decisions about what individual learners have achieved in a teaching/learning context but also to advance our understanding of the processes of vocabulary acquisition. Secondly, in the absence of much recent interest in vocabulary among language testers, acquisition researchers have often had to deal with assessment issues themselves as they devised the instruments for their research. The third reason is that the results of their research can contribute to a better understanding of the nature of the construct of vocabulary ability, which – as I explained in the previous chapter – is important for the validation of vocabulary tests.

Although the amount of research on second language vocabulary acquisition has increased in recent years, the field has tended to lack coherence. As Meara (1993) pointed out, there have been many one-off studies by researchers who then moved on to other areas; only a handful of scholars have built a sustained record of research on second language vocabulary. I do not attempt to carry out a comprehensive review of the field here (for overviews, see Harley, 1995; Coady and Huckin, 1997; Schmitt and McCarthy, 1997), but rather I have selected four topic areas which have been extensively researched and offer insights on vocabulary assessment. In dealing with each area, I first survey some of the significant studies and then consider the assessment issues that arise.

The first two topics are complementary in that they represent two major processes by which learners add new words to their vocabulary. One involves systematic procedures to memorise the form and meaning of words, usually based on lists of L2 words together with their translation equivalents in the learners' L1. It is a form of learning that went out of fashion – among language teachers, if not learners – with the advent of communicative approaches to language teaching. The other process is incidental vocabulary learning, by which learners acquire knowledge of new words incrementally as they encounter them in context through their reading and listening activities. This is presumed to be the main way that native speakers of a language expand their vocabulary knowledge.

The third topic is linked to the second one. It focuses on the extent to which learners can infer the meaning of unknown words when they read or hear them. Two significant issues here are what kind of contextual clues are available and whether learners can be trained to use those clues to make successful guesses about the meaning of unknown words. The fourth topic is learners' use of communication strategies to cope with situations where they lack the vocabulary to put across the meanings that they want to express. The third and fourth topics are complementary in the sense that both are concerned with ways that learners can overcome their limited vocabulary knowledge when they are using the target language for communicative purposes.

There are two other research areas which could have been included in this chapter but, since they primarily involve the development of particular kinds of vocabulary tests, I have chosen to discuss them in Chapter 4. These are estimating learners' vocabulary size and the assessment of quality (or depth) of vocabulary knowledge.

Systematic vocabulary learning

Given the number of words that learners need to know if they are to achieve any kind of functional proficiency in a second language, it is understandable that researchers on language teaching have been interested in evaluating the relative effectiveness of different ways of learning new words.

The starting point for research in this area is the traditional approach to vocabulary learning, which involves working through a list of L2 words together with their L1 glosses/translations and memorising the word–gloss pairs. A great deal of research has been motivated by two questions arising from this kind of learning from lists:

1 What characteristics of the words – and the way they are presented to the learners – tend to make learning easier or more difficult?
2 Surely there are better techniques than rote memorisation for committing these items to memory?

The findings of studies that address both of these issues have been reviewed by a number of authors (e.g. Higa, 1965; Nation, 1982; Cohen, 1987; Nation, 1990: Chapter 3; Ellis and Beaton, 1993b, Laufer, 1997b). In brief, some of the significant findings are as follows:

- Words belonging to different word classes vary according to how difficult they are to learn. Rodgers (1969) found that nouns are easiest to learn, following by adjectives; on the other hand, verbs and adverbs were the most difficult. Ellis and Beaton (1993b) confirmed that nouns are easier than verbs, because learners can form mental images of them more readily.
- Mnemonic techniques are very effective methods for gaining an initial knowledge of word meanings in a second language (Cohen, 1987; Hulstijn, 1997). One method in particular, the keyword technique, has been extensively researched (see, for example, Paivio and Desrochers, 1981; Pressley, Levin and McDaniel, 1987). It involves teaching learners to form vivid mental images which link the meanings of an L2 word and an L1 word that has a similar sound. This technique works best for the receptive learning of concrete words.
- In order to be able to retrieve L2 words from memory – rather than just recognising them when presented – learners need to say the word to themselves as they learn it (Ellis and Beaton, 1993a).
- Words which are hard to pronounce are learned more slowly than ones that do not have significant pronunciation difficulty (Rodgers, 1969; Ellis and Beaton, 1993b).
- Learners at a low level of language learning store vocabulary according to the sound of words, whereas at more advanced levels words are stored according to meaning (Henning, 1973).
- Lists of words which are strongly associated with each other – like

opposites (*rich, poor*) or word sets (*shirt, jacket, sweater*) – are significantly more difficult to learn than lists of unrelated words, because of the cross-association that occurs among the related words (Higa, 1963; Tinkham, 1993).

- More generally, learners commonly confuse L2 words which look and sound alike (Laufer, 1997b).

In his surveys of the field of L2 vocabulary acquisition, Meara (1980; 1994) has pointed out the limitations of this area of research. It can be seen as part of a wider tradition of psychological research on the role of memory in language processing. Researchers have generally used some form of experimental design to investigate the effects of particular variables on the learning of words in a second language under laboratory conditions. Quite apart from defects that can be identified in the design of specific studies, Meara questions whether the research findings as a whole tell us much that is useful about how real language learners go about learning new words. The subjects have typically been university students with no prior knowledge of the language to which the target words belong and no intention of studying it. The learning activity takes place over a short period of time and involves a relatively small number of words. The range of memorising techniques investigated also tends to be limited.

A broader issue is whether real language learners – as distinct from the subjects of vocabulary learning experiments – should be encouraged to learn sets of words by means of memorising techniques. As we saw in Chapter 2, there is much more to vocabulary knowledge than just having an associative link between an L2 word and an equivalent word or phrase in L1. This is one reason why the trend in the 1990s is for many language teachers to discourage learners from memorising lists of isolated words, on the basis that vocabulary should always be learned in context. Nevertheless, research shows that systematic learning of individual words can provide a good foundation for vocabulary development, especially in foreign-language environments where learners have limited exposure to the language outside of the classroom. Nation (1982) made a careful analysis of various arguments that could be put forward to support the learn-in-context view, as applied to the initial learning of new words, and concluded that it was a statement of belief rather than a principle supported by the research evidence. Similarly, Carter (1987: 168–169) acknowledged that it:

has not been convincingly demonstrated that the information
learners obtain from meeting words in a variety of contexts is
more beneficial, either in terms of knowledge of forms or meanings of lexical items, than either translation or simply looking up
the word in a dictionary.

Whatever the merits of memorising words from lists, the fact is that
most of the research evidence we have about systematic vocabulary
learning comes from controlled experiments that focus on a particular
strategy. However, a small number of studies have gone beyond the
experimental paradigm by, for example, looking at vocabulary learning over a more extended period of time (Cohen and Aphek, 1981;
Schmitt, 1998c) or investigating the strategies that learners themselves use to add new words to their vocabulary in or out of the
classroom (Ahmed, 1989; Lawson and Hogben, 1996). The latter two
studies both involved presenting learners with a set of L2 words and
requiring them to think aloud as they went through the process of
learning each one in preparation for a test. A range of strategies were
identified and both studies found that good vocabulary learners ac-
tively employ a larger number of different strategies than those who
are poor learners. Sanaoui (1995) undertook more naturalistic research, asking adult learners of English and French in Canada to
report their vocabulary learning activities over several weeks. She
found that while some learners spend a lot of time independently
listing, memorising and practising new words, others rely mostly on
classroom work to build their vocabulary knowledge. In another
recent project, Schmitt (1997) surveyed a large sample of Japanese
learners of English concerning their use of 40 different vocabulary
learning strategies. The most popular one was using a bilingual dictionary, while other strategies that the learners frequently used and
also found helpful were written repetition, oral repetition, saying the
word aloud, studying the word's spelling and taking notes in class.
There was some evidence that learners change their strategies as they
progress from junior high school to learning as adults.

Assessment issues

As for the assessment implications, the design of tests to evaluate how
well students have learned a set of new words is straightforward,
particularly if the learning task is restricted to memorising the asso-

ciation between an L2 word and its L1 meaning. It simply involves presenting the test-takers with one word and asking them to supply the other-language equivalent. However, as Ellis and Beaton (1993b) note, it makes a difference whether they are required to translate into or out of their own language. For example, English native speakers learning German words find it easier to supply the English meaning in response to the German word (i.e. to translate into the L1) than to give the German word for an English meaning (i.e. to translate into the L2). In the former case, it is 'receptive' knowledge that is being assessed and, in the latter, 'productive' knowledge. I have more to say about this distinction as it applies to vocabulary-test design in Chapter 6.

This, then, is the classic situation in which a discrete, selective and context-independent vocabulary test is the appropriate measure to use. Since the learning task is limited, the test format is similarly limited in its demands on the test-taker and in what we can infer from the test results. Conventional discrete-point vocabulary tests of the kind that I illustrated in Chapter 1 are suitable for the purpose (see also Madsen, 1983: Chapter 2; Heaton, 1988: Chapter 5). Test items can be designed to assess not only the basic meaning of a word, but also its derived forms, its spelling, its synonyms and other words associated with it; they can also be designed to assess the grammatical structures into which a word fits.

Incidental vocabulary learning

Since the early 1980s a number of reading researchers have focused on vocabulary acquisition by native speakers of English. While there is a great deal of variation in the estimates of the number of words known by native speakers of various ages and levels of education, there is general agreement that vocabulary acquisition occurs at an impressivly fast rate from childhood throughout the years of formal education and at a slower pace on into adult life. On the face of it, a large proportion of these words are not taught by parents or teachers, or indeed learned in any formal way. The most plausible explanation for this is that native speakers acquire words 'incidentally' as they encounter them in the speech and writing of other people.

The term **incidental** often causes problems in the discussion of research on this kind of vocabulary acquisition. In practice it usually means that the research subjects are given a reading or listening task without being told to focus on the vocabulary in the input and without being warned that they will be taking a vocabulary test after completing the task. It does not mean that any vocabulary learning which occurs is 'unconscious' from the learner's point of view. Applied linguists have different views on whether unconscious learning is even possible. Schmidt (1990), who has published influential work on consciousness in second language acquisition, argues that learners do not acquire knowledge of words or any other elements of language unless they ('consciously') notice them in some sense. On the other hand, Ellis's (1997) position is that, while the semantic aspects of vocabulary are consciously acquired, we learn word forms and how they collocate with other words in a largely unconscious way.

Research with native speakers

The first step in investigating this kind of vocabulary acquisition was to obtain evidence that it actually occurs. Teams of reading researchers in the United States (Jenkins, Stein and Wysocki, 1984; Nagy, Herman and Anderson, 1985; Nagy, Anderson and Herman, 1987) undertook a series of studies with native-English-speaking school children. The basic research design involved asking the subjects to read texts appropriate to their age level that contained unfamiliar words. The children were not told that the researchers were interested in vocabulary. After they had completed the reading task, they were given unannounced at least one test of their knowledge of the target words in the text. Then the researchers obtained a measure of vocabulary learning by comparing the test scores of the students who had read a particular text with those of other students who had not. The results showed that, in these terms, a small, statistically significant amount of learning had indeed occurred. In their 1985 study, Nagy, Herman and Anderson estimated that the probability of learning a word while reading was between 10 and 25 per cent (depending how strict the criterion was for knowing a word), whereas in the 1987 study they calculated a probability of just 5 per cent. One reason for the discrepancy was that in the latter study the test was administered six days after the children did the reading task rather than immediately afterwards.

I have given a simplified description of the research design because the full details need not concern us here. You may be thinking of some of the questions raised by this kind of research, most of which have been addressed in at least one of the studies. How do we know that the subjects did not already have some knowledge of the target words? Do the texts provide clues as to the meaning of the words? How adequate is the multiple-choice format as a way of assessing knowledge of the words? What does it really mean to say that a word has been 'learned'? Has learning occurred in any meaningful sense if the subjects are tested as soon as they have finished reading the text?

We will return to the assessment aspects of this research later but first let me mention a couple of ways in which the basic findings have been extended. In a recent study modelled on Nagy, Anderson and Herman (1987), Shu, Anderson and Zhang (1995) found that school children in Beijing reading texts in Chinese exhibited the same kind of learning of unfamiliar words that American children reading in English did. And Elley (1989) has shown that incidental learning also occurs through listening. He tested young New Zealand school children after they had listened to a story read aloud to them by teachers. When the children were absorbed and entertained by the story, they made significant gains in knowledge of the target words, even when the teacher gave no explanation of them at all. Moreover, the gains were maintained for a three-month period after the experimental treatment.

Second language research

Now, how about incidental learning of *second* language vocabulary? In a study that predates the L1 research in the US, Saragi, Nation and Meister (1978) gave a group of native speakers of English the task of reading Anthony Burgess's novel *A Clockwork Orange*, which contains a substantial number of Russian-derived words functioning as an argot used by the young delinquents who are the main characters in the book. When the subjects were subsequently tested, it was found on average that they could recognise the meaning of 76 per cent of the 90 target words. Pitts, White and Krashen (1989) used just excerpts from the novel with two groups of American university students and also found some evidence of vocabulary learning; however, as you might expect, the reduced scope of the study resulted in fewer target words being correctly understood: an average of only two words out of 30 tested. If you have read the novel yourself, you may recall how you were able to gain a reasonable understanding of what most of the Russian words meant by repeated exposure to them as the story progressed. Of course, since Burgess deliberately composed the text of the novel to facilitate this kind of 'incidental acquisition', it represents an unusual kind of reading material that is significantly different from the prose that learners normally encounter.

Other researchers have obtained evidence of incidental vocabulary learning using a variety of shorter texts. I can mention here the study by Day, Omura and Hiramatsu (1991) involving Japanese university students reading a fictional story in English set in Africa, and the one by Dupuy and Krashen (1993) where American students of French read part of a French film script containing colloquial expressions that they were unlikely to be familiar with.

Such experiments show that there is incidental learning of vocabulary in the sense that learners who are set a reading task without being told to pay attention to vocabulary nonetheless demonstrate some understanding of a few previously unknown words in the text when they are given a test shortly after they have completed the reading. As Horst, Cobb and Meara (1998: 208–210) point out, this is a limited finding because there are various weaknesses in the way the studies were designed and carried out. In addition, it gives us no insight into the way that the learners process the words in the text psycholinguistically as they read. It does not tell us whether any of the words have been retained by the learners in their mental lexicon and will be remembered when they are encountered again on some future occasion. Furthermore, we need to know which variables affect the probability that particular words will be acquired and, as a more practical goal, how teachers and learners can enhance vocabulary acquisition through reading and listening activities.

There is no model of the process of vocabulary acquisition that we can turn to for guidance in considering these issues. However, some of the research provides useful insights into certain aspects. Hulstijn (1992) reports on a series of experiments on incidental learning during reading that he conducted in Holland. In these studies the learning was incidental in the sense that the subjects were not informed in advance that they would be tested on their vocabulary knowledge. However, the focus on vocabulary was made salient by the fact that in the experimental conditions various kinds of assistance were provided in the margin of the text to help the learners understand the target words. Hulstijn found evidence for his hypothesis that the amount of mental effort that learners put into understanding an unknown word would positively influence their chances of retaining its meaning. When the subjects were provided with a cue designed to encourage them to work out the meaning for themselves, they remembered it better than if they were simply given a synonym or translation.

Other research has looked at the effects of giving learners access to dictionaries while they read. Luppescu and Day (1993) found that Japanese learners who were allowed to use a bilingual dictionary scored higher on a vocabulary post-test than students who were not allowed to. In this case, the researchers were not able to observe or record the extent to which the dictionary group actually made use of their dictionaries. However, new technology offers ways of overcoming the problem. Current computer programs can provide dictionary entries online by means of hypertext links, which means that learners reading a text on the screen can click on an unknown word and a definition appears. In addition, the computer can be programmed to keep an unobtrusive record of which entries the learners consult and how often they do it. Taking advantage of these features, Knight (1994) confirmed Luppescu and Day's finding: students with access to the computerised dictionary (the experimental group) demonstrated more vocabulary knowledge after reading than those who did not. Within the experimental group, students of low ability seemed to gain more from using the dictionary entries than those with high ability. Hulstijn (1993) found no significant difference in post-test vocabulary scores between students who looked up many words and those who looked up only a few. A further development, in studies by Chun and Plass (1996), is the use of multimedia programs, in which definitions can be provided not only in textual form but also as pictures and video clips. In this case, there was evidence that access to these multiple annotations of words meant that the students engaged in more active learning behaviour and achieved higher scores in the vocabulary post-test.

Vocabulary learning from listening has received much less attention than learning through reading, but there are a couple of recent research projects that have explored this area. One is a study by Brown (1993) in an American-university intensive-English course, where she investigated the students' acquisition of vocabulary used in the videodisc program *Raiders of the Lost Ark*. She was particularly interested in factors that influenced the learning of unfamiliar words. It appeared that, in terms of frequency, learning was associated with the general frequency of words in the language rather than how often they occurred in that particular text. In addition, she found that words were more likely to be learned if they were salient, in the sense of being important for understanding a specific part of the program.

The other listening study, by Ellis (1995), drew on earlier work reported in Ellis, Tanaka and Yamazaki (1994). In this research Japanese high-school students listened to a set of directions in English about how to locate various objects in a picture of a kitchen. One group heard directions which had been modified in advance to make them easier for non-native speakers to understand. The other group heard the directions in a form that was more suitable for native speakers, but they also had the opportunity to ask for clarification while they were listening. The results showed that the latter group gained consistently higher post-test scores. However, since they took much longer to complete the task – because of the time taken to respond to their questions – their rate of acquisition (in words per minute of input time) was much slower than that of the group which heard the premodified directions. Another important distinction made by Ellis in his analysis was between comprehension (ability to locate objects correctly in the picture while listening) and acquisition (retention of some knowledge of what the names of the objects meant for a period of time after the listening task was completed). He found only a weak relationship between the two: 'there were many cases where comprehension was high but acquisition low . . . and, conversely, cases where comprehension was quite low but acquisition high' (Ellis, 1995: 424–425). A third finding of interest was that the range of contexts (i.e. number of directions) in which a word occurred was positively related to acquisition. As in the Brown (1993) study, simple frequency of the words in the input was not a significant variable.

Assessment issues

Now, what are the testing issues that arise from this research on incidental vocabulary acquisition? One concerns the need for a pre-test. A basic assumption made in these studies is that the target words are not known by the subjects. To some extent, it is possible to rely on teachers' judgements or word-frequency counts to select words that a particular group of learners are unlikely to know, but it is preferable to have some more direct evidence. The use of a pre-test allows the researchers to select from a set of potential target words ones that none of the subjects are familiar with. Alternatively, if the learners turn out to have knowledge of some of the words, the test results can provide a baseline against which post-test scores can be evaluated. The problem, however, is that if a vocabulary test is given before the learners undertake the reading or listening task, they will be alerted to the fact that the researchers are interested in vocabulary and thus the 'incidental' character of any learning that occurs may be reduced, if not lost entirely.

Various solutions to this problem have been adopted. In some of the research where the subjects were reading texts in their first language, the type of target items used could be assumed to be unfamiliar without giving a pre-test. For example, the researchers who used *A Clockwork Orange* had only to ensure that none of their subjects had studied Russian. And in the two experiments by Hulstijn (1992) that involved subjects who were reading in their first language, the target items were 'pseudo-words' created by the researcher. An L2 study that did not involve a pre-test is the one by Dupuy and Krashen (1993), who relied instead on the highly colloquial nature of the target items, plus the fact that a control group of learners who were at a more advanced level of proficiency than the experimental subjects showed very little familiarity with the items. Where a pre-test has been used, the researchers have taken steps to reduce the possibility that it would affect the incidental nature of the vocabulary learning. Nagy, Herman and Anderson (1985) and Shu, Anderson and Zhang (1995) gave the children the pre-test one week in advance, and it contained a variety of other items in addition to the target words. The pre-test in Ellis's (1995) study, which was administered one month before the listening task, was used to select 18 target items that were unknown to any of the subjects.

Timing is also relevant to the post-tests used in these studies. The issue here is what is really meant by vocabulary 'learning'. A test given immediately after the completion of the reading or listening task could be said to measure whether the learners have some understanding of the vocabulary items while the text is still fresh in their

minds but it does not give an indication of whether they will remember them on a longer term basis. If the concept of learning
includes the notion of retention over time, the administration of the
post-test needs to be delayed for a period after the subjects have been
exposed to the input material. Thus, studies in which only immediate
post-tests were given (for example, Dupuy and Krashen, 1993; Luppescu and Day, 1993; Shu, Anderson and Zhang, 1995) can be said to
have assessed vocabulary learning only in a limited sense. In contrast,
Ellis (1995) clearly distinguished between 'comprehension', as measured by responses made by the subjects as they listened, and 'acquisition', which was assessed in three subsequent tests given two days,
one month, and two and a half months later.

One interesting phenomenon observed in a few of the studies was
that the learners gained a slightly higher mean score in a later post-
test than in an earlier one. Chun and Plass (1996) found that this
applied to words for which a picture was used to annotate the
meaning but not to words with textual or video annotations. They
explained this result by reference to a 'hypermnesia effect', by which
good static images are recalled better over time, whereas words and
transient images tend to be forgotten. In Ellis's (1995) study, a verbal–
visual distinction was also relevant. His first two post-tests involved
translation of decontextualised words, whereas the last one required
the subjects to label the same pictures that had been used for the
listening task itself. Ellis suggests that the pictures triggered recall in a
way that the target words by themselves did not. Thus, apart from the
timing issue, these findings highlight the need to consider the format
of the tests to be used as dependent measures in experiments of this
kind and in particular the form of the stimulus material.

But probably the most important testing issue that comes out of the
work on incidental vocabulary learning is how to conceptualise and
measure the gains in knowledge that occur as a result of the learners'
reading or listening activities. Typically in these studies the learning
of the experimental subjects is expressed in terms of getting a larger
number of items in the post-test correct, as compared with a control
group of learners. Another way of stating this is to say that a small
number of the target words change from being 'unknown' to 'known'
after the subjects have read or heard the text. However, as I noted in
Chapter 2, native speakers and learners alike have varying levels of
knowledge of the vocabulary that they have acquired and it seems
unreasonable to assume that words will be 'fully known' by a learner

after being encountered in a single text on just one occasion. It is more realistic to expect that learners will acquire a degree of partial knowledge of some of the target words. Given the lack of a model of second language vocabulary development that would guide us in devising suitable measures of partial knowledge, scholars who have addressed this issue have adopted essentially pragmatic solutions using two kinds of instrument: rating scales and specially constructed multiple-choice items.

To see what has been done, let us return first to Nagy, Herman and Anderson (1985), which was a ground-breaking study in a number of respects. In their research with eighth-grade American students reading in English, they used two tests that were designed to measure even small increases in vocabulary knowledge. The first was an interview conducted shortly after the reading task, in which the subjects were asked to explain the meaning of the target words. Their explanations were rated on this four point scale:

0 – no correct knowledge
1 – minimal partial knowledge
2 – incomplete answer which displayed substantial partial knowledge
3 – totally correct answer

The second test of partial knowledge consisted of a set of multiple-choice items. Each target word was tested by three items at varying levels of difficulty, determined by how specific the correct answer was and how closely the distractors were related in meaning to it. For example, in the case of the word *gendarme*, the Level One (easy) item was:

gendarme means:

a) to trick or trap someone
b) policeman
c) spoken as if one was out of breath or having trouble breathing
d) the secret collection of information about another country
e) the illegal transportation of goods across a border
f) don't know

On the other hand, the difficult (Level Three) item looked like this:

gendarme means:

a) policeman
b) bellboy
c) bodyguard
d) spy
e) waiter
f) don't know

It is clear from these examples that the subjects needed a rather more precise understanding of the word to answer the difficult item correctly as compared with the easy one. In constructing the test, the researchers took steps to separate the three items for each word, in order to reduce the possibility that responding to the easy item would assist the students in answering the more difficult ones.

In the second language research, the same idea was adopted in a more limited way by Dupuy and Krashen (1993). They used multiple-choice items in which one of the two distractors shared semantic features with the correct answer. In one analysis of the results, subjects who chose that distractor were given partial credit for knowing the target word.

One significant feature of Nagy, Herman and Anderson's (1985) study was that more than one kind of test was used to capture evidence of partial vocabulary learning. Following their lead, Joe (1995) adopted three different ways of measuring what adult L2 learners gained from reading an expository text and then retelling the information to a listener who had not read it. One was a test consisting of easy and difficult multiple-choice items for each of the target words in the text. Secondly, there was an interview in which each learner was asked to explain the meaning of the words, and their responses were rated using a modified version of Paribakht and Wesche's (1993) Vocabulary Knowledge Scale (see Chapter 5). The third measure involved an analysis of the transcripts of the learners' retelling of the text to see how 'generatively' they used the target words in their own speech. That is to say, the learners were considered to have acquired more knowledge of the word if they used it in a novel way and in a different context from which it occurred in the source text.

Inferring word meanings from context

We move on now to consider the more practical concern in second language teaching of how learners deal with unknown words as they encounter them through reading or listening. As with incidental learning, the primary focus of the learner is on understanding spoken or written discourse but, especially in natural communication situations, there are inevitably unfamiliar lexical items, some of which may be crucial for adequate comprehension, and the learner should have ways of finding out what they mean. Teachers are aware of this problem in the classroom context and have a variety of techniques at their disposal to address it with texts that they use in class, such as pre-teaching the unknown words, providing glosses adjacent to the text or giving a quick oral translation of the word. However, learners also need to be able to apply their own strategies for dealing with unknown words outside of class. First, there is the metacognitive strategy of evaluating whether it is worth trying to figure out what the unknown lexical item is and, if not, simply ignoring it. If it does seem necessary to understand the item, the learner may look it up in a dictionary or ask someone to explain what it means, but the most important strategy is inferring the meaning from information available in the text itself. Inferencing is a desirable strategy because it involves deeper processing that is likely to contribute to better comprehension of the text as a whole and may result in some learning of the lexical item that would not otherwise occur.

A number of writers (e.g. Chandrasegaran, 1980; Clarke and Nation, 1980; Bruton and Samuda, 1981) have developed strategies for guessing words in context that can be taught to learners. The Clarke and Nation strategy, for instance, includes steps such as identifying the word class of the unknown word, scanning the surrounding sentence for other words that collocate with it, looking for cohesive devices that link the sentence with the other sentences in the text and analysing the structure of the word itself into prefix, root and suffix.

Questions about lexical inferencing

This topic is not purely a pedagogical concern. Inferencing by learners is of great interest in second language acquisition research and there are several types of empirical study that are relevant here. In reviewing this work, I find it helpful to start with five questions that seem to follow a logical sequence:

1 What kind of contextual information is available to readers to assist them in guessing the meaning of unknown words in texts?
2 Are such clues normally available to the reader in natural, unedited texts?
3 How well do learners infer the meaning of unknown words without being specifically trained to do so?
4 Is strategy training an effective way of developing learners' lexical inferencing skills?
5 Does successful inferencing lead to acquisition of the words?

Let us look briefly at each of these in turn before going on to consider what assessment issues arise from this area of research.

(1) There is a lengthy series of studies since the 1940s that set out to identify and classify the contextual clues that can assist both first and second language readers to make inferences about unknown words. In the L1 case, one influential framework is that developed by Sternberg and Powell (1983). They proposed a theory of learning from context that distinguishes between the *external* and *internal* context of the unknown word. The major components of their theory are presented in Table 3.1. The external context is categorised according to the kinds of semantic information that is available in the text surrounding the target word. Looking at their own example, 'At dawn, the *blen* arose on the horizon and shone brightly', we can see that 'At dawn' provides a temporal clue, 'arose' and 'shone brightly' give functional descriptive clues and 'on the horizon' offers a spatial clue. They identify a total of eight clue types of this kind. On the other hand, the internal context is simply the morphological structure of the word: prefix, stem and suffix. Thus, confronted with the word *thermoluminescence*, a native speaker of English may be able to identify *thermo-* as a prefix referring to heat, *luminesce* as a verb that probably means 'producing light' and *-ence* as a suffix that creates an abstract noun. This analysis, combined with some knowledge of the world, could lead to the correct inference that the word refers to the kind of light given off by heated objects.

One important component of Sternberg and Powell's theory is that, for each kind of context, there is a set of mediating variables which determine how effectively the reader is able to take advantage of the clues that are available. In the case of external context, an unknown word is more likely to be guessable if it occurs numerous times in a variety of contexts within the text, if it is clearly an important word to

Table 3.1 *Components of a theory of learning words from context (from Sternberg and Powell, 1983)*

EXTERNAL CONTEXT

Contextual cues

Temporal cues	When/how often/for how long does X (the unknown word) occur?
Spatial cues	Where can X be found?
Value cues	How valuable or desirable is X? What do people feel about it?
Stative descriptive cues	What are the physical features of X (size, shape, colour, odour, feel, etc.)?
Functional descriptive cues	What are the purposes of X? What is it used for?
Causal/enablement cues	What causes X or enables it to occur?
Class membership cues	What class of things does X belong to?
Equivalence cues	What does X mean? What does it compare or contrast to?

Mediating variables

The number of occurrences of the unknown word

The variability of contexts in which multiple occurrences of the unknown words appear

The density of unknown words

The importance of the unknown words to understanding the context in which it is embedded

The perceived helpfulness of the surrounding context in understanding the meaning of the unknown word

The concreteness of the unknown word and the surrounding context

The usefulness of prior knowledge in cue utilisation

INTERNAL CONTEXT

Contextual cues

Prefix cues

Stem cues

Suffix cues

Interactive cues (where two or three word parts convey information in combination)

Mediating variables

The number of occurrences of the unknown word

The density of unknown words

The density of decomposable unknown words

The importance of the unknown word to understanding the context in which it is embedded

The usefulness of previously known information in cue utilisation understand and if the context provides several useful clues. Related to the last point is the question of how many words in the text the reader does not know or, to put it another way, what the density of unknown words is. The mediating variables for internal context are similar. One that is significant is whether there are a number of words in the text that can be analysed internally into interpretable morphemes; if so, that would presumably encourage the reader to apply this strategy where possible to unknown words. You can imagine, for example, that the technical terms in a science text might often provide good internal clues to someone with a knowledge of word parts derived from Greek or Latin.

Although the Sternberg and Powell framework is comprehensive, it is by no means exhaustive. One category of clues that it does not cover are those that relate to the structure of the text, as revealed in the research by Ames (1966), who asked subjects to report what clues they actually used to make inferences about unknown words. Structural clues may be syntactic or discoursal. On a syntactic level, the reader needs to identify what part of speech the target word is and to search for grammatical clues in the clause and sentence where the word occurs. At the discourse level, the reader can look for expressions of language functions such as definition, comparison and contrast, cause–effect, question–answer and main idea–details.

Turning now to the work on second language reading (e.g. Carton, 1971; Honeyfield, 1977; Nation and Coady, 1988), we find that most of the variables that apply to L1 readers are considered relevant to the L2 case as well. One mediating variable that applies specifically to L2 readers is level of proficiency in the language. If the reader has a limited knowledge of the target-language vocabulary, this means that she or he will encounter a large number of unknown words. As a consequence, the reader may be unable to make use of contextual clues that are available in the text because the words which provide such clues for a particular target word are themselves unknown. In Sternberg and Powell's terms, the density of unknown words is typically higher for a second language reader than for a native speaker. Laufer (1992; 1997a) claims that second language readers of English need to have a vocabulary of at least 3000 word families in order to have some knowledge of 95 per cent of the running words in a text. With that kind of vocabulary size, the density of unknown words is reduced, on average, to 1 in 20.

An obvious source of clues that second language readers can use is knowledge of the vocabulary of their first language, and indeed of other languages that they have acquired, especially if the two languages are related or one has borrowed lexical items extensively from the other. Seibert (1945), who was a pioneer in writing about lexical inferencing in a second language, noted how the large number of cognate words shared by Western European languages allowed speakers of one language to guess the meaning of many words in one of the others. One of her English-speaking subjects who also knew French was able to guess 41 per cent of the words in a Spanish text correctly, without having ever studied Spanish.

(2) Writers on lexical inferencing often give the impression that, with such a wide range of contextual clues being available, every unknown word will have some clues, if only the reader knows how to find and interpret them. This optimistic view is reinforced by the common practice, both in research studies and in course books for learners, of presenting target words in contexts which have been chosen, edited or even specially written to offer clues that are aimed to give the learners a reasonable chance of guessing the words successfully. This approach may be justifiable if the primary objective is to train learners in the strategy of inferencing and to convince them it is worthwhile to apply the strategy to their own reading. However, the results of some of the research suggest the need for caution. For example, in their study of lexical guessing by students studying English as a foreign language at a university in Israel, Bensoussan and Laufer (1984) selected 70 target words from an unedited text of about 600 words. When the researchers themselves analysed the context for each target word, they discovered that there were no contextual clues for 29 (41 per cent) of them, while only 13 (19 per cent) of the remaining ones could be said to be clearly cued by the surrounding text.

Further evidence comes from two experiments by Schatz and Baldwin (1986) involving American senior high-school students in Florida. The researchers randomly selected paragraphs containing low-frequency words from novels, textbooks and periodicals and tested the students' understanding of the words by means of multiple-choice items (Experiment 1) and a definition-writing task (Experiment 2). They found that students who were given the words in context performed no better in the tests than a control group who responded to the words in isolation. Schatz and Baldwin do not report any analysis of the extent to which their paragraphs provided clues for each of the target words and there are other limitations to their study. For instance, they restricted the context in their test items to the sentence containing the target word, plus two adjacent ones. Nevertheless, the basic point is that we should not assume that the presence of context necessarily makes it easier for readers to understand the meaning of words that are unfamiliar to them.

(3) The third question that I posed about lexical guessing is how successful learners are if they have not been specifically trained to do it. Several researchers (Bensoussan and Laufer, 1984; Haynes, 1984; Laufer and Sim, 1985b) have set a guessing task which learners responded to in writing and then analysed how correct the guesses were. The general finding is that learners very frequently make wrong guesses – if in fact they guess at all. In Bensoussan and Laufer's (1984) study, the most common reaction to an unknown word was to make no attempt to guess. Wrong guesses resulted from giving the wrong meaning of a word that had several meanings, translating the individual morphemes of a word (*inconstant* rendered as 'internal constant'), mistranslating an idiom (*on the grounds* became 'on the earth') and confusing the target word with one that looked or sounded similar (*uniquely* translated as 'unequally'). More generally, learners have been found to make guesses on some narrow basis, producing an inferred meaning that has little relation to the wider context of the text.

On a more optimistic note, Liu and Nation (1985) reported that their learners could successfully guess most of the unknown words that they encountered in context. However, these 'learners' were in fact experienced teachers, including a few native speakers, who were taking a postgraduate course in teaching English as a second language. In addition, they were asked to guess mostly known English words that had been replaced by non-words in the text for the purposes of the research. Liu and Nation estimated that at least 85 per cent of unknown words could be guessed by a class of learners working together to pool their relevant knowledge and skills. The authors acknowledge that most learners would need considerable practice in class, with the guidance of a teacher, before being able to guess successfully while reading alone.

Other scholars have focused on the processes that foreign-language learners engage in when they infer the meanings of unknown words in a text. Van Parreren and Schouten-Van Parreren (1981) asked Dutch learners of various foreign languages to think aloud in Dutch as they dealt with unfamiliar words in a reading passage. The authors identified four linguistic levels at which the learners could operate:

- syntactic: the structure of the sentence in which the word occurred;
- semantic: meaning found in the immediate and wider context of the word;
- lexical: the form of the word;
- stylistic: the exact usage of the word in this context.

They found that the levels were ordered from syntactic as the lowest to stylistic as the highest. What this meant was that learners could not operate at a higher level if they lacked lower level skills. For instance, a learner who had difficulty identifying the word class of the unknown item was also hampered in picking up semantic clues or analysing the parts of the word. Furthermore, those learners who were good at inferring meanings initially decided which was the most appropriate level to work on and then if necessary adjusted their strategy by moving up or down a level.

Another research procedure, adopted by Haastrup (1987, 1991) and Schouten-Van Parreren (1992), was to form pairs of learners matched according to their proficiency in the foreign language. The learners worked together to infer the meanings of unknown words, thus producing introspective 'think-aloud' accounts of their reasoning processes. Haastrup, whose subjects were Danish secondary students learning English, analysed the clues they used into three categories:

- interlingual: drawing on L1 and languages other than English;
- intralingual: drawing on knowledge of English; and
- contextual: drawing on the content of the text and knowledge of the world.

She noted that many of the introspective accounts were incomplete or difficult to interpret and so about half of the subjects were also interviewed individually as soon as they had completed the inferencing task, in order to clarify what they had said. Schouten-Van Parreren focused on differences between 'strong' and 'weak' learners among her Dutch secondary students. She found that weak students generally had more limited sources of knowledge to draw on and more difficulty in integrating information from different sources.

The evidence, then, is that lexical guessing is not an easy task to perform, even when contextual information is readily available. Learners can be led astray by inferences that are based on partial knowledge and by their failure to check their preliminary guesses against the wider context of the text.

(4) Given this evidence that many learners lack the skill to infer the meaning of unknown words correctly, there has been surprisingly little research on whether they can be successfully trained to apply it in their reading. Writers such as Clarke and Nation (1980) do not report any empirical evaluation of the guessing procedure that they recommend. Van Parreren and Schouten-Van Parreren (1981) refer to a few experiments 'which convincingly demonstrate that the guessing skill is trainable' but they give no details and also hint that the skill is not easily acquired.

In the literature on learner strategies (for reviews, see Skehan, 1989: Chapter 5; O'Malley and Chamot, 1990; Oxford, 1993; McDonough, 1995), there are reports of projects to teach strategies to groups of learners. Normally this has involved training the learners or their teachers in the application of a package of strategies so that – while vocabulary learning strategies have commonly been included – it is difficult to evaluate the effectiveness of training in lexical inferencing in isolation from other strategies related to reading comprehension, and from the overall success of the project. Oxford (1993) identifies a number of methodological problems that have affected investigations of L2 strategy training, such as having too short a training period, emphasising the intellectual aspects of language learning too much, not taking account of the kind of attitudes and motivation that learners bring to the training and not integrating the strategy training into normal class work. It is clear that strategy training is a complex activity and specialists in this area are just beginning to understand how to enhance the learning strategies of particular groups of students in the most effective way.

(5) One final point needs to be made. Even if learners successfully infer the meaning of an unknown word in a reading text, it does not mean that they will necessarily acquire knowledge of the word. This is something I noted earlier with regard to studies of incidental vocabulary learning. Logically, one can figure out what a word means for immediate comprehension purposes without retaining any long-term memory of the meaning or even the form of the word, once the reading task is completed.

A study by Mondria and Wit-De Boer (1991) addresses this issue directly. They set out to test Schouten-Van Parreren's theory that guessing the meaning of words presented in context (especially a 'pregnant' one offering a range of clues) is an effective strategy for vocabulary learning. The theory was that the cognitive activity generated by guessing would create useful associations for the word and, in addition, the learner would gain positive affective feedback from verifying that the guess was correct. For their experiment with Dutch learners of French, Mondria and Wit-De Boer chose eight target words and wrote series of sentences in which the pregnancy of the context was systematically varied. An example of a pregnant sentence (with an English translation given below) was:

> Le jardinier remplit un <u>arroisoir</u> pour donner de l'eau aux plantes.
> 'The gardener filled a watering can to water the plants.'

By contrast, a non-pregnant sentence for the same word was this:

> Je cherche un <u>arroisoir</u> pour finir mon travail.
> 'I am looking for a watering can so I can finish my work.'

As expected, subjects who were presented with the words in a pregnant context were significantly better at guessing what they meant than those who did not have the benefit of contextual clues, especially when the adverbial phrase at the end of the sentence was pregnant (e.g. *pour donner de l'eau aux plantes*). However, when the subjects were tested for their retention of the word meanings two or three days later, the pattern was reversed: it was the learners who had the *non-*pregnant adverb phrases who remembered the words better. The researchers explained their finding by suggesting that having contextual clues available made it easy for the learners to understand the word and did not encourage them to put any effort into making a mental association between the word-form and its meaning which could be applied in other contexts. The generalisability of the findings in this case is limited by the small number of target words and the artificial nature of the sentences. Nevertheless, the relationship between lexical inferencing and vocabulary learning is another area which requires further investigation.

Assessment issues

As in any test-design project, we first need to be clear about what the purpose of a lexical inferencing test is. The literature I have just reviewed above indicates at least three possible purposes:

1 to conduct research on the processes that learners engage in when they attempt to infer the meaning of unknown words;
2 to evaluate the success of a programme to train learners to apply lexical inferencing strategies; or
3 to assess learners on their ability to make inferences about unknown words.

The design of the test should be influenced by which of these purposes is the applicable one.

There are two possible starting points for the test design. The first approach is to select a set of words which are known to be unfamiliar to the test-takers and then create a suitable context for each one in the form of a sentence or short paragraph. This strategy allows the tester to control the nature and amount of the contextual clues provided but at the risk of producing unauthentic contexts that may be unnaturally pregnant. The alternative is to take one or more texts as the starting point and to choose certain low-frequency words within them as the target items for the test. There are drawbacks in this case as well: there may be too many unfamiliar words or conversely too few; and the text may not provide any usable contextual information for a particular word, or again may provide too much.

A second design issue is how to select the target words and in what form to present them to the test-takers. The essential requirement – as in the case of research on incidental vocabulary learning – is that the test-takers should have little if any knowledge of the words before they take the test. Administering a pre-test is one way to determine whether any of the proposed words are already known; otherwise it may be necessary to rely on word-frequency data, teacher judgements and other indirect methods of identifying words that are unfamiliar to the learners. An alternative strategy – to be considered when the test-takers have an advanced level of proficiency in the language – is to replace the target words with non-words or pseudo-words. This means that the learners cannot rely on recognising the form of the word and must make use of contextual information to decide on their response. However, if non-words are being used because of the likelihood that the test-takers will have some knowledge of the real words that they replace, this somewhat changes the nature of the test task from making inferences about what an unknown item might mean to figuring out what the missing – but possibly known – word is.

One final issue is what form the test-takers' responses should take.

Research studies that focus on the process of inferencing normally require elaborated responses from the subjects, reflecting the thinking that they engage in as they try to work out the meaning of the unknown word. On the other hand, for practical assessment purposes, it may be necessary to use test items that can be given a score more easily. One obvious method is to have multiple-choice items in which the test-takers select the option that fits most closely their inference about what each word means. However, this and other types of objective-test item may work against the spirit of what the learners are being asked to do when they make inferences, particularly if it implies that there is one correct answer for each word. There is a case for encouraging the test-takers to construct a response that expresses what they have inferred about the target word. This in turn means that, especially with lower proficiency learners, they should have the opportunity to respond in their first language rather than through L2. Thus, the convenience of scoring objective test items has to be balanced against the more time-consuming process of rating responses composed by the test-takers themselves. It can be argued that the latter approach would yield results that more validly reflect the quality of the learners' inferences. This is a clear example of a decision about test design that has to be taken in the light of the assessment purpose.

Communication strategies

When compared with the amount of research on ways that learners cope with unknown words they encounter in their reading, there has been less investigation of the vocabulary difficulties they face in expressing themselves through speaking and writing. However, within the field of second language acquisition, there is an active tradition of research on communication strategies. Although the scholars involved have not seen themselves as vocabulary researchers, a primary focus of their studies has been on how learners deal with **lexical gaps**, that is words or phrases in the target language that they need to express their intended meanings but do not know. It is therefore appropriate for us to consider what the findings have been and what their possible implications for vocabulary assessment are. Chapelle's (1994) model of vocabulary ability, which I discussed in Chapter 2, includes strategies of vocabulary use as one of the three components, and the literature on communication strategies is an obvious place to look for guidance as to their nature and function.

The most influential early research on communication strategies was carried out by Tarone (1978). She took a small group of inter-mediate-level ESL learners and presented them with three pictures, which they were asked to describe both in their first language and in English. The pictures included objects such as a balloon, a water-pipe (hookah) and a caterpillar, things for which the learners generally did not know the English names. Tarone wanted to find out how her subjects would cope with the problem of identifying objects they could not directly name in the target language.

Her classification produced a taxonomy of five communication strategies, some of which were divided into subtypes (see Table 3.2). According to her analysis, there were five ways of dealing with lexical gaps that were open to her subjects. The first was simply to avoid referring to something that they could not name. Secondly, they could use other words in the target language (L2) to explain what they wanted to refer to, perhaps in a rather roundabout way. A third strategy was to draw on the vocabulary of their first language, either by literal translation or by actually using the equivalent L1 term. Another way was to ask the person they were speaking to for help in supplying the required word for them. Finally, they could resort to non-verbal means of communication, using gestures or acting out what they wanted to express.

Other researchers have developed their own typologies, in which they have added elements or classified the strategies according to other criteria. In Chapter 2 I referred to the work of Blum-Kulka and Levenston (1983), who explicitly linked the strategies to vocabulary use. The process of expanding the range of devices covered by the term communication strategies has reached the point where, in a recent review article, Dörnyei and Scott (1997) listed 33 of them, some of which were further sub-classified. On the other hand, some re-searchers have sought to reduce the complexity by proposing a much smaller number of general categories. For example, Faerch and Kasper (1983b: 52–53) classified them into two broad groups:

- Reduction (or avoidance) strategies: topic avoidance, message abandonment, etc.
- Compensatory (or achievement) strategies: circumlocution, word coinage, L1 transfer, etc.

Table 3.2 *A typology of communication strategies (Tarone, 1978)*

Paraphrase

Approximation	Use of a single target-language vocabulary item or structure, which the learner knows is not correct, but which shares enough features with the desired item to satisfy the speaker (e.g., *pipe for waterpipe*)
Word coinage	The learner makes up a new word in order to communicate the desired concept (e.g., *airball* for *balloon*)
Circumlocution	The learner describes the characteristics or elements of the object or action instead of using the appropriate target-language structure (*She is, uh, smoking something, I don't know what's its name. That's, uh, Persian, and we use in Turkey, a lot of*)

Transfer

Literal translation	The learner translates word for word from the native language (e.g., *He invites him to drink* for *They toast one another*).
Language switch	The learner uses the nataive-language term without bothering to translate (e.g., *balon* for *balloon* or *tirtil* for *caterpillar*).

Appeal for assistance	The learner asks for the correct term or structure (e.g., *What is this?*).

Mime	The learner uses non-verbal strategies in place of meaning structure (e.g., clapping one's hands to illustrate applause).

Avoidance

Topic avoidance	Occurs when the learner simply does not talk about concepts for which the vocabulary or other meaning structure is not known.
Message abandonment	Occurs when the learner begins to talk about a concept but is unable to continue due to lack of meaning structure, and stops in mid-utterance.

The essential difference between them is that, in the first case, speakers faced with communication difficulties change what they originally intended to say, whereas in the second case they proceed to express their intended meaning as best they can.

Part of the reason for the expansion in the list of communication strategies is that various authors have defined their scope differently. From early on, researchers recognised that the strategies were not used just by learners with limited language knowledge. As I noted in Chapter 2, native speakers employ them as well to deal with difficult or challenging communication situations, often because it is the *listener* rather than the speaker who lacks the necessary knowledge of the language. Blum-Kulka and Levenston (1983) go even further. In their discussion of the general strategy of lexical simplification, they identify no fewer than six contexts in which it may be observed:

- in the speech and writing of second language learners;
- in the speech of children acquiring their first language;
- in the speech of adult native speakers addressing children, foreigners, learners and even other less (lexically) competent native speakers;
- in the writing of simplified reading texts;
- in pidgin languages; and
- in the work of translators.

Thus, the strategies employed by learners can be seen as part of a much broader phenomenon in linguistic communication. How, then, can we restrict their scope? Here are two widely quoted definitions:

> [C]ommunication strategies are potentially conscious plans for solving what to an individual presents itself as a problem in reaching a particular communicative goal.
>
> (Faerch and Kasper, 1983b: 36)

> The term [communication strategy] relates to a mutual attempt of two interlocutors to agree on a meaning in situations where requisite meaning structures do not seem to be shared.
>
> (Tarone, 1983: 65)

As Bialystok (1990: 3–5) points out, these definitions and others incorporate three key features:

- Language users employ strategies as attempts to solve a communication *problem*.
- They apply them *consciously*.
- They make an *intentional* choice of a particular strategy to deal with a specific communication situation.

Although Bialystok herself questions whether these criteria are the right ones to delimit the scope of communication strategies, they are the ones that are generally used in definitions.

One interesting characteristic of the research on communication strategies from our point of view is that, despite the references to broad concepts like 'communicative goals' and 'meaning structures' in the definitions, most studies have concentrated on lexical problems. Kasper and Kellerman (1997b: 7–11) give various reasons to justify this emphasis.

- Learners are much more aware of making choices about which words to use than about the grammatical features of their speech, because the vocabulary carries the main information load in a communicative situation. This means that in a research study they are able to tell the researchers afterwards what they intended to say and why they chose particular strategies.
- As I have already stated, all of us from time to time encounter lexically challenging situations requiring the use of communication strategies (even if it's just having a word 'on the tip of my tongue') and so lexical strategies represent an important component of strategic competence for all language users.
- There is a close link between the use of compensatory-type lexical strategies and the development of vocabulary knowledge. By using the strategies, learners build connections in their minds between the words they already know: Which are opposites? Which are synonyms? Which refer to general classes of things? They can also develop skill in word formation: compound words, derived forms, using a noun as a verb and so on. Another benefit of using lexical strategies effectively is that learners can sustain conversations with more proficient speakers of the target language and thus have many opportunities to acquire new words in a meaningful communicative context.

The third point raises the issue of whether communication strategies should be taught to learners. Some researchers (Bialystok, 1990; Kellerman, 1991) have argued against the idea in principle, on the basis that the strategies reflect underlying cognitive processes that the learners have already developed through their first language. Kellerman and his colleagues at the University of Nijmegen found that Dutch learners used very similar strategies in performing a task (describing graphic designs) in both Dutch and in English, leading to the conclusion that the subjects were transferring their first language strategic skills to the second language and thus strategy training was unnecessary. However, numerous other scholars (Tarone, 1984; Willems, 1987; Dörnyei, 1995) have favoured the teaching of communication strategies as part of a communicative, task-based approach to language learning, so that learners can take advantage of the kind of benefits identified by Kasper and Kellerman in their third point.

Only a small amount of research has been conducted to evaluate the effectiveness of strategy training. A relatively large experimental study was carried out by Dörnyei (1995) with learners of English in five Hungarian secondary schools. The experimental subjects received training over a six-week period in three communication strategies:

- topic avoidance and replacement;
- circumlocution; and
- the use of conversational fillers (like *well, as a matter of fact*).

Circumlocution, which was taken in this study as the ability to provide a good definition of a word, was the strategy that most obviously involved vocabulary knowledge and use. The results showed that, at the end of the strategy training, the experimental subjects were able to provide significantly better definitions than the students in the control group did. Overall, the effects of the training programme were not very clear-cut, but there were indications that it could have positive results over a longer period. I noted in the previous section some of the problems encountered in training students to develop learning strategies such as lexical inferencing. Presumably the same constraints apply to the teaching of communication strategies.

Assessment issues

There are two possible approaches to the assessment of lexical communication strategies. One would be to have an embedded, comprehensive measure of the learners' performance of a speaking task, such as participating in an interview or telling a story. The measure might take the form of a scale on which raters judged the learners' effectiveness in using strategies to communicate their meanings. An indication of how this might be done is found in the ACTFL Proficiency Guidelines (American Council on the Teaching of Foreign Languages, 1986), which are widely used in the United States for the assessment of foreign-language learners in high schools and colleges. The Guide-lines comprise descriptions of nine levels of proficiency from 'Novice-Low' to 'Superior'. Some of the higher level descriptions for speaking include statements about the learners' use of communicative strategies:

- Intermediate-High: . . . Limited vocabulary still necessitates hesita-tion and may bring about slightly unexpected circumlocution . . .
- Advanced: . . . Circumlocution which arises from vocabulary or syntactic limitations is very often quite successful, though some groping for words may still be evident . . .
- Advanced-High: . . . The Advanced-Plus speaker shows a well devel-oped ability to compensate for an imperfect grasp of some forms with confident use of communication strategies, such as para-phrasing and circumlocution . . .

These statements do not strictly form an embedded measure in the sense that I am using the term, because they are incorporated in quite wide-ranging descriptions of performance, and the raters are not asked to make a separate assessment of the strategies. However, the authors of the ACTFL Guidelines evidently consider that circumlocu-tion is frequent and salient enough in the speech of learners to provide one kind of evidence of their proficiency level.

Leaving this possibility aside, though, the research indicates that embedded, comprehensive measures are not practicable unless the speaking task is designed to create communication problems of a specific kind. Identifiable communication strategies do not necessa-rily occur very often in normal speech, and in fact one of the issues debated by the researchers is what criteria to use for identifying them (Kasper and Kellerman, 1997b: 3–4). In many cases there are obser-vable signs, such as hesitations, gestures or the use of L1 words, but the application of avoidance strategies or skilful circumlocution may not be noticeable at all to a listener. Since one of the defining features of a communication strategy is that it is employed *consciously* by a speaker, some researchers have asked their subjects to listen to a recording of their spoken performance afterwards and report whether they were aware of dealing with communication problems at various points. This would not be feasible, however, if learners were being assessed for decision-making purposes in a high-stakes test.

Thus, it seems that a more promising approach to assessment is to have discrete, selective test tasks which require learners to use at least one kind of communication strategy. The most popular kind of task in the research studies has been to describe an object or explain a concept which the subject cannot name in the target language. I have already given some examples from Tarone's (1978) study. Paribakht (1985) asked her subjects to communicate to an interlocutor concepts associated with words that were both concrete (like *abacus, hammock, lantern*) and abstract (like *fate, martyrdom, flattery*). A larger-scale study was the Nijmegen project in the Netherlands, in which Dutch learners of English performed four different tasks. They were required to:

1 refer to 20 photographed objects, for which they did not know the conventional English names (such as a bib or a fly-swat);
2 describe 12 novel graphic designs both in Dutch and in English;
3 retell in English four one-minute stories told to them in Dutch; and
4 have a 15-minute conversation with a native speaker of English.
   (Poulisse, 1993: 165)

In all of the tasks, except perhaps the last one, the content of the subjects' speech was carefully controlled and chosen to create lexical challenges for them. These are the kinds of task that would be suitable for assessment purposes, in that they will elicit numerous examples of communication strategies and allow the performance of different learners to be compared on a common basis.

However, assessment involves more than just eliciting performance. Whereas the researchers have used the tasks primarily to produce a range of strategies for classification and analysis according to their theoretical stances, language teachers and testers presumably want to make judgements about how well the learners use the strategies. One specific method of assessment is illustrated by a measure used in Dörnyei's (1995) strategy training experiment. In order to assess the quality of the experimental subjects' definitions, he asked judges to read a transcript of each definition and guess which word was being defined. The subjects then received a score based on how many times the judges were able to identify the target words correctly. A similar method was used in the Nijmegen project to evaluate the effectiveness of communication strategies used in the story retelling task, but the researchers concluded that 'it does not make much sense to speak of more or less effective CS [communication strategy] types, because the comprehensibility of a particular CS depends so heavily on the amount of specific information contained in the CS itself and on the informativeness of the context in which it is embedded' (Poulisse, 1993: 166). It appears, then, that a relatively context-independent test is required if the effectiveness of a communication strategy is to be judged in its own right.

Another basis for assessment is suggested by Yule and Tarone's (1997) work. They report on a study in which they asked both native speakers and learners of English to describe objects such as a coffee pot and a tape dispenser. The native-speaker responses provided a baseline for the evaluation of the learners' efforts to refer to the same objects. In the case of the dispenser, all the native speakers were able to name it correctly, whereas the learners produced quite a variety of responses. Yule and Tarone observed that the responses could be ranked from clearly unsuccessful to relatively successful, as in the following examples:

> . . . I don't know what this name
> . . . an object designed to put another object
> . . . this is object, the measure is approximately three inch length
> and one half inch height . . .
> . . . a device to put Scotch tape
>
> (Yule and Tarone, 1997: 24)

On the other hand, in describing the metal inner part of the coffee pot, the two groups were not nearly so distinguishable:

> NATIVE SPEAKER: a sort of a I don't know what it is but on top had
> a round thing
> LEARNER: the thing that you close has a round thing in the top
>
> (Yule and Tarone, 1997: 23)

Thus, although there appears to be some potential here for rating the quality of learners' communication strategies on a scale, further investigation is required to find suitable test items and to establish whether learner responses can be rated on a reliable basis.

The assessment of communication strategies, and of strategic competence generally, is an undeveloped area of study. A question that arises then is the following: For what purposes might we want to assess learners' vocabulary strategies? One obvious situation is in a study like Dörnyei's (1995), where researchers set out to evaluate the effectiveness of programmes to train learners in the use of the strategies. Less formally, classroom teachers may want to assess their learners' progress in developing strategies that will allow them to take advantage of opportunities for use – and further acquisition – of the target language outside the classroom. In both these cases, a discrete, selective test is appropriate. It is discrete in the sense that it is designed just to assess a component of vocabulary ability, and selective in that it elicits the performance of one or more specific strategies chosen in advance by the test designer.

Although vocabulary strategies are also required when learners perform less structured speaking tasks, the prospects for developing embedded, comprehensive measures of strategic competence for use in proficiency tests do not look so good. The ACTFL Guidelines suggest that paraphrasing and circumlocution may be strategies that are suitable for the purpose. Certainly, as I mentioned in Chapter 2, there is a need for more research on ways in which test-takers' use of communication strategies in an interview may affect how their speaking ability is rated.

Conclusion

Let us review the assessment procedures discussed in this chapter in terms of the three dimensions of vocabulary assessment I presented in Chapter 1. Research on second language vocabulary acquisition normally employs discrete tests, because the researchers are investigating a construct that can be labelled 'vocabulary knowledge', 'vocabulary skill' or 'vocabulary learning ability'. This applies even to the research on communication strategies. Despite the apparently broad scope of the topic area, most researchers have focused very specifically on lexical strategies and designed tests that oblige learners to deal with their lack of knowledge of particular vocabulary items. Embedded measures make sense in theory, but it remains to be seen whether they can be used as practical tools for assessing communication strategies.

Secondly, selective rather than comprehensive measures are used in vocabulary acquisition research, at least in the areas covered in this chapter. Tests assess whether learners have some knowledge of a series of target words and/or specific vocabulary skills that the researcher is interested in. However, comprehensive measures may have a limited role in the development of incidental learning or inferencing tests. In order to have access to the contextual information required to gain some understanding of the unknown or partially known target words, the test-takers need to have a reasonable knowledge of most of the words in the input text. A comprehensive measure of the non-target vocabulary – say, in the form of a readability formula – would therefore be a useful guide to the suitability of a text for this kind of test.

As for context dependence, there is variability according to what aspect of vocabulary is being investigated. Tests of systematic vocabulary learning are normally context independent, with the words being presented in isolation or in a limited sentence context. In the case of research on incidental learning, subjects are certainly presented with the target words in context as part of the experimental treatment, but knowledge of the words is assessed afterwards in a context-independent manner, in that the subjects cannot refer to what they read or heard while they are taking the vocabulary test. By contrast, context dependence is an essential characteristic of the test material in studies of lexical inferencing. In order for the items to be truly context dependent, the test-writer needs to ensure both that contextual clues are available for each target word and that the test-takers have no prior knowledge of the words.

....

CHAPTER FOUR

Research on vocabulary assessment

Introduction

In the previous chapter, we saw how tests play a role in research on vocabulary within the field of second language acquisition (SLA). Now we move on to consider research in the field of language testing, where the focus is not so much on understanding the processes of vocabulary learning as on measuring the level of vocabulary knowledge and ability that learners have reached. Language testing is concerned with the design of tests to assess learners for a variety of practical purposes that can be summarised under labels such as placement, diagnosis, achievement and proficiency. However, in practice this distinction between second language acquisition research and assessment is difficult to maintain consistently, because, on the one hand, language testing researchers have paid relatively little attention to vocabulary tests and, on the other hand, second language acquisition researchers working on vocabulary acquisition have often needed to develop tests as an integral part of their research design. Thus, some of the important work on how to measure vocabulary knowledge and ability has been produced by vocabulary acquisition researchers rather than language testers; the latter have tended either to take vocabulary tests for granted or, in the 1990s, to be interested in more integrative and communicative measures of language proficiency.

Other significant contributors to our understanding of vocabulary assessment are researchers on reading English as a first language. There is a long tradition of vocabulary work in reading research because of the strong, well-documented association between good vocabulary knowledge and the ability to read well. Since the late 1970s this line of research has gained fresh impetus, especially from the innovative studies conducted by Richard Anderson, William Nagy and their associates at the University of Illinois in the United States. In this chapter I draw on theoretical concepts and research results related to first language reading and second language vocabulary acquisition to supplement the limited amount of work on vocabulary assessment in the field of language testing.

For the most part, what I am covering here are vocabulary tests of the conventional kind, made up of a set of items that present the test-takers with a selected number of words in isolation from a broader context and require them to demonstrate some understanding of each word. To use the terminology introduced in Chapter 1, we are talking about discrete vocabulary tests which are selective and context independent. It may seem self-evident that tests of this sort are measures of vocabulary knowledge, but there is a small amount of research that shows it is difficult to distinguish even such discrete 'vocabulary' tests from tests of 'grammar'. The issue of how meaningful it is to separate vocabulary knowledge from other aspects of language ability arises even more when we consider embedded lexical measures. Towards the end of the chapter, I go on to discuss the family of language tests known collectively as the cloze procedure. Although cloze tests are not normally regarded as vocabulary measures, at least not primarily so, they have been extensively investigated by language testing researchers and I want to explore whether they may function as embedded vocabulary tests that are selective and context dependent. In other words, to what extent is it possible to show that scores in a cloze test reflect the test-takers' vocabulary knowledge and ability? Other embedded lexical measures are considered in Chapter 7.

Objective testing

The history of vocabulary assessment in the twentieth century is very much associated with the development of **objective testing**, especially in the United States. Objective tests are ones in which the learning material is divided into small units, each of which can be assessed by means of a test item with a single correct answer that can be specified in advance. Most commonly these are items of the multiple-choice type. The tests are objective in the sense that they can be scored without requiring any judgement by the scorer as to whether an answer is correct or not. In his book *Measured Words*, Spolsky (1995) explains how **psychometrics**, the science of mental measurement that gave rise to objective testing, came to have a dominant influence on assessment in all areas of the American school curriculum during the period after the First World War, so that the new tests progressively displaced traditional essay examinations from the 1930s on. The first modern language tests, for Latin, French and German, were published in the US by Daniel Starch in 1916 (Spolsky, 1995: 40). These tests assessed vocabulary knowledge by presenting learners with a list of foreign words to be matched with their English translations. Other early tests used multiple-choice items in a similar way, with an L2 word in the stem and four or five L1 words as the options.

It is easy to see how vocabulary became popular as a component of objective language tests.

- Words could be treated as independent linguistic units with a meaning expressed by a synonym, a short defining phrase or a translation equivalent. As a result, it was relatively straightforward to write a set of multiple-choice items consisting of a word followed by four or five possible meanings, or a matching test comprising jumbled lists of words and short definitions.
- There was a great deal of work in the 1920s and 1930s to prepare lists of the most frequent words in English, as well as other words that were useful for the needs of particular groups of students. According to Lado (1961: 181), similar though more limited work was done on the vocabulary of major European languages. These lists provided a large stock of vocabulary items that could be conveniently sampled to select the target words for a test.
- Multiple-choice vocabulary tests proved to have excellent technical characteristics, in relation to the requirements of psychometric theory. Well-written items could discriminate effectively among learners according to their level of ability, and thus the tests were highly reliable. Reliability was the great virtue of a psychometric test.
- Rather than simply measuring vocabulary knowledge, objective vocabulary tests seemed to be valid indicators of language ability in a broad sense. As Anderson and Freebody (1981: 78–80) noted, one of the most consistent findings in L1 reading research has been the high correlation between tests of vocabulary and reading compre-

hension. The same has been shown to apply in second language assessment (e.g. Pike, 1979). Furthermore, '[t]he strong relationship between vocabulary and general intelligence is one of the most robust findings in the history of intelligence testing' (Anderson and Freebody, 1981: 77).

Given these considerations, it is quite understandable that objective vocabulary tests came to form an integral part of **the discrete-point approach** to second language testing, in which the assessment of learners focused primarily on their knowledge of individual structural elements of the language. The classic statement of this approach is found in Lado's (1961) pioneering book *Language Testing*. Other books on testing published in the 1960s and 1970s (Valette, 1967; Harris, 1969; Clark, 1972; Heaton, 1975) followed Lado's lead, with substantial sections on the testing of vocabulary items, along with speech sounds, grammatical points and other discrete elements of the language. The authors recommended the use of objective test items such as multiple-choice, matching, picture labelling, blank-filling and word translation.

These books were written as handbooks for teachers, so the authors drew on their practical experience of test-writing and some basic concepts in making their recommendations, rather than referring to any research findings on vocabulary testing. When we turn to the research journals, though, we find that surprisingly few studies have been conducted throughout the twentieth century on aspects of second language vocabulary assessment. One exception is the significant amount of research related to the vocabulary items in the Test of English as a Foreign Language (TOEFL), which we look at in some detail in Chapter 5.

Multiple-choice vocabulary items

Although the multiple-choice format is one of the most widely used methods of vocabulary assessment, both for native speakers and for second language learners, its limitations have also been recognised for a long time. Wesche and Paribakht summarise the criticisms of these items as follows:

1 They are difficult to construct, and require laborious field-testing, analysis and refinement.

2 The learner may know another meaning for the word, but not the one sought.

3 The learner may choose the right word by a process of elimination, and has in any case a 25 per cent chance of guessing the correct answer in a four-alternative format.

4 Items may test students' knowledge of distractors rather than their ability to identify an exact meaning of the target word.

5 The learner may miss an item either for lack of knowledge of words or lack of understanding of syntax in the distractors.

6 This format permits only a very limited sampling of the learner's total vocabulary (for example, a 25-item multiple-choice test samples one word in 400 from a 10,000-word vocabulary).

Wesche and Paribakht, (1996: 17)

However, the authors conclude that multiple-choice items will continue to be popular with test developers – for vocabulary as well as other aspects of language proficiency – because they are so convenient to administer and there are well-established procedures for analysing them. In spite of their widespread use, though, there is little ongoing research on such tests, especially as applied to second language learning.

One aspect that has been investigated in a small number of studies can be summed up in the question: can we identify variables that influence the difficulty of multiple-choice vocabulary items for second language learners? For example, Goodrich (1977) undertook a study that can be seen as related to Wesche and Paribakht's (1996) fourth criticism above. He focused on the relative effectiveness of eight types of distractor in multiple-choice items for Arabic-speaking learners of English. The target words were presented in a sentence in the stem of the item, and the most attractive distractors turned out to be words that either fitted the context or were semantically related to the correct answer (including antonyms). By contrast, the test-takers were generally not attracted by false cognates, by arbitrarily chosen distractors or by words with similar spelling to the correct answer (e.g. *beard* for *bread*). When he compared a version of his test containing only effective distractor types with one loaded with ineffective types, Goodrich found some evidence that the former version was a better measure of the learners' proficiency. These results can be interpreted as supporting the criticism that distractors have too much influence on the way that multiple-choice items measure vocabulary knowledge.

Two other studies have investigated what features of the target words, rather than the distractors, influence the difficulty of multiple-choice vocabulary items. The assumption is that test-takers perform better on items assessing words which are easier to learn and have thus been acquired early. An example of this approach is found in the analysis by Perkins and Linnville (1987) of the vocabulary section of the Michigan Test of English Language Proficiency, containing 40 multiple-choice items in which again the target words occurred in the context of a stem sentence. These researchers were interested in exploring whether learners at different levels of proficiency had distinctive profiles of vocabulary knowledge. They therefore administered the test to learners at two levels in an intensive-English programme as well as a group of native-speaking undergraduates. To analyse the results, they first identified numerous features of each of the target words: its frequency and range of use, how abstract it was, its length, the kind of connotations it evoked and how many synonyms it had. Then they used the statistical procedure of regression analysis to find out which of the target-word features were the best predictors of the test-takers' performance on the test items.

From a number of separate analyses, Perkins and Linnville found that several features functioned as significant predictors. The most common ones were frequency, number of syllables and abstractness. These results seem reasonable because you would expect that items involving words that are frequent, short and concrete would be easier to answer than those with longer, less frequent and more abstract words. The authors also noted that there was a tendency for different predictors to emerge at the three levels of proficiency, although this is by no means clear-cut in their analyses.

The second study, by McQueen (1996), involved not a vocabulary test as such but the reading section of an elementary test of Chinese as a foreign language administered to secondary school students in Australia and New Zealand. Using multiple-choice items, the test assesses comprehension of a variety of simple texts written in both characters and the Romanised Pinyin script. The scores are grouped into three band levels, based on the number of items correctly answered, and the candidates receive a descriptive statement of their performance like this one for Level 1:

A typical student at this level can read Pinyin and understand some everyday words and phrases, such as names of family members, numbers and time, and pick out simple information from a short piece of writing or dialogue.

(McQueen, 1996: 152)

The descriptors are written to reflect the reading skills required for the items that test-takers at each level answered correctly most of the time. McQueen wanted to investigate whether the level descriptions validly reported what was involved in answering the relevant items. She argued that, particularly at the elementary level of language learning, vocabulary knowledge plays a crucial role in reading comprehension and therefore for each test item she identified a key phrase in the stimulus text or in the item itself. The key phrases were analysed in terms of a set of variables similar to those used by Perkins and Linnville, and then the relationship between these variables and the difficulty of the test items was calculated. She found that these variables were significantly associated with item difficulty:

- how easy the words were to pronounce;
- whether they had been presented in the students' textbook and, if so, in which unit (an earlier or more recent one); and
- whether they were written in characters or Pinyin in the source text.

The lexical analysis thus provided an empirical basis for more complete descriptors to report the learners' performance on the test.

The studies by Perkins and Linnville and by McQueen are useful in that they present ways of linking vocabulary-test performance to the learners' progress in vocabulary learning or, to put it more generally, give us clues as to what vocabulary-test items are actually measuring. It is disappointing, then, to find that there are so few studies of this kind conducted with second language learners.

Validating tests of vocabulary knowledge

Writers on first language reading research over the years (Kelley and Krey, 1934; Farr, 1969; Schwartz, 1984) have pointed out that, in addition to numerous variations of the multiple-choice format, a wide range of test items and methods have been used for measuring vocabulary knowledge. Kelley and Krey (cited in Farr, 1969: 34) identified 26 different methods in standardised US vocabulary and reading tests. However, as Schwartz puts it, 'there does not appear to be any rationale for choosing one measurement technique rather than another. Test constructors sometimes seem to choose a particular measurement technique more or less by whim' (1984: 52). In addition, it is not clear that the various types of test are all measuring the same ability; this calls into question the validity of the tests.

A number of early studies (e.g. Sims, 1929; Kelley, 1933; Tilley, 1936) addressed these issues by administering two or more vocabulary tests to a group of students and then comparing the results by means of correlation. Typically, one of the tests was considered a criterion measure and the others were judged to be valid according to how highly they correlated with the criterion. Alternatively, as in Hurlburt's (1954) study, a merely moderate correlation between a multiple-choice test and a completion (fill-in-the-blank) test was interpreted to mean that recognising a word is a somewhat different vocabulary skill from recalling it. From a modern perspective, simple correlational procedures like this have limited value and more sophisticated analyses are now available for test validation, as we will see later in this chapter.

Regardless of what statistical procedures are used, though, another important aspect of validation is to try to clarify conceptually what a vocabulary test is supposed to be measuring. If we assume that conventional (discrete, context-independent) vocabulary tests are designed to assess learners' knowledge of individual word meaning, it is useful to distinguish two dimensions of that knowledge, as defined by Anderson and Freebody:

> The first may be called 'breadth' of knowledge, by which we mean the number of words for which the person knows at least some of the significant aspects of meaning . . . [There] is a second dimension of vocabulary knowledge, namely the quality or 'depth' of understanding. We shall assume that, for most purposes, a person has a sufficiently deep understanding of a word if it conveys to him or her all of the distinctions that would be understood by an ordinary adult under normal circumstances.
>
> (Anderson and Freebody, 1981: 92–93)

I have applied this distinction in my own earlier writing on second language vocabulary testing (Read, 1993; 1998) and others have followed suit (e.g. Wesche and Paribakht, 1996), although Meara (1996a: 44) finds the terms breadth and depth confusing in this context. Another way to label the two dimensions is vocabulary size and quality of vocabulary knowledge respectively, and in the following discussion I use the two sets of terms interchangeably. A great deal of both L1 and L2 vocabulary testing research can be seen as addressing one or other of these dimensions.

Measuring vocabulary size

Let me first sketch some educational situations in which consideration of vocabulary size is relevant and where research has been undertaken.

- Reading researchers have long been interested in estimating how many words are known by native speakers of English as they grow from childhood through the school years to adult life. It represents one facet of research into the role of vocabulary knowledge in reading comprehension as it develops with age. As Anderson and Freebody (1981: 96–97) noted, the results of such research have important implications for the way that reading programmes in schools are designed and taught. Reliable estimates of the number of words acquired by children at different age levels would provide a better basis for decisions about how many new words should be introduced in each unit of a learning programme and, indeed, whether it is worthwhile for the teacher to do any direct teaching of vocabulary at all.
- Estimates of native-speaker vocabulary size at different ages provide a target – though a moving one, of course – for the acquisition of vocabulary by children entering school with little knowledge of the language used as the medium of instruction. Let us take the case of children from non-English-speaking backgrounds who migrate with their families to Canada. Cummins (1981) analysed the vocabulary-test results of foreign-born students in the Toronto school system and found that those who arrived in the country at the age of six or older took five to seven years to achieve scores that were comparable to those of native-born students at their grade level. Similarly, research on the learning needs of migrant students in schools in the United States (e.g. Saville-Troike, 1984; Harklau, 1994) has shown the significant role that vocabulary knowledge plays in their academic achievement.
- International students undertaking upper secondary or university education through a new medium of instruction simply do not have

time to achieve a vocabulary size that comes close to that of a native speaker. For them the focus of vocabulary research shifts to the question of what minimum number of words they need to know to cope with the language demands of their studies. For example, Sutarsyah, Nation and Kennedy (1994) found that knowledge of 4000 to 5000 words would be a prerequisite for understanding an undergraduate economics textbook written in English. On a broader scale, Hazenberg and Hulstijn (1996) estimated that a non-native speaker of Dutch entering a university in the Netherlands needs a vocabulary of 10,000 Dutch words to be able to deal with first-year reading materials.

- In numerous countries where English is a foreign language, university students are taught through the medium of the national language but they need to read English texts related to their field of study. Examples of such countries are Indonesia and Thailand, where a primary objective of English teaching in secondary school is to prepare students to meet their reading needs at the university level. As with the international students above, it is useful to calculate a realistic minimum vocabulary size for these learners. Scholars work on the assumption that, in order to read independently, learners should know at least 95 per cent of the running words in a text. This means that on average only one word in 20 will be unfamiliar to them. Nation (1990: 24) and Laufer (1992; 1997a) argue that a vocabulary of at least 3000 word families is necessary to achieve this level of coverage. However, two studies of the vocabulary knowledge of first-year university students in Indonesia have found that typically they fall well short of the target, even after six years of high-school English study. In the late 1960s Quinn (1968) made an estimate of less than 1000 words, whereas 30 years later Nurweni and Read (1999) produced a figure of about 1200 words on average.

Scholars who carry out research on vocabulary size are not claiming that learners can meet their language needs simply by increasing the number of words they know. Obviously reading comprehension involves grammatical competence, an understanding of how texts are organised, background knowledge of the subject matter and other abilities in addition to vocabulary knowledge. Rather, the point is that adequate knowledge of words is a prerequisite for effective language use. Learners whose vocabulary is below a certain threshold level struggle to decode the basic elements of a text, to the extent that they find it hard to develop any higher level understanding of the content.

If we accept that vocabulary size has significant uses as a concept, the question is how to measure it. One characteristic of the literature on vocabulary size is the wide variation in the estimates that have been made of the number of words known by specific groups of native speakers. For example, the figures produced for students in US universities range from 15,000 to 200,000 (Anderson and Freebody, 1981: 96). The reasons for such discrepancies have been recognised since the early days of research in this field by some scholars (Thorndike, 1924; Lorge and Chall, 1963; Anderson and Freebody, 1981; Nation, 1993b), but others have undertaken studies on vocabulary size without really understanding the pitfalls. Essentially the issues that need to be addressed can be summed up in these three questions:

1 What counts as a word?
2 How do we choose which words to test?
3 How do we find out whether the selected words are known?

Let us look at each of these in turn.

What counts as a word?

This is an issue that I discussed in Chapter 2. The larger estimates of vocabulary size for native speakers tend to be calculated on the basis of individual word forms, whereas more conservative estimates take word families as the units to be measured. Remember that a word family consists of a base word together with its inflected and derived forms that share the same meaning. For example, the word forms *extends*, *extending*, *extended*, *extensive*, *extensively*, *extension* and *extent* can be seen as members of a family headed by the base form *extend*. The other members of the family are linked to *extend* by simple word-formation rules and all of them share a core meaning which can be expressed as 'spread or stretch out'. A person who knows the meaning of *extend* (or perhaps the meaning of any one member of the family) should be able to figure out what the other word forms mean by applying a little knowledge of English suffixes and getting some assistance from the context in which the word occurs. Thus, it seems overly generous to credit someone with knowing all eight forms of *extend* as separate items when they are so closely related both in form and meaning.

On the other hand, we can also find multiple words derived from a single base which have quite a range of meanings and thus seem to form more than one word family. I gave the example in Chapter 2 of these words: *social, socially, sociable, unsociable, sociability, socialise, socialisation, socialism, socialist, socialite, sociology, sociologist, sociological* and *societal*. The problem is how to separate them into families. Nagy and Anderson (1984) faced this difficulty in their study to estimate how many words American children are exposed to in the books that they read in school. They recognised that many words in their sample were semantically related to varying degrees and they developed a scale of relatedness to help sort out whether two word forms belonged to the same family or to different ones. The key question here is whether, having learned the meaning of a base word, the learner is able to work out what a derived form means when it is encountered in context. At Level 1 the meaning of the derived word can be inferred with minimal context (e.g. *various – vary, geneticist – genetic, sunbonnet – sun*). At Level 3 some aspects of the meaning of the derived word cannot be inferred except with considerable help from context (e.g. *collarbone – collar, visualize – visual, conclusive – conclusion*), while at Level 5 the meaning of the base word does not assist the learner at all in learning or remembering the derived word (*dashboard – dash, prefix – fix, peppermint – pepper*).

The Nagy and Anderson scale is not entirely satisfactory, since it involved a significant amount of subjective judgement by the researchers and was based on untested assumptions about what children find easy or difficult in interpreting the meanings of words. Bauer and Nation (1993) outline an alternative approach to defining membership of word families, using criteria such as the regularity, productivity and frequency of the prefixes and suffixes that are added to base words.

Thus, the identification of the units to be counted is an important step in research on vocabulary size. Apart from the problem of distinguishing base and derived words, researchers have to make decisions about how to deal with homographs, abbreviations, proper nouns, compound words, idioms and other multi-word units.

How do we choose which words to test?

For practical reasons it is impossible to test all the words that the native speaker of a language might know. Researchers have typically started with a large dictionary and then drawn a sample of words representing, say, 1 per cent (1 in 100) of the total dictionary entries. The next step is to test how many of the selected words are known by a group of subjects. Finally, the test scores are multiplied by 100 to give an estimate of the total vocabulary size.

It seems a straightforward procedure but, as Nation (1993b) pointed out in some detail, there are numerous traps for unwary researchers. For example, dictionary headwords are not the most suitable sampling units, for the reasons I gave in response to the first question. A single-word family may have multiple entries in the dictionary, so an estimate of vocabulary size based on headwords would be an inflated one. Second, a procedure by which, say, the first word on every sixth page is chosen will produce a sample in which very common words are overrepresented because these words, with their various meanings and uses, take up much more space in the dictionary than low-frequency words. Third, there are technical questions concerning the size of sample required to make a reliable estimate of total vocabulary size. As Meara (1996a: 40) noted, it is hard to estimate an indefinitely large quantity – probably numbering tens of thousands of items – from a small sample of just a few hundred words.

Measuring the vocabulary size of second language learners may be less problematic in the sense that they generally know a lot fewer words in the target language than native speakers do. In addition, the words they know are likely to be common, high-frequency ones. These are reasonable assumptions in a foreign-language environment where language learning takes place mainly in the classroom; however, learners who use the target language for communicative purposes outside the language classroom are much more likely to acquire the vocabulary that serves their various needs. For example, Harklau (1994: 255) observed that an Asian migrant student studying in a California high school knew the word *silhouette* but not *sleeve* or *snake*. Similarly, international students undertaking postgraduate study generally know the technical terms in their field of study but may lack a lot of vocabulary for everyday conversation.

Despite these observations, the few studies that have estimated the vocabulary size of learners of English (e.g. Quinn, 1968; Harlech-

Jones, 1983; Meara and Jones, 1988; Nurweni and Read, 1999) have used lists of high-frequency words such as the *Teacher's Word Book* (Thorndike and Lorge, 1944) or the *General Service List* (West, 1953) as the basis for their sampling. It is a relatively straightforward matter to draw a sample of words from an established list, and the sample usually represents a much higher proportion of the items in a list containing a few thousand words than does a sample taken from a large dictionary.

A limited word list may not include all the vocabulary that learners have some knowledge of but, as I indicated in introducing this section on vocabulary size, studies of learners have a different focus from research on native speakers. With learners, the issue may not be so much what their vocabulary size is in absolute terms but how much they know of the high-frequency words that they are most likely to encounter and need in their use of the language.

How do we find out whether the selected words are known?

Once a sample of words has been selected, it is necessary to find out – by means of some kind of test – whether each word is known. In studies of vocabulary size, the criterion for knowing a word is usually quite liberal, because of the large number of words that need to be covered in the time available for testing. The following test formats have been commonly used:

- multiple-choice items of various kinds;
- matching of words with synonyms or definitions;
- supplying an L1 equivalent for each L2 target word;
- the checklist (or yes–no) test, in which test-takers simply indicate whether they know the word or not.

I have already outlined earlier in this chapter the criticisms that can be made of tests using multiple-choice vocabulary items. For the purposes of testing vocabulary size, they are time-consuming to construct and the test-takers' performance is too dependent on the choice of distractors.

Although the next two tests are simpler to construct than multiple-choice ones, they represent a low level of word knowledge: the ability to associate each target word with another word or phrase that has the 'same' meaning. Such tests do not give any indication of whether the learners will understand the word when they encounter it in use, especially if it has a different meaning from the one they have learned. With an L2 to L1 translation task there is the additional drawback that the test-takers may produce a range of answers that have to be scored subjectively, which takes more time than for a more objective test format.

Nonetheless, these item types have been used with some success in measures of vocabulary size. In Chapter 5, we look in some detail at Nation's (1990: 261–272) Vocabulary Levels Test, which incorporates a matching test format. Also, Nurweni's study (Nurweni and Read, 1999) of the English vocabulary knowledge of Indonesian university students is a recent example of research in which a translation procedure was used.

The checklist test is really the simplest possible format for testing vocabulary and, according to Melka Teichroew (1982: 7), it has been used with native speakers at least since 1890. In comparison with other test items, Anderson and Freebody saw its simplicity as a virtue, in that 'it strips away irrelevant task demands that may make it difficult for young readers and poor readers to show what they know' (1983: 235). However, researchers have come to different conclusions about its validity as a measure of children's vocabulary knowledge. Sims (1929) found that a checklist test did not correlate well with three other methods of testing knowledge of a set of words and concluded that it was measuring the children's familiarity with the words from having seen them in books, rather than how well they understood them. On the other hand, Tilley (1936) obtained a high correlation between a checklist and a standardised multiple-choice test in his investigation of the relative difficulty of words for students at three different grade levels.

The obvious criticism of the checklist in its classic form is that there is no way of knowing how validly the test-takers are reporting their knowledge of the words. They can have a different idea from the researcher as to what 'knowing a word' means and may be genuinely mistaken about particular words, confusing one with another and so on. To address this problem, Anderson and Freebody (1983) prepared a vocabulary checklist containing a high proportion (about 40 per cent) of items that were not real English words. The researchers created these items either by changing letters in real words (e.g. *porfame* from *perfume*) or by combining word parts in novel ways to form 'pseudowords' (e.g. *observement*). If children ticked a number of the non-words, it was taken as evidence that they were likely to be overrating their knowledge of the real words and their scores were adjusted accordingly by applying a simple correction formula. The corrected scores correlated much more highly with the results of an interview procedure than did scores from a multiple-choice test of the words. In later studies, Anderson and his colleagues (Nagy, Herman and Anderson, 1985; Shu, Anderson and Zhang, 1995) have used pseudowords along with complete non-words like *ferlinder, werpet* and *ushom*.

These studies of children's first language vocabulary have been concerned with their knowledge of particular sets of words rather than total vocabulary size. However, the same approach was adopted by Meara and his associates (Meara and Buxton, 1987; Meara and Jones, 1988) in work on estimating the vocabulary size of second language learners. The original focus of the research was to produce a computerised vocabulary measure that would serve as an efficient placement test for language schools. This led to the publication of the Eurocentres Vocabulary Size Test (Meara and Jones, 1990a), which is one of the tests that I look at as a case study in Chapter 5. Meara and other scholars have continued work with both computer-based and pen-and-paper checklist tests. In a recent discussion of research with these tests in a number of settings, Meara (1996a: 42–44) notes that the effectiveness of the format depends on various factors: the proficiency level of the learners, their language background and whether they have a strong tendency to claim wrongly that they know a word.

The simple nature of the checklist test is obviously appealing to researchers on vocabulary size, who need to present learners with several hundred words in order to have a reliable basis for making their estimates. For some purposes, the format produces satisfactory results. However, in other situations, particularly when learners are being individually assessed rather than acting as the subjects of research, it is necessary to obtain some direct evidence that the words are indeed known in some sense; this can be achieved by using test formats such as multiple-choice or matching.

Overall, making good estimates of vocabulary size is a complex task. At all three levels – defining the units to be counted, selecting a sample and deciding on a test format – there are challenging questions to be resolved before a reliable measure can be obtained. Beyond that is the broader validity question, which takes us back to the various reasons for measuring vocabulary size that I outlined at the beginning of this section.

Assessing quality of vocabulary knowledge

Whatever the merits of vocabulary-size tests, one limitation is that they can give only a superficial indication of how well any particular word is known. In fact this criticism has long applied to many objective vocabulary tests, not just those that are designed to estimate total vocabulary size. Dolch and Leeds (1953) analysed the vocabulary subtests of five major reading and general achievement test batteries for American school children and found that

1 only the commonest meaning of each target word was assessed; and
2 the test-takers were required just to identify a synonym of each word.

Thus, the test items could not show whether additional, derived or figurative meanings of the target word were known, and it was quite possible that the children had learned to associate the target word with its synonym without really understanding what either one meant. Dolch and Leeds designed items that would measure what they called 'depth of meaning' of target words. Here are two examples:

A cow is an animal that	A disaster is ruin that happens
a. is found in zoos	a. suddenly
b. is used for racing	b. within a year's time
c. gives milk	c. to all people
d. does not have calves	d. gradually

Notice that the items include a synonym (*animal, ruin*), but then probe further the test-takers' understanding of the specific meaning of the target word. In an exploratory test of this kind given to university students and school teachers, the researchers found that less than 60 per cent of the subjects had a 'deep' knowledge of words like *shower, portal* and *dahlia*.

In general, though, research on depth – or quality – of vocabulary knowledge is quite limited, even in studies involving native speakers of English. As Anderson and Freebody put it:

> Through some quirk of the sociology of science, the in-depth study of word knowledge has been the special province of psycholinguists studying language development in young children. There is a substantial body of literature on selected vocabulary of children from about two through eight years of age. The literature involving older children and adults is meager.
>
> (Anderson and Freebody, 1981: 94)

Despite the relative lack of research, studying the quality of learners' word knowledge seems to have value for a variety of purposes:

- The conventional psychometric approach to validating tests involves correlating them with a criterion measure that can be considered valid. In first language vocabulary testing studies (e.g. Sims, 1929; Kelley, 1933; Corson, 1985), the criterion has often been performance in an individual interview, in which the subjects are required to demonstrate their understanding of each word by giving an explanation, providing a definition and/or using the word in a sentence. The interviewer has the opportunity to probe the subject's knowledge of the word in some depth, and the assumption is that a less direct measure like a multiple-choice, matching or checklist test is valid to the extent that its scores are consistent with the interview results.
- A second purpose was covered in Chapter 3: measuring partial knowledge of words in the context of research on incidental vocabulary learning. Among the studies that have used interviews to measure the quality of vocabulary knowledge after a period of learning are those by Nagy, Herman and Anderson (1985), Paribakht and Wesche (1993), Joe (1995) and Schmitt (1998c).
- A third situation is that of children from migrant communities being educated through their second language. In the Netherlands, for instance, bilingual children from Turkish and Moroccan backgrounds have relatively low levels of achievement in school, and linguistic research has shown that their vocabulary size in Dutch is significantly smaller than that of their monolingual Dutch-speaking peers, just as Cummins (1981) found in his work on vocabulary knowledge of immigrant children in Canadian schools. Verhallen and Schoonen (1993) provided another perspective on this situation by investigating the quality of Turkish children's knowledge of common Dutch words. Taking just six words, like *neus* ('nose'), *geheim* ('secret') and *haar* ('hair'), the researchers conducted inten-

sive interviews to elicit from the children every possible aspect of meaning that they might associate with each target word. The results clearly showed that the Turkish children knew fewer and less varied aspects of the words than monolingual children of the same age. This lag in the bilingual children's lexical development in Dutch was interpreted as a strong contributing factor to their low level of educational achievement.

- For my own work on measuring depth of vocabulary knowledge (Read, 1993; 1998), the basic rationale was that students studying English for academic purposes need to have a thorough knowledge of words that occur frequently in different academic texts. Since these words have a range of uses in academic contexts, it makes sense to assess whether the learners know more about them than just synonyms or general L1 equivalents. Nurweni and Read's (1999) study of the English vocabulary of Indonesian university students included two measures of depth of knowledge to complement the test of vocabulary size.

There are two questions that I want to focus on in the rest of this section on quality of vocabulary knowledge: how to conceptualise it, and how to measure it?

How to conceptualise it?

The Dolch and Leeds (1953) test items with which I introduced this section of the chapter essentially assess *precision* of knowledge: do the test-takers know the specific meaning of each target word, rather than just having a vague idea about it? This represents one way to define quality of knowledge, but it assumes that each word has only one meaning to be precisely known. Of course, words commonly have several different meanings – think of *fresh*, as in *fresh bread, fresh ideas, fresh supplies, a fresh breeze* and so on. If we take this aspect into account, we need to add a dimension of *range* of meaning, in addition to precision.

Going a step further, vocabulary knowledge involves more than simply word meaning. As we saw in Chapter 2, Richards (1976) and Nation (1990) list multiple components of word knowledge, including spelling, pronunciation, grammatical form, relative frequency, collocations and restrictions on the use of the word, as well as the distinction between receptive and productive knowledge. To add to the complexity, alternative frameworks for analysing the scope of vocabulary knowledge, such as Cronbach's (1942), are often quoted in the literature. It is not surprising, then, that a reader can become quite confused by the different ways that authors and researchers use terms such as 'depth', 'precision' and 'quality' of knowledge.

In a recent paper, Henriksen (1999) has attempted to clarify matters by proposing that we should recognise three distinct dimensions of vocabulary knowledge:

1 partial–precise knowledge: Vocabulary-size measures, which we looked at in the last section, tend to be located towards the 'partial' end of this continuum, whereas the Dolch and Leeds' items quoted above are nearer to the 'precise' end.
2 depth of knowledge: This is where the various types of knowledge identified by Richards (1976) and Nation (1990) fit in. Since there are many components involved in this dimension, it cannot really be conceived as a single continuum in the way that the partial–precise one may be. Henriksen sees it more as a process whereby learners build a network of links between one word and other words in their minds.
3 receptive–productive: The distinction here is between having some knowledge of a word and being able to use it in speech or writing. It is often seen as a continuum, although there are difficulties in defining how and at what point words become available for productive use. I will discuss this dimension in some detail in Chapter 6.

Henriksen's analysis goes some way towards providing a better basis for conceptualising quality of vocabulary knowledge and for sorting out what aspects of the construct are being measured in particular research studies. However, the fact remains that vocabulary knowledge is an inherently complex concept.

How to measure it?

A common assessment procedure for measuring quality of vocabulary knowledge is an individual interview with each learner, probing how much they know about a set of target words. For instance, in their work with bilingual and monolingual Dutch children, Verhallen and Schoonen (1993) wanted to elicit all aspects of the target word meaning that the children might know, in order to make an elaborate semantic analysis of the responses. Therefore, they asked a whole series of questions:

> What does [book] mean?
> What is a [book]?
> How would you explain what a [book] is?
> What do you see if you look at a [book]?
> What kinds of [book] are there?
> What kind of thing is a [book]?
> What can you do with a [book]?
> Can you make three sentences with the word [book]?
>
> (Verhallen and Schoonen, 1993: 350)

After responding to each of the first six questions, the children were given a further prompt ('Can you tell me more?') and so there were at least 13 questions for each word. It is not surprising, then, only a small number of target words (just six) were covered in each inter-view. There is clearly a trade-off between how much can be elicited about each word and how many different words can be included.

Interviews with adults are subject to the same constraint, and others as well. Schmitt (1998c) took two hours to interview each of his subjects about five aspects of their knowledge of 11 words. From my own experience of conducting such interviews (Read, 1989), I have found that they can be affected by the degree of rapport established between interviewer and interviewee. Adult learners may be embar-rassed to admit that they do not really know what a word means. Besides, it is difficult to achieve consistency from one interview to the next unless the procedure is carefully structured.

Thus, for practical purposes it is necessary to explore alternatives to the interview as ways of assessing depth of vocabulary knowledge. Two recent initiatives along these lines are featured in later chapters of the book. In Chapter 5, one of the case studies is Paribakht and Wesche's Vocabulary Knowledge Scale, a measure designed to eval-uate how well students gain knowledge of target words through reading. And I discuss the development of my own word associates format as a case of vocabulary-test design in Chapter 6.

The construct validity of vocabulary tests

In the discussion so far I have assumed we can accept at face value that tests labelled 'vocabulary' are measures of lexical knowledge and not anything else. However, the distinction between vocabulary tests and other tests of language ability is not easy to establish by means of statistical analysis. In a review of measurement issues in first language reading research, Farr and Carey (1986: 103) noted that researchers have found a high degree of overlap between tests of vocabulary and the other subskills involved in reading. As we saw earlier in the chapter, correlational procedures have often been used to validate vocabulary tests, but generally this has meant correlating one vocabulary measure with another. To show that vocabulary knowledge is a separate component of language ability, it is necessary to have a systematic procedure to investigate the relationships between vocabulary tests and other language tests, and this involves the most fundamental kind of research that language testers undertake: construct validation of tests.

As I explained in Chapter 1, the term construct refers to the particular kind of knowledge or ability that a test is designed to measure. Most conventional vocabulary tests are intended to assess knowledge of the meaning of a specific set of words. In this case, the relationship between the test content and the construct may seem quite straightforward. After all, what else could the test be measuring if it presents the test-takers with a set of words with little if any context and requires them to select the correct synonym or definition? And it seems self-evident that a 'vocabulary' test of that kind is measuring something different from a 'grammar' test in which the learners have to recognise a context where the present perfect form of a verb must be used or identify the preposition to be used after *similar*.

Nevertheless, distinguishing between tests in this way – and showing that they do indeed tap different underlying constructs – is not as straightforward as it appears. Let us look at some specific test items to help make the point.

(1)   [*Choose the best answer, from the four choices given.*]

After the heavy rain, many parts of the city were ____ .
a. flooded   b. washed   c. drowned   d. watered

(2)   [*Write the missing word in the space provided.*]

At last the climbers reached the s_____ of the mountain.

(3)   [*Choose the correct answer, from the four choices given.*]

We could see the place ____ she had the accident.
a. which   b. where   c. whether   d. what

(4) [*Rewrite the sentence in another way, beginning with the words given.*]

It was difficult to play on the wet field.
Playing ――――――――――――――― .

On the face of it, (1) and (2) are items testing vocabulary knowledge, whereas the other two items are assessing knowledge of grammar. Thus, we might expect that a test composed of items like (1) would be strongly related to a test with items like (2), since they are both measuring the same construct; similarly, the two grammar tests should have a close relationship with each other. And, if two distinct constructs are involved, tests (1) and (2) should give a different pattern of results from tests (3) and (4). What complicates the comparisons, though, is the fact that we also need to take account of the test task. It is a well-established finding in testing research that the choice of test item to assess a particular skill or ability has an influence on the scores obtained. From this point of view, we might expect test (1) to give somewhat similar results to test (3), on the basis that the scores will at least partly reflect the test-takers' expertise at answering multiple-choice items while, on the other hand, tests (2) and (4) have in common the fact that both require the test-takers to compose a response rather than select one.

Therefore, we have to recognise two major sources of influence on test scores: the knowledge or ability represented by the construct and the testing task. In construct validation, these are generally referred to by the terms **trait** and **method** respectively. Two American educational measurement specialists, Campbell and Fiske (1959), developed a methodology known as **multitrait multimethod (MTMM)** construct validation, which provides a way of evaluating separately the contributions of traits and methods to test scores. Such studies are complex and time-consuming because a substantial number of carefully planned tests must be given to a reasonably large number of test-takers. It is perhaps not surprising, then, that few such studies have been carried out in language testing. However, there are two MTMM studies that have investigated the construct of vocabulary knowledge, and it is to these we now turn.

Both studies set out to investigate whether it was possible to distinguish statistically between knowledge of vocabulary and of grammar. In the first one, Corrigan and Upshur (1982) devised three vocabulary and three grammar tests, each assessing knowledge of the same language items using a different test method. For example, in method 1 the language item (the word or structure) was presented aurally on tape; in method 2, it was presented in a printed sentence; and in method 3, it was cued by a picture. The response required by the test-takers was similarly varied. The tests were administered to adult ESL learners from a variety of language backgrounds studying at a university in the US.

The MTMM procedure involved a systematic comparison of the correlations between the six tests. The general principle is that, in order to establish that vocabulary knowledge was an independent trait, it was necessary to show that the vocabulary tests correlated with each other more highly on average than did the pairs of tests where the traits and methods were mixed, or 'crossed' (e.g. the picture-based vocabulary test and the aural grammar test). In this case, the average correlation between the pairs of vocabulary tests (0.216) was lower than that for the tests in which traits and methods were crossed (0.257). It was also lower than the mean correlation of the tests which used the same method, for example picture-based vocabulary vs. picture-based grammar (0.358). This meant that Corrigan and Upshur could not produce evidence for the construct validity of their tests of vocabulary knowledge. Vocabulary did not emerge from their test results as a distinct trait, because the type of item used had a greater influence on the learners' performance than whether it was a vocabulary test or not.

If you know anything about correlations, you will have observed that they were rather low overall in the Corrigan and Upshur study. As Arnaud (1989) noted, this reflected the low reliabilities of the individual tests. Arnaud attempted to obtain more conclusive results by running a similar study, using tests that were tailored for a more homogeneous group of English learners: first-year students at a French university. Again the traits were vocabulary and grammar, assessed by three test methods: picture-cued multiple-choice, French-to-English translation and error recognition. Although Arnaud's tests were substantially more reliable than the ones in the earlier research, he too was unable to show that vocabulary – or grammar, for that matter – existed as a separate construct. Some of the correlations involving the same test method (e.g. vocabulary-error recognition and grammar-error recognition: 0.57) were higher than ones for the same hypothesised trait (e.g. vocabulary multiple-choice and vocabulary-error recognition: 0.32).

Arnaud concluded in a somewhat pessimistic vein that it might never be possible to demonstrate that vocabulary knowledge is a distinct trait by employing the MTMM methodology. He pointed out how difficult it was to find three separate test methods that could be satisfactorily used to assess both vocabulary and grammar. Another issue raised by Arnaud, to which I have already alluded, is the effect of the personal characteristics of the learners who are the subjects in this type of research. Arnaud's subjects were homogeneous in terms of first language, educational background and experience of formally studying English as a foreign language. In contrast, Corrigan and Upshur's sample of learners was more diverse in their language backgrounds and levels of proficiency in English. In the latter case, there was a greater chance that the subjects' vocabulary knowledge was distinguishable from their grammatical competence. And in fact the American researchers did find evidence in their results both that the grammar items were easier than the vocabulary ones, and that grammar was a distinct trait. There has apparently been no follow-up research, however, to clarify these points.

Nevertheless, the inconclusive results of the MTMM studies are consistent with other research findings. I noted in Chapter 2 the way that the work of corpus linguists like Sinclair (1991) is challenging our conventional view of the separateness of vocabulary and grammar. Another illustration of the point comes from a survey by Dieterich, Freeman and Crandall (1979) of tests used by schools in the United States to assess the English proficiency of students from non-English-speaking backgrounds. The researchers identified numerous linguistic problems in the tests which meant that test users were likely to make faulty inferences about the children's ability in English. One problem was that tests intended to assess control of grammatical structures often seemed just to test knowledge of word meanings. Here is an example from among the several given by the authors:

> In [one] test . . . the person must choose the correct response to a passive sentence ('The forks are held by both children'). Since only one of the three pictures shows two children with forks, the test taker can get the answer right simply by knowing the two words *fork* and *children*. We know no more about the person's ability to understand passive sentences than we did before.
>
> (Dieterich, Freeman and Crandall, 1979: 539)

Although you might consider this to be just a case of poor item writing, it illustrates the difficulty of isolating particular elements of the language for assessment purposes. Furthermore, it highlights the point that we need to be cautious in making assumptions about what aspect of language is being assessed just on the basis of the label that a test has been given.

The role of context

Whether we can separate vocabulary from other aspects of language proficiency is obviously relevant to the question of what the role of context is in vocabulary assessment. In the early years of objective testing, many vocabulary tests presented the target words in isolation, in lists or as the stems of multiple-choice items. It was considered that such tests were pure measures of vocabulary knowledge. In fact, the distinguished American scholar John B. Carroll wrote in an un-published paper in 1954 (quoted in Spolsky, 1995: 165) that test items containing a single target word were the only ones that should be classified as vocabulary items. Any longer stimulus would turn the item into a reading-comprehension one.

One practical difficulty with testing vocabulary in isolation was re-cognised early on: a word can have different meanings and be used as more than one part of speech. When the word form is presented by itself, there is no indication as to which meaning or use of the word the test-writer intends to assess. Sims (1929) addressed the problem in his research by not testing any word that had more than one meaning; however, this is obviously not a feasible solution in normal assessment situations. Another approach, one which has generally been recom-mended in the handbooks on language testing, was to present the word in a short phrase or sentence to cue the intended usage. For instance, Clark (1972: 49–50, 99–100) emphasised the need to provide a 'neutral' context for the target words in vocabulary-test items. He gave as an illustration a listening item to assess knowledge of the French word *marteau* ('hammer'). According to Clark, the stimulus sentence *Voici un marteau* ('Here is a hammer') is suitably neutral, whereas a sen-tence like *Pierre enfonce des clous avec un marteau* ('Pierre drives in some nails with a hammer') might give away the correct answer to a test-taker who knew the word *clou* but not the intended target word.

It is interesting to note in passing that this view of the role of context neatly complements the concerns of vocabulary researchers discussed in Chapter 3. Whereas designers of traditional vocabulary tests have sought to create items that did not provide any contextual clues as to the meaning of a word not known by the test-taker, researchers on second language vocabulary acquisition have often deliberately planted such clues in stimulus sentences or texts, in order to investigate the ability of learners to make inferences about unfamiliar words that they encounter in their reading or listening.

There has been little research that explicitly addresses the role of context in assessing knowledge of individual words. One study, by Stalnaker and Kurath (1935), compared two methods of testing knowledge of German vocabulary. One (the 'Best-answer' test) consisted of multiple-choice items, with each target word presented in isolation, like this:

> 1. bekommen   1-become   2-arrive   3-accept   4-escape
>   5-receive . . . __
> 2. versuchen   1-attempt   2-search   3-request   4-conceal
>   5-visit . . . __

For a second ('Context') test, a reading passage was constructed containing all 100 of the same target words and the test-takers had to supply the English equivalent of each underlined word, as in the following excerpt:

> Ein Mann hatte drei <u>erwachsene</u>   erwachsene ___ ;
> Söhne. Diese arbeiteten <u>fast</u> nie,   fast ___ ;
> <u>obgleich</u> der Vater ihnen <u>befohlen</u>   obgleich ___ befohlen ___ ;
> hatte, ihr eigenes Brot zu <u>verdienen</u>,   verdienen ___ ;
> und <u>böse</u> wurde, wenn sie nicht auf   böse ___ ;
> ihn <u>achteten</u>. . . .   achteten ___

When the two tests were administered to students of German at the University of Chicago, they produced remarkably similar results. They were highly correlated with each other and had very similar correlations with two other measures of the students' ability: teacher ratings of their achievement in German and intelligence-test scores. Thus, the researchers concluded that the two tests were equally valid measures of essentially the same ability. Although they made no recommendation as to which type of test should be preferred, the implication was that there was no real advantage in testing words in context.

However, my distinction between context-independent and

context-dependent tests is relevant here. Stalnaker and Kurath's Context test was, as noted above, based on a text that was especially written to contain all 100 of the pre-selected target words, in the style of a graded reader. Although the authors stated that each response 'had to fit into the context in which it appeared' (1935: 438), it is likely that at this elementary level of language learning the students could treat each underlined word as an isolated item in most cases, without needing to refer to the context to arrive at the correct answer. To the extent that this was true, the Context test was in fact a context-independent measure of the test-takers' knowledge of the target words.

The Test of English as a Foreign Language (TOEFL), which is one of the case studies in Chapter 5, offers another interesting illustration of a contextualised vocabulary test that could be considered context independent in practice.

Nevertheless, despite the lack of research evidence on the role of context in vocabulary assessment, it has become almost an article of faith among both language teachers and testers that vocabulary should always be presented in context. In the shift away from decon-textualised discrete-point tests in the 1970s, one type of test that received a great deal of attention was the **cloze procedure**. Although it may be past its heyday now, cloze tests of various kinds are still widely used and there is continuing research on what they measure. It is true that the cloze has never been seen primarily as a lexical measure, but presumably test-takers need to draw strongly on their vocabulary knowledge in making their responses. Following from this, in the next section we review the literature on the cloze to see what we can learn about the assessment of vocabulary.

Cloze tests as vocabulary measures

A standard cloze test consists of one or more reading passages from which words are deleted according to a fixed ratio (e.g. every seventh word). Each deleted word is replaced by a blank of uniform length, and the task of the test-takers is to write a suitable word in each space. Some authors (e.g. Weir, 1990: 48; Alderson, 2000) prefer to restrict the use of the label **cloze** to this kind of test, but the term is commonly used to include a number of modifications to the standard format. One modified version is the selective-deletion (or **rational**) cloze, where the test-writer deliberately chooses the words to be deleted, preferably according to principled criteria. A second modification is the **multiple-choice cloze**. In this case, each deleted word is incorporated into a multiple-choice item and, instead of writing in the word, the test-takers have to choose which of the three or four options is the one that fills the blank. A third alternative is the **C-test**, in which a series of short texts are more radically mutilated by deleting the second half of every second word. The two scholars in Germany who devised the C-test, Klein-Braley and Raatz (1984), argued that it is based on the same principles as the standard cloze and at the same time overcomes what they see as some problems with the original format.

Cloze tests have been used for a variety of purposes. The researcher in the US who is usually credited with inventing the procedure, Wilson Taylor (1953), presented it initially as a means of evaluating the readability of texts for particular groups of students. Subsequently, it has been widely used to measure L1 reading-comprehension ability. In second language testing the scholar who most vigorously promoted the use of cloze tests was John Oller (see, for example, Oller, 1973; 1979). He saw the standard fixed-ratio cloze as a highly effective way of testing learners' overall second language proficiency, as distinct from their knowledge of particular vocabulary items or grammatical elements.

In order for the cloze to be valid for this purpose, there seemed to be two crucial requirements. The first was that a good range of word types should be deleted from the text, including both content words (nouns, main verbs, adjectives) and function words (articles, prepositions, auxiliary verbs, conjunctions). Oller argued that this was achieved satisfactorily by deleting about 50 words from a suitable text according to the fixed-ratio method. The second requirement was that, in a large proportion of cases, the test-takers should have to look beyond the immediate environment of the blank – beyond the clause or sentence in which it occurred – to be able to figure out what the missing word was.

This second point became a source of controversy among researchers on the cloze procedure. Oller and his associates (Oller, 1975; Chihara, Oller, Weaver and Chávez-Oller, 1977) conducted studies in which they scrambled the order of sentences in a cloze text and found that this made it much more difficult for test-takers to fill in the blanks than when the sentences were presented in their proper sequence. This, they argued, demonstrated that the discourse structure of the text made a substantial contribution to performance in the cloze test. Other scholars (for example Alderson, 1979; Shanahan, Kamil and Tobin, 1982; Porter, 1983), employing a variety of research methods, produced evidence that most cloze blanks could be successfully completed by referring only to the immediate linguistic context and they concluded that the cloze procedure basically assessed just knowledge of 'local' grammar and vocabulary rather than higher-level reading skills beyond the individual sentence. These studies have been criticised (by, for example, Cziko, 1983; Jonz and Oller, 1994) on methodological grounds and a further series of studies (Brown, 1983; Bachman, 1985; Jonz, 1987; 1990) have kept alive the debate on the meaning of cloze-test scores.

A large proportion of L2 cloze research, then, focuses the validity of the total score in a cloze test as a measure of the test-taker's overall proficiency as a reader or a user of the target language. However, if we are particularly interested in vocabulary, we want to know to what extent lexical knowledge has contributed to the test-takers' performance in the test and also which particular items can be seen as assessing vocabulary rather than something else. Another question is whether we can modify the cloze procedure to make it more a measure of vocabulary ability. There are some studies that provide evidence that is relevant to answering such questions and it is best to review them according to the type of cloze test that was investigated.

The standard cloze

Let us first look at the standard, fixed-ratio cloze. A popular way of exploring the validity of cloze tests in the 1970s was to correlate them with various other types of test. In numerous studies the cloze correlated highly with 'integrative' tests such as dictation or composition writing and at a rather lower level with more 'discrete-point' tests of vocabulary, grammar and phonology. This was interpreted as evidence in support of Oller's claim that the cloze was a good measure of overall proficiency in the language. However, as I discussed earlier in this chapter, simple correlations are not an adequate means of establishing what a test is measuring, especially when the correlation is a moderate one, say, in the range of 0.50 to 0.80. Tests differ not only in what they are designed to measure (the trait) but also in the task that they set the test-taker (the method). For example, filling in the blanks in a cloze passage is a rather different task from writing a composition or selecting the correct options in a multiple-choice vocabulary test. From a modern perspective, it is necessary to take a more sophisticated approach to the interpretation of correlations, one that will allow us to predict the relative size of the correlations between a number of tests, according to both the kind of ability being measured and the type of task.

A study that adopted such an approach is the one by Chapelle and Abraham (1990), who compared scores on four different types of cloze test with the results of various components of a placement test battery. After analysing what was involved in each test, the researchers predicted that the fixed-ratio cloze would have the strongest correlation with the writing test, relatively weaker relationships with the reading and vocabulary tests and the lowest correlation with the listening test. The latter three tests all used the multiple-choice format. The actual correlations were indeed ranked in this order, although none of them was very high in absolute terms. We need to be cautious about drawing conclusions from the results of this study because the student sample was relatively small and some of the tests were not very reliable, but the design of the research illustrates how such studies should be carried out. We consider other results of this study below.

Another way to explore what a standard cloze test measures is to make a detailed analysis of what is involved in responding correctly to each item. Where are clues to be found that will help the test-taker to arrive at the correct answer? Obviously, this is a similar sort of question to the one we discussed in Chapter 3, concerning the clues available for inferring the meaning of unknown words in a text. For this purpose, Bachman (1985) made a four-way classification of the level of context required:

1 within the clause in which the blank occurs;
2 outside the clause, but within the same sentence;
3 beyond the sentence, but somewhere in the text; and
4 outside the text.

All four levels may require the application of vocabulary knowledge, as well as other aspects of linguistic competence. Bachman suggested that, in any fixed-ratio cloze test, the proportion of items in each of these four categories would be about the same.

Taking up Bachman's suggestion, Jonz (1990) chose eight standard cloze texts which had been used by various researchers and analysed the types of context required to fill in the blanks. He found a high level of consistency in the percentages of items assigned to each type of context, whether he used Bachman's four-category classification or modified systems that he devised himself. From our point of view, the most interesting modification was a five-part system in which he divided Bachman's within-the-clause category into two; he called these clause-level syntax and clause-level lexis. On average, over the eight cloze passages, Jonz found the following percentages for the five categories:

Clause-level syntax	24.1%
Clause-level lexis	33.0%
Within the sentence	10.9%
Within the text	23.2%
Outside the text	8.9%

(Jonz, 1990: 70)

The two categories that obviously involve vocabulary knowledge are Clause-level lexis and Outside the text. The latter group consisted mostly of blanks to be filled by content words for which there were few if any clues provided in the text. If we add these categories, we get a figure of 42 per cent for fixed-ratio cloze items that explicitly draw on vocabulary. This almost certainly underestimates the lexical contribution to successful performance in a cloze test because the third and fourth categories (within the sentence and within the text) also involve, in many cases, links between vocabulary items.

A word of caution is necessary here since, although he carefully defined his categories, Jonz's figures represent purely his judgement as to what kind of contextual information was required to fill in each blank correctly. He himself noted that, as a preliminary step in his research, he re-classified the items in the cloze text that Bachman used in his 1985 study and found that he put 14 of the 30 items in a different category from the one chosen by Bachman. Most of the discrepancies were the result of the different ways that they interpreted the extratextual category. Bachman used this category more frequently than Jonz did because he included in it items where the test-taker had to draw on background knowledge of the subject matter to make the connection between the missing word and another word in the text which provided a clue (Oller and Jonz, 1994:

333). Jonz suggests that more is involved than just inconsistencies in the rating process: 'I take these discrepancies to indicate that the constraints on response for any cloze item might, in fact, vary in principled ways from one person to the next' (1990: 72).

Thus, both the correlational approach (Chapelle and Abraham) and subjective judgements about individual items (Bachman; Jonz) offer ways to investigate the role of vocabulary knowledge in learner performance. Both methods show that vocabulary makes a substantial contribution, but it is difficult to say precisely how large it is because the various components of language ability are interrelated. It is also very likely that there are individual differences that affect the way that test-takers go about responding to cloze items, so that some may draw more on their vocabulary knowledge than others do.

The rational cloze

Although Oller has consistently favoured the standard fixed-ratio format as the most valid form of the cloze procedure for assessing second language proficiency, other scholars have argued for a more selective approach to the deletion of words from the text. In his research, Alderson (1979) found that a single text could produce quite different tests depending on whether you deleted, say, every eighth word rather than every sixth. He also obtained evidence that most cloze blanks could be filled by referring just to the clause or the sentence in which they occurred. (There is of course some confirmation of this in the figures from Jonz's (1990) research quoted above: 68 per cent of the items could be answered from within the clause or the sentence. The issue hinges then on what we mean by 'most'.) From these results, Alderson concluded that the standard cloze procedure measured what he called lower-order skills, particularly those involving vocabulary and sentence structure. And it did so somewhat unpredictably, according to which particular words ended up being deleted from the text. This led him to the view that '[p]erhaps the principle of randomness needs to be abandoned in favour of the *rational* selection of deletions, based upon a theory of the nature of language and language processing' (1979: 226; emphasis added).

Alderson's view has been influential, especially among British scholars (see, for example, Johnson, 1981; Hughes, 1989; Weir, 1990), but there has been only a small amount of research that has investigated the rational cloze in a systematic way with second language learners. Bachman (1982; 1985) conducted two studies in which he selected items that focused primarily on cohesive links within and between the sentences of the text. Chapelle and Abraham (1990) chose items that matched the types of items in a fixed-ratio cloze based on the same text. None of the published studies has involved a rational cloze designed just to measure vocabulary, but once you accept the logic of selective deletion of words from the text, it makes sense to use the cloze procedure to assess the learners' ability to supply missing content words on the basis of contextual clues and, at a more advanced level, to choose the most stylistically appropriate word for a particular blank.

For their rational cloze, which was designed to form part of a university entrance examination in Israel, Bensoussan and Ramraz (1984) selected items according to three levels of meaning in the text:

1 the micro-level: focusing on the lexical choice of words and their interaction with other words in the context (12 items);
2 the pragmatic level: which is extra-textual and draws on the reader's general knowledge of the world (2 items); and
3 the macro-level: dealing with the functions of the sentences and the structure of the text as a whole (7 items).

(Bensoussan and Ramraz, 1984: 231)

Clearly these three selection criteria, which were derived from the theory of discourse analysis, have a strong lexical orientation and a lot in common with Bachman and Jonz's categories for types of context. An effort was made to choose individual words or short phrases not so much as vocabulary items in their own right but rather as carriers of 'the thought sequence' or 'the weight of the argument'. In one of their experiments with the cloze, Bensoussan and Ramraz correlated the scores with various subsections of the English test battery in the entrance examination. However, those subtests consisted of quite small numbers of items (there were only nine vocabulary items, for example), so it is not surprising that the correlations were quite modest and difficult to interpret.

The largest research project to date to investigate the use of the rational cloze with ESL learners was conducted by Hale, Stansfield, Rock, Hicks, Butler and Oller (1989) as part of the ongoing research programme on the Test of English as a Foreign language (TOEFL). The objective was to see whether the cloze procedure, with selective deletion of items and a multiple-choice response format, could be used in the TOEFL context as an effective measure of reading ability for students from a wide variety of language groups. In this case, the researchers were interested in looking at the respective contributions of vocabulary knowledge, grammar knowledge and reading comprehension ability to test-takers' performance on the cloze. However, recognising that these three aspects of language ability were interrelated, they developed four categories of items. The first two required the test-takers to understand the text beyond the clause in which the item was located. Then they were distinguished according to whether knowledge of grammar or knowledge of vocabulary was most needed:

1) Reading Comprehension/Grammar (RG)

   Example: A ballad is a folk song; however, a folk song is not a ballad [because / if / whether / unless] it tells a story.

2) Reading Comprehension/Vocabulary (RV)

   Example: . . . known as the Lost Sea. It is listed in the Guinness Book of World Records as the world's largest underground [water / body / lake / cave].

The other two types of item were ones that could be answered just by using the information available in the clause where the item was found. Again they were differentiated on the basis of requiring grammatical or lexical knowledge:

3) Grammar/Reading Comprehension (GR)

   Example: It is generally understood that a ballad is a song that tells a story, but a folk song is not so [easy / easily / ease / easier] defined.

4) Vocabulary/Reading Comprehension (VR)

   Example: In fact, there are folk songs for many occupations – railroading, [following / mustering / concentrating / herding] cattle, and so on.

A cloze test was developed consisting of three short texts, with a total of 50 multiple-choice items spread across the four categories. The test was administered at the end of a scheduled TOEFL test session to more than 11,000 candidates from nine different language groups.

To analyse the results, the researchers first intercorrelated the four types of cloze item and found that they had a similar, moderate level of relationship among them. There was no clear evidence, for example, that the RV and VR items (both supposedly drawing on vocabulary knowledge) were more closely associated with each other than they were with the RG or GR items. Then the authors looked at the correlations between the cloze items and the various subtests of the TOEFL. The RV and VR items tended to correlate more highly with the vocabulary and reading comprehension sections of TOEFL, whereas the RG and GR items had a somewhat stronger relationship with the structure and written expression (i.e. error detection) items in the TOEFL battery. However, the differences were not large and, indeed, the TOEFL subtests had high intercorrelations among themselves.

Thus, although the words to be used for the cloze items had been carefully selected by the combined efforts of several distinguished American applied linguists, the results of this study provided further evidence of how difficult it is to isolate the distinct contribution of vocabulary knowledge to test performance – at least by means of the correlational procedures employed here. As Hale *et al.* put it, 'Perhaps the kind of text processing required by MC [multiple-choice] cloze items is more holistic in character than current linguistic analyses might suggest' (1989: 65).

The multiple-choice cloze

In the preceding discussion of the rational cloze, we have already looked at the Hale *et al.* (1989) test, which used the multiple-choice item format as well. Let us now focus on this form of the cloze procedure.

There have been various reasons given for using multiple-choice items in a cloze test rather than the standard blanks to be filled in. Porter (1976) and Ozete (1977) argued that the standard format requires writing ability, whereas the multiple-choice version makes it more a measure of reading comprehension. Jonz (1976) pointed out that a multiple-choice cloze could be marked more objectively because it controlled the range of responses that the test-takers could give. In addition, he considered that providing response options made the test more student-centred – or 'learner-friendly', as we might say these days. For Bensoussan and Ramraz (1984), multiple-choice items were a practical necessity, because their cloze test formed part of an entrance examination for two universities in Israel, with 13,000 candidates annually. The same would be true, of course, of the Hale *et al.* (1989) multiple-choice cloze that we just discussed above, if it had been adopted for use in the TOEFL, which has candidates numbering in the hundreds of thousands each year. One further advantage, exploited by Bensoussan (1983) and Bensoussan and Ramraz (1984), was the opportunity offered by the multiple-choice format to create items where more than one word – and even as much as a whole sentence – was deleted from the original text. This allows the test designer to move beyond a view of vocabulary as being composed of single word forms to cover larger lexical units as well.

Multiple-choice items have been used with both fixed-ratio and selective-deletion cloze tests. Jonz (1976) began the development of his multiple-choice cloze by administering a standard open-ended test with every seventh word deleted. He then performed an item analysis to select the items that were of moderate difficulty and discriminated well. This meant that he discarded about half of the items, while the remaining ones were converted into the multiple-choice format; the most frequently supplied acceptable response was accepted as the correct option and the three most common unacceptable responses as the distractors. The resulting 33-item test was administered, at the same time as a placement examination, to ESL students at a university in the US. The cloze had a correlation of 0.54 with the vocabulary subtest in the examination. This was relatively low, compared to the correlation of 0.61 with the reading subtest, 0.70 with the structure test and 0.80 with the composition.

Chapelle and Abraham (1990) found an even lower correlation between their multiple-choice cloze and a multiple-choice vocabulary test (0.18), whereas the cloze correlated highly with a reading-comprehension test (0.86). They had predicted that the two correlations would be about the same and were at a loss to explain the discrepancy. More generally, from this and a later re-analysis of their data (Abraham and Chapelle, 1992), the researchers concluded that the multiple-choice version of the cloze procedure functioned quite differently from the fill-in format. For one thing, the items based on content words in the text were significantly easier in the multiple-choice version than items based on function words, whereas researchers working with conventional fill-in tests have consistently found the reverse. This makes sense because there are commonly a lot more possible answers when a noun, adjective or verb has been deleted than when the missing word is an article, a preposition or a conjunction. As Abraham and Chapelle point out, the multiple-choice format has the effect of reducing the range of possibilities for a content-word item, which presumably makes it easier to respond to. It is likely, too, that the presence of the distractors in each item changes the nature of the task in ways that have not yet been properly investigated. This would be consistent with the criticisms of the role of the distractors in multiple-choice vocabulary items that I reported earlier in the chapter.

The C-test

At first glance the C-test – in which a series of short texts are prepared for testing by deleting the second half of every second word – may seem to be the version of the cloze procedure that is the least promising as a specific measure of vocabulary. For one thing, its creators intended that it should assess general proficiency in the language, particularly for selection and placement purposes, and that the deletions should be a representative sample of all the elements in the text (Klein-Braley, 1985; 1997: 63–66). If that is the intention, there is no question of using only content words as items. Second, the fact that just the second half of a word is deleted might suggest that knowledge of word structure is more important in this kind of test than, say, the semantic aspects of vocabulary knowledge – especially if the language being tested has a complex system of word endings.

However, Chapelle and Abraham (1990) found that their C-test correlated highly with their multiple-choice vocabulary test ($r = 0.862$). The correlation was substantially higher than with the other parts of the placement test battery, including the writing test (0.639) and the reading test (0.604). Looking at it the other way, the vocabulary test had a stronger association with the C-test than with any of the other three versions of the cloze procedure that Chapelle and Abraham administered. The researchers interpreted this as evidence that the C-test was particularly good as a measure of what Alderson would call 'lower-level' knowledge of lexical and grammatical elements, while at the same time it also drew on 'higher-level' textual competence, as indicated by the substantial correlations with the reading and writing subtests.

In their research on the C-test with Hungarian learners of English, Dörnyei and Katona (1992) confirmed the usual finding with fill-in type cloze tests that structure-word items were significantly easier for the test-takers than content-word items were. Then they took the distinction a step further by comparing the performance on the test of learners in university and at secondary school. For the university students, who found the C-test quite easy, the content-word items were a better measure of their general proficiency in the language, whereas in the case of the secondary school students, for whom the test was really too difficult, the structure-word items alone correlated better with the proficiency test battery that was used as a criterion measure. This suggested that lexical knowledge has more influence on C-test performance as learners become more proficient in the language. Perhaps the same also applies to other forms of the cloze procedure.

Singleton and Little (1991) used the C-test as a research instrument, rather than an assessment tool, in order to provide evidence about the nature of vocabulary knowledge in a second language. They administered a version of the test to university students in Ireland who were studying French and German as foreign languages and made an analysis of their responses, especially the incorrect ones. The researchers argued that most of the incorrect answers showed that the students were able to draw on semantic clues in the text and figure out what meaning needed to be expressed by the mutilated word. What the students tended to lack was knowledge of the exact word form. This meant that they would either use a possible but incorrect form of the word or create a plausible but non-existing form. For example, in one of the German C-tests, one item was

... *der kleinen südsch* _____ *Gemeinde* ...
'of the small southern Scottish community'

and several students wrote *südschottlandischen* instead of the correct form *südschottischen*. Singleton and Little were making two claims: one was that the C-test was a suitable way of gaining an insight into the vocabulary knowledge of second language learners; and the other was that learners' knowledge of L2 words was organised on a semantic basis rather than a phonological one, as the earlier work of Meara (1984: 232–234) and others might suggest.

It is beyond the scope of this book to discuss the second claim here, but the first one was challenged by Chapelle (1994), who weighed up the arguments for and against considering the C-test as a valid measure in second language vocabulary research. Using Messick's (1989) framework for test validity, she found that students' responses to certain items in a C-test could reveal aspects of their L2 vocabulary knowledge. However, analysing the errors could not show how they arrived at the answers they wrote in each blank: did they automatically come up with a response, or was conscious thinking involved? She argued that, if teachers or researchers wanted to use the C-test specifically as a vocabulary measure, then they would need to abandon the principle of fixed-ratio deletion (the second half of every second word) and select particular words in the text to be mutilated, as in a rational cloze test. This would involve choosing just content words and, in particular, words that could be restored by making use of contextual clues.

As we have seen, there are two methods of investigating what cloze tests measure. One is to look at the correlations between a cloze test and tests of various aspects of language ability, including vocabulary tests. The correlations are quite variable, to the extent that it is difficult to say how important vocabulary knowledge is in influencing learners' performance on the cloze. Part of the difficulty here is that conventional discrete vocabulary tests measure just one aspect of the learners' lexical ability, especially if they are highly context independent. They assess knowledge of individual words but not the ability to use contextual clues to determine which particular word fits a blank.

The second approach to the validation of the cloze is to explore what is involved in responding to individual items. The published research has largely relied on the judgements of native-speaker experts, especially the researchers themselves, as to the amount of context and type of clues required to complete a blank successfully. Chapelle (1994) pointed to the need to obtain introspective evidence from learners by asking them to 'think aloud' as they respond to items in a cloze test. Although a small number of researchers (Feldmann and Stemmer, 1987; Singleton, 1994) have conducted such studies with C-tests, the results they report are restricted in scope and provide only limited indications of the role of vocabulary in C-test performance. Regardless of whether it is native speakers or learners who provide the data, the research on cloze-test items highlights the problems of trying to distinguish the contribution of vocabulary from other aspects of language knowledge.

In both cases, we need to recognise that there are different ways of viewing cloze tests as measures of vocabulary.

- One view is that the cloze procedure provides a means of assessing – in a contextualised way – learners' knowledge of particular content words that occur in the text. As I noted in the discussion of the rational cloze, we can seek to maximise the extent to which the cloze functions in this way by selectively deleting content words which the learners are assumed to have some knowledge of. Thus, we produce a discrete, selective, context-dependent vocabulary test. Following this logic, we can say that the test score is a measure of the test-takers' knowledge of the deleted words.
- However, the fact that the test is context dependent means that the test-takers also need to know many of the undeleted content words, because these form a major part of the context and provide the clues required to figure out what the deleted words are. Thus, a second view is that a cloze-test score is a comprehensive measure of how well learners know a large proportion of the content words in the text, though with a particular focus on the deleted words.
- A third perspective, already implicit in the second view above, is that cloze-test performance is based not just on knowledge of individual words but on vocabulary skills, especially inferencing. Obviously there is a great deal in common between responding to items in a cloze test and the skill of guessing the meaning of unknown words in a reading text, which we discussed in Chapter 3. The skill of inferencing draws not just on word meanings but also knowledge of spelling, word parts, sentence structure, paragraph organisation and so on. Thus, although the goal may be to identify a missing content word, the test-taker needs various kinds of language knowledge to do so successfully.
- Finally, we can adopt a broad view of vocabulary that goes beyond the individual word level. Cloze texts may include idiomatic expressions and other multi-word phrases that the proficient reader recognises as whole lexical units. For example, 'The fifth year, don Ramiro decided ___ put an end to the foolishness ___ and for all.' (Jonz, 1975, quoted in Oller and Jonz, 1994: 338). If the test-taker is able to identify such a unit, it is relatively easy to supply any word within it that has been deleted to form a cloze item.

It is not surprising, then, that the research on cloze tests gives such an unclear picture of how much they measure vocabulary knowledge or ability. We can say that a cloze tends to make a very *embedded* assessment of vocabulary, to the extent that it is difficult to unearth the distinctive contribution that vocabulary makes to test performance.

Conclusion

Discrete, selective, context-independent vocabulary tests have been an important part of the educational measurement scene for almost the whole of the twentieth century. They have all the virtues of an objective language test and became so well established that for a long time they were almost taken for granted. Multiple-choice vocabulary items are still very much in use, generally using a more contextualised form in the 1990s, with the target words presented at least in a sentence if not a broader linguistic context. At the same time, the prevailing view in language testing is that discrete vocabulary measures are no longer a valid component of tests designed to assess the learners' overall proficiency in a second language. Vocabulary knowledge is assessed indirectly through the test-takers' performance of integrative tasks that show how well they can draw on all their language resources to use the language for various communicative purposes.

Nevertheless, researchers and language-teaching specialists with a specific interest in vocabulary learning have a continuing need for assessment tools. Much of their work can be classified as focusing on either vocabulary size (breadth) or quality of vocabulary knowledge (depth). Vocabulary size has received more attention because, despite the fact that the tests may seem superficial, they can give a more representative picture of the overall state of the learners' vocabulary than an in-depth probe of a limited number of words. Measures of quality of vocabulary knowledge also have value but for quite specific purposes.

The construct validation studies by Corrigan and Upshur (1982) and Arnaud (1989) challenge the notion that vocabulary can be assessed as something separate from other components of language knowledge, even when individual words are tested in relative isolation. This is consistent with other evidence of the integral part that vocabulary plays in language ability, such as the strong relationship between vocabulary tests and measures of reading comprehension.

Such findings lend support to the view that vocabulary should always be assessed in context. However, as the research on the various members of the cloze family of tests shows, the more we contextualise the assessment of vocabulary, the less clear it may be to what extent it is vocabulary knowledge that is influencing the test-takers' performance.

....

CHAPTER FIVE

Vocabulary tests: four case studies

Introduction

In this chapter I discuss four tests that assess vocabulary knowledge as case studies of test design and validation. I have referred to all four of them in earlier chapters, especially Chapter 4, and so the case studies give me the opportunity to explore issues raised earlier in greater depth, in relation to particular well-known language tests.

The four tests are:

- The Voluntary Levels Test;
- The Eurocentres Vocabulary Size Test (EVST);
- The Vocabulary Knowledge Scale (VKS); and
- The Test of English as a Foreign Language (TOEFL)

These tests do not represent the full range of measures covered by the three dimensions of vocabulary assessment which I presented in Chapter 1. Three of them are discrete, context-independent tests and all four are selective rather than comprehensive. However, I have chosen them because they are widely known and reasonably well documented in the literature. More specifically, there is research evidence available concerning their validity as assessment procedures for their intended purpose. They also represent innovations in vocabulary assessment and serve to highlight interesting issues in test design. However, there is a limited number of instruments that I could have considered for inclusion as case studies in this chapter, which reflects the fact that, despite the upsurge in second language vocabulary studies since the early 1980s, the design of tests that could function as standard instruments for research or other assessment purposes has been a neglected area.

The first two tests, the Vocabulary Levels Test and the Eurocentres Vocabulary Size Test, are both measures of vocabulary size, whereas the Vocabulary Knowledge Scale is designed to assess depth of vocabulary knowledge. The fourth test to be considered is the Test of English as a Foreign Language (TOEFL), which is certainly not a discrete vocabulary test but rather a well-researched proficiency-test battery that has incorporated vocabulary items in a variety of interesting ways throughout its history.

The Vocabulary Levels Test

The Vocabulary Levels Test was devised by Paul Nation at Victoria University of Wellington in New Zealand in the early 1980s as a simple instrument for classroom use by teachers in order to help them develop a suitable vocabulary teaching and learning programme for their students. He has distributed copies freely and made it available in two publications (Nation, 1983; 1990), and it has been widely used in New Zealand and many other countries. It has proved to be a useful tool for diagnostic vocabulary testing of migrant or international students when they first arrive at a secondary school in an English-speaking country. Moreover, in the absence of any more sophisticated measure, it has been used by researchers who needed an estimate of the vocabulary size of their non-native-speaking subjects. Meara calls it the 'nearest thing we have to a standard test in vocabulary' (1996a: 38). Thus, it is certainly a test that deserves attention in a book on vocabulary assessment.

The design of the test

The test is in five parts, representing five levels of word frequency in English: the first 2000 words, 3000 words, 5000 words, the University word level (beyond 5000 words) and 10,000 words. The levels were defined by reference to the word-frequency data in Thorndike and Lorge's (1944) list, with cross-checking against the General Service List (West, 1953) (for the 2000-word level) and Kučera and Francis (1967). The odd-level-out is the University word level. The inclusion of this level reflects the fact that the test was originally developed in the context of an intensive English course for international students preparing for university studies in New Zealand. Words for this level were taken from a specialised list compiled by Campion and Elley (1971), which is based on a frequency count of words in university textbooks. Since Campion and Elley excluded from their list words that occurred in the first 5000 of Thorndike and Lorge's list, Nation located the University word level after the 5000-word level in the test.

Each level is intended to relate to specific vocabulary learning objectives. According to Nation (1990: 261), the 2000- and 3000-word levels contain the high-frequency words that all learners need to know in order to function effectively in English. For instance, it is difficult for learners to read unsimplified texts unless they know these words. The 5000-word level represents the upper limit of general high-frequency vocabulary that is worth spending time on in class. Words at the University level should help students in reading their textbooks and other academic reading material. Finally, the 10,000-word level covers the more common lower-frequency words of the language.

As for the format, the test involves word–definition matching although, in a reversal of the standard practice, the test-takers are required to match the words to the definitions. That is, the definitions are the test items rather than the words. At each level, there are 36 words and 18 definitions, in groups of six and three respectively, as in this example from the 2000-word level:

1	apply	
2	elect	____ choose by voting
3	jump	____ become like water
4	manufacture	____ make
5	melt	
6	threaten	

This unconventional format was designed to involve as little reading as possible while at the same time minimising the chances of guessing correctly. Although there are only 18 words at each level, Nation argues that 36 words are tested because the test-takers need to check every word against the definitions in order to make the correct matches. Observation of test-takers during the development of the test confirmed that they did adopt such a strategy, but only in sections of the test that they found difficult; with easy items they focused directly on the correct words and largely ignored the distractors.

All the words in each group belong to the same word class, in order to avoid giving any grammatical clue as to the correct definition. On the other hand, apart from the correct matches, care was taken not to group together words and definitions that were related in meaning. The test was intended as a broad measure of word knowledge, without requiring the test-takers to distinguish between semantically related words.

The words for each level were selected on a random basis (but with proper nouns and compound words excluded), so that the results of the test give a reasonable indication of what proportion of the total number of words at each frequency level the learner has some knowledge of. Nation (1990: 262–263) gives guidelines for teachers on interpreting the results and deciding on the kind of learning activities that are appropriate for the learners' vocabulary level.

Validation

Given the widespread use and influence of the test, there has been surprisingly little research until recently to establish its validity. One way to validate the test as a measure of vocabulary size is to see whether it provides evidence for the assumption on which it is based: words that occur more frequently in the language are more likely to be known by learners than less frequent words. I investigated this question (Read, 1988) by analysing the results of 81 students who took the test during a three-month intensive course in English for academic purposes. The students ranged in proficiency from low-intermediate to advanced. They were given the test shortly after they began the course, and a summary of their results is presented in the upper part of Table 5.1.

If we look at the mean scores across the five levels, we can see a consistent pattern of declining scores from the highest frequency level to the lowest. In other words, the test-takers as a group knew almost all of the words at the 2000-word level, but little more than a third of those at the 10,000-word level – and progressively fewer of those in between.

The test was administered again to the same students at the end of their course, even though it was not originally intended to assess achievement in vocabulary learning. If our intention had been to measure learning gains in a formal way, it would have been preferable

Table 5.1 *Results of the Vocabulary Levels Test*

First administration (beginning of course)

Level	2000	3000	5000	University	10,000	Total
Number of items	18	18	18	18	18	90
Mean	16.4	15.7	12.3	11.6	6.7	62.8
Standard deviation	2.3	3.3	4.3	4.7	3.5	15.3

Second administration (end of course)

Level	2000	3000	5000	University	10,000	Total
Number of items	18	18	18	18	18	90
Mean	17.0	16.6	13.9	14.1	8.8	70.3
Standard deviation	1.1	2.3	3.6	3.8	3.6	11.7

to use an alternate form of the test, if one had been available. Nevertheless, as the lower part of Table 5.1 shows, the mean scores were uniformly higher at the end of the course and the same general pattern of declining scores was found across the frequency levels – with one exception. There was a slightly higher mean for the University-word level than for the 5000-word level (14.1 vs. 13.9). This can be cautiously interpreted as reflecting the effects of learning during the course, because a considerable amount of attention was paid in class to the learning of non-technical academic vocabulary. However, there are other factors that may have had an effect, like the fact that the University word level does not exactly fit into the sequence formed by the other four frequency levels, and of course measurement error could have played a part.

Another question that arises in looking at the test results is whether the individual scores for the five levels form an **implicational scale**. For example, if a student scores well at the 5000-word level, can we assume that that person has obtained good scores at the 2000- and 3000-word levels as well? We would expect this to be the case if vocabulary knowledge is cumulative across the frequency levels in the way that the test design assumes. To evaluate the scalability of the test, it was first necessary to set a criterion (or mastery) score for each level. For the analysis of this test, the criterion was set at 16 out of 18. In other words, a student who scored at least 16 on a particular level

Table 5.2 *A hypothetical 'perfect' implicational scale*

| | | Levels of the test | | |
Student	2000	3000	5000	University	10,000
A	12 (−)	9 (−)	5 (−)	2 (−)	0 (−)
B	16 (+)	14 (−)	11 (−)	7 (−)	6 (−)
C	17 (+)	15 (−)	13 (−)	11 (−)	10 (−)
D	18 (+)	16 (+)	14 (−)	14 (−)	9 (−)
E	18 (+)	18 (+)	17 (+)	15 (−)	14 (−)
F	18 (+)	16 (+)	16 (+)	14 (−)	11 (−)
G	17 (+)	18 (+)	17 (+)	15 (−)	15 (−)
H	18 (+)	18 (+)	17 (+)	16 (+)	14 (−)
I	18 (+)	17 (+)	18 (+)	18 (+)	15 (−)
J	18 (+)	18 (+)	18 (+)	17 (+)	16 (+)

of the test was considered to know more or less all of the words at that frequency level. Then a **Guttman scalogram analysis** (Hatch and Farhady, 1982: 176–187) was carried out. This kind of analysis looked at the extent to which the test scores formed a pattern like the one in Table 5.2. The table shows a made-up set of results for ten students which have been sorted into an order where they form a perfect implicational scale. The plus (+) sign means that the student has obtained at least the criterion score (16/18) at that level; the minus (−) sign represents a score of less than the criterion. If you look across each row of the table, you will see that there is no case where someone has reached the criterion at a lower word-frequency level without having achieved it at the preceding higher frequency level(s).

In practice, this kind of perfect scaling is not usually achieved. It is common to find that, no matter how carefully the test-takers are sorted, there are some 'errors' that do not conform to the implicational pattern. For example, a test-taker may have obtained a score of 16/18 at the 5000-word level but not at the 3000 level. In my study of the Levels test, there were 18 scaling errors in the first administration at the beginning of the course, and 25 errors when the test was given again at the end.

The Guttman scalogram analysis produces a summary statistic called the **coefficient of scalability**, which indicates the extent to which the test scores truly form an implicational scale, taking into account the number of errors as well as the proportion of correct responses. According to Hatch and Farhady (1982: 181), the coefficient should be well above 0.60 if the scores are to be considered scalable. In my analysis, the scores from the beginning of the course yielded a coefficient of 0.90, with the five frequency levels in their original order, as in the upper part of Table 5.1. For the end of course scores, I obtained the best scalability, 0.84, by reversing the order of the 5000 and University levels, following the pattern of the mean scores in the lower part of Table 5.1. Thus, the statistics showed a high degree of implicational scaling, but by no means a perfect one. The kind of vocabulary learning encouraged by teachers in the English course apparently had some influence on the scaling by the end of the three-month programme.

Of course, looking at all 81 students as a single population tends to obscure some obvious differences among subgroups. For instance, one group consisted of teachers of English from South Pacific island nations who were to undertake a programme in Teaching English as a Second Language during the following academic year. At the beginning of the course, these teachers tended to score higher at the 5000-word level than the University level, reflecting their familiarity with general English, including literary works, and their relative lack of familiarity with academic or technical registers. On the other hand, there was a small group of Latin American students who were native speakers of Spanish and Portuguese preparing for postgraduate studies in engineering or agriculture. These students almost all had substantially higher scores at the University word level than the 5000-word level. This partly reflects their previous experience of academic study but more especially the fact that a high proportion of University level words are derived from Latin and have cognate forms in Spanish and Portuguese. In fact, Nation suggests that the test 'is not suitable for learners whose mother tongue is a language which has been strongly influenced by Latin' (1990: 262). This is probably too strong a statement, but certainly the results of test-takers from a Romance language background need to be interpreted with caution.

New versions

For ten years or so after it was first developed, only one form of the Vocabulary Levels Test existed, but there have been some further developments in recent years. Schmitt (1993) wrote three new forms of the test, following the original specifications and taking fresh samples of words for each level. This new material was used by Beglar and Hunt (1999), but they concentrated on the 2000- and University-word levels, treating them as separate tests. Their rationale was that, according to Laufer's (1992; 1997a) work, these levels correspond to a knowledge of 3000 word families which is the approximate threshold required to be able to read academic texts in English relatively independently. Beglar and Hunt administered all four forms of either the 2000-Word-Level or the University-Word-Level Tests to nearly 1000 learners of English in secondary and tertiary institutions in Japan. Based on the results of this trial, they selected 54 of the best-performing items to produce two new 27-item tests for each level. The two pairs of tests were then equated statistically, so that they could function as equivalent measures of learners' vocabulary knowledge at the two frequency levels. The authors have obtained various forms of evidence to support their case that – within the limitations of the test format and the relatively small number of items – the new test forms produce satisfactory estimates of vocabulary size, at least for the Japanese learners on whom they were trialled.

Schmitt himself (personal communication, 1998) has undertaken a somewhat similar test-development project with the four full forms of the test. He administered all four forms to 106 non-native-speaking British university students and used the item statistics to create two longer versions which were statistically equivalent. The revised versions have 30 items at each level, instead of the original 18. At the time of writing, he was piloting these two forms of the test as a prelude to a large-scale validation study.

Research of the kind conducted by Beglar and Hunt and now by Schmitt was overdue. Although it has proved its worth as an informal diagnostic tool for teachers, the Vocabulary Levels Test needs to meet higher standards of analysis and validation if it is to be used as an instrument in vocabulary research and as a basis for more formal decisions about learners.

One further development is Laufer's 'active' version of the test (Laufer and Nation, 1995; 1999). The active version has the same overall structure as the original test and the same target words; however, instead of matching words and definitions, the test-takers are presented with a set of sentences including a blank and required to write the missing target word in each blank, as in the following examples from the 5000-word level:

> The picture looks nice; the colours bl_____ really well.
> Nuts and vegetables are considered who_____ food.
> The garden was full of fra_____ flowers.

A variable number of initial letters are provided for each blank in an attempt to ensure that only the target word correctly fits it. However, this means that in some cases most of the word stem is included:

> Many companies were manufac_____ computers.
> They need to spend less on adminis_____ and more on production.

Laufer and Nation (1995) used this blank-filling version to provide one kind of evidence for the validity of their Lexical Frequency Profile (LFP), a comprehensive measure of the range of vocabulary used in learners' written compositions (see Chapter 7 for further discussion of the profile). Subsequently, Laufer (1998) has worked with both versions of the Levels Test, along with the LFP, to investigate the development of learners' vocabulary knowledge over time.

However, it is not clear just what the blank-filling test is measuring. Laufer (1998) found that the scores were lower than those for the original matching version of the test, which is what you would normally expect when test-takers are required to supply a response rather than selecting one from those provided. At the same time, the blank-filling test items appear to be quite variable in the demands they make on the learners because of the differing number of letters given to cue the target word. This means that some test items require more word knowledge – and more use of contextual information – than others do, which complicates the issue of what the test as a whole measures. In a recent study, Laufer and Nation (1999) offer as their main evidence for the validity of the blank-filling test the fact that learners at higher levels of proficiency obtained significantly better scores than lower proficiency learners did. Again, though, this finding does not give any specific insight into the meaning of the test scores.

Laufer herself (Laufer, 1998; Laufer and Nation, 1999) describes the blank-filling version of the test as a measure of 'active' or 'productive' vocabulary knowledge (she uses the two terms interchangeably in her articles). In the studies just cited, she distinguishes it from the two other measures used as follows:

- Levels Test – original matching version: receptive knowledge
- Levels Test – blank-filling version: controlled productive knowledge
- Lexical Frequency Profile (LFP): free productive knowledge

According to this classification, the blank-filling version is associated with the ability to use vocabulary in writing (which is what
the LFP sets out to measure), and in fact Laufer and Nation (1999)
assert that the blank-filling test scores can be interpreted in terms
of the approximate number of words at a particular frequency level
which are 'available for productive use' (1999: 41). However, they
have limited evidence to support this interpretation. In an earlier
study (Laufer and Nation, 1995: 317) they found some moderate
correlations between sections of the blank-filling Levels Test and
corresponding sections of the LFP. On the other hand, Laufer's
(1998: 264) intercorrelations of the three measures produced some
contradictory evidence. Whereas there were substantial correlations
between the two versions of the Levels Test, there was no significant relationship between either version and a measure based on
the LFP. Thus, the blank-filling version may simply be an alternative way of assessing receptive knowledge rather than a measure of
productive ability.

One problem here, I believe, is a widespread confusion concerning
the nature of the receptive–productive distinction. I will discuss this
issue in more detail in Chapter 6.

The Eurocentres Vocabulary Size Test

Like the Vocabulary Levels Test, the Eurocentres Vocabulary Size
Test (EVST) makes an estimate of a learner's vocabulary size using
a graded sample of words covering numerous frequency levels.
However, there are several differences in the way that the two
tests are designed and so it is worthwhile to look at the EVST in
some detail as well. As I noted in Chapter 4, the EVST is a checklist test which presents learners with a series of words and simply
requires them to indicate whether they know each one or not. It
includes a substantial proportion of non-words to provide a basis
for adjusting the test-takers' scores if they appear to be overstating their vocabulary knowledge. Another distinctive feature of
the EVST is that it is administered by computer rather than as a
pen-and-paper test. Let us now look at the test from two perspectives: first as a placement instrument and then as a measure of
vocabulary size.

The EVST as a placement test

The original work on the test was carried out at Birkbeck College, University of London by Paul Meara and his associates (Meara and Buxton, 1987; Meara and Jones, 1988). In its published form (Meara and Jones, 1990a) the test was commissioned by Eurocentres, a network of language schools in various European countries, including the UK. The schools ran many short intensive courses each year and thus needed an efficient and accurate placement procedure to be able to assign students to classes with a minimum of administrative effort.

The vocabulary test addresses this need in a variety of respects. The test is individually administered on a computer and typically takes less than ten minutes. A series of words is presented, each appearing one by one on the screen, accompanied by the question 'Do you know the meaning of this word?' The test-taker simply presses one key to signal 'Yes' and a different one for 'No'. The test-taker is warned that not all of the items are real English words; a certain proportion of them are non-words. Thus, if the student claims to know some non-words, the final score is reduced. The computer program automatically scores the test, so that the student's result – in the form of an estimate of vocabulary size – is available immediately on completion of the test. Meara (1996a: 42) reports that this was one feature which made the test very popular with the learners who took it. The software package also contains a utility program that can sort the results of a whole group of students and present them to the course administrator in a way that is convenient for placement purposes.

These are the practical virtues of the test, but is it a valid placement test? The assumption here is that vocabulary knowledge is a crucial component of language proficiency and that the number of words learners know is directly related to their level of proficiency (Meara and Jones, 1988: 80; 1990b: 1). The validity of the assumption depends partly on the amount of emphasis given to vocabulary learning in the language teaching programme that the students are about to enter. In the final analysis, though, a placement test is valid if it allows students to be assigned to classes with only a minimum number of misplacements. Meara and Jones (1988) report a validation study of the EVST in language schools in Cambridge and London using two criterion measures. First, the scores were correlated with the scores obtained in the existing Eurocentres placement test, which yielded an overall coefficient of 0.664 for the Cambridge learners and 0.717 for those in London. The second approach was to review – after one week of classes – the cases of students who had apparently been assigned to the wrong class by the existing placement test. Although there were not a large number of misplaced students, in the majority of cases the vocabulary-test scores were more in accord with the teachers' assessments than the placement test scores were. These results were encouraging but they suggest that further evaluation is needed to confirm the validity of the EVST for this purpose.

Of course, it is unwise to base any significant decision on one single-format language test. The user's guide recommends that, in addition to the EVST, an oral interview should be used as part of the placement procedure for a language school (Meara and Jones, 1990b: 3).

The EVST as a measure of vocabulary size

If the Eurocentres test is to have a wider application than just as a placement tool for language schools, we also need to consider its validity as a measure of vocabulary size, and for this we should look into various aspects of its design:

- the format of the test and, in particular, the role of the non-words;
- the selection of the words to be tested; and
- the scoring of the test.

The first thing to consider is the test format, which allows a large number of words to be covered within a short time. The format is a version of the long-established checklist procedure, discussed in Chapter 4. In essence, the test-takers are asked to indicate whether they recognise each of a set of words as being an English word. Unlike the matching format used in the Vocabulary Levels Test, this one does not include any direct check on their understanding of individual words. It assumes that most students carry out the task in an honest and realistic manner. However, there is a built-in means of checking the validity of the responses, because about a third of the items presented are 'non-words': forms that have the appearance of English words but do not in fact exist in the language. Thus, the test-takers are presented with a sequence of words and non-words, as in the following extract from a pen-and-paper checklist test prepared by Meara (1992a):

1 dring	2 take in	3 majority
4 modest	5 vowel	6 easy
7 swithin	8 obsolation	9 foundation
10 receipt	11 annobile	12 resident
13 impatient	14 phase	15 transparent
16 dyment	17 grand	18 album
19 mudge	20 weate	21 cockram
22 expostulant	23 wine	24 christian

If the test-takers claim to know non-words, this is taken as evidence that they are overstating their vocabulary knowledge and their scores are adjusted accordingly.

The role of the non-words in the test has emerged as an area requiring further investigation. When the test was first devised, the non-words were designed to be as similar as possible in spelling and morphology to the real words. However, in practice it seems that the non-words are not linguistically neutral. Meara and Jones note that 'some of the imaginary words are easier to handle than others: some can be rejected instantaneously while others cause even native speakers of English to puzzle for a long time' (1988: 85–86).

The indications are that the test-takers' language background influences their reactions to non-words. Obviously it would have been undesirable to have included items that were non-words in English but were real words in the L1 of potential test-takers. Beyond that, particular non-words have proved to be more attractive to speakers of some languages than others. Meara and Buxton (1987: 148) give the example of the form *observement*, which resembles a real word in French or Italian but not in German. Thus, it should be easier for a German speaker to reject it than for a speaker of a Romance language. This 'cognate effect' appears to have an influence on the results obtained in the test by speakers of different language backgrounds. Meara (1996a: 43) notes that this is a particular problem in administering the test to speakers of French because of the close relationship between the vocabularies of English and French.

The second aspect of the design that we need to look at is the selection of the words for the test. Like the Vocabulary Levels Test, the EVST assumes that there is a direct relationship between the frequency of a word in the language and the probability that a learner will know it. Using the frequency statistics in Thorndike and Lorge's (1944) list, the test samples words from ten frequency bands, starting with the first thousand words and proceeding in sequence to the tenth thousand words. Within each 1000-word band, the computer program presents a random sample of 20 words. If the test-taker achieves a criterion level of performance, the program proceeds to the next level; if not, it is assumed that the test-taker has reached the upper limit of her or his vocabulary knowledge and so the program presents a further set of 50 words from that frequency level in order to estimate the learner's vocabulary size more closely.

Clearly, the test will not give an accurate estimate of vocabulary size if the learner's knowledge of English words is quite different from the frequency profile that is assumed. According to the User's Guide (Meara and Jones, 1990b: 3), most students fit this pattern quite closely. However, we saw in the analysis of the Vocabulary Levels Test that there are group differences influenced by language background and educational experience, and Meara (1990) acknowledges that there are problems in interpreting the vocabulary size estimate in such cases. This would need to be considered in making any decision about the appropriateness of the test for particular groups of learners.

We come now to the scoring of the test. A straightforward way to produce a score would be simply to take the number of 'Yes' responses to the real words and calculate what proportion of the total inventory of 10,000 words they represent. For a good percentage of test-takers, this is in fact what happens, because they do not claim to know any of the non-words and so their responses are taken at face value (Meara and Jones, 1990b: 2). However, when the test-taker has responded 'Yes' to non-words, a more complex calculation is required. The calculation is based on statistics from signal detection theory, which was originally developed in a military context to evaluate the success of sonar operators at correctly locating enemy submarines from information displayed on their screens. The statistics measure two aspects of a person's performance: the ability to discriminate (in this case, between words and non-words) and the response bias (i.e. the test-taker's preference for choosing 'Yes' or 'No'). Therefore, the number of non-words that the student claims to know is taken into account in addition to the number of real words correctly identified. This means that those who respond cautiously and press the 'Yes' key only when they are sure that they know the word are not unduly disadvantaged in comparison to those who are more willing to give themselves the benefit of the doubt. The practical effect of the calculation is to reduce the vocabulary-size estimate according to the number of non-words claimed. In the extreme case, if the 'Yes' response is given to an equal number of real words and non-words, the learner's score will be zero. This is not to say that the learner knows no English vocabulary but rather that the test responses provide no basis for making a meaningful estimate of her or his vocabulary size. According to Meara (1996a: 43–44), there are consistently a certain number of learners who obtain very low scores for precisely this reason.

Thus, experience with the EVST and other checklist tests in English indicates that they can give a valid estimate of the vocabulary size of most second language learners, with certain exceptions. First, learners at a low level of proficiency lack a good basis for distinguishing words from non-words and tend to respond in inconsistent and unpredictable ways. The second problematic group are speakers of French, whose knowledge of cognate words has a significant effect on their scores. There are also individual learners whose pattern of vocabulary acquisition has been unconventional and others for whom the non-words prove to be just too attractive to say no to.

Meara and other scholars have continued work with both computer-based and pen-and-paper checklist tests, but particularly the latter. Meara (1992a) produced a whole book of tests, covering the 1000- to the 5000-word levels in English. Each test contains 40 real words along with 20 non-words and can be completed in about three minutes. The fact that 20 tests are provided for each frequency level means that a more reliable estimate can be obtained by giving learners two or more tests at a given level. Shillaw (1996) administered a series of pen-and-paper tests to Japanese university students learning English and analysed the scores using the Rasch Model, a widely used method of test-item analysis. His results show that a checklist containing a suitable set of real words produces a highly reliable measure of vocabulary knowledge without any need for non-words. The words form a series of items that fit very well along a single measurement scale. In addition, Rasch analysis provides a way of identifying learners who may be overestimating their vocabulary knowledge because their responses tend not to fit the overall pattern of item difficulty. Thus, Shillaw argues that not only are non-words unnecessary but they also detract from the measurement quality of a checklist test. As always, further research is required to evaluate the validity of these findings in other testing contexts.

Meara (1996a: 44) expresses optimism that the problems with

checklist tests can be overcome and that they can provide satisfactorily reliable estimates of vocabulary size for research studies investigating the development of L2 word knowledge at advanced levels of proficiency. The great attraction of the checklist format in the estimation of vocabulary size is how simple it is both to construct the test and for the test-takers to respond. The simplicity of the task means that a large number of words can be covered within the testing time available, which is important for achieving the sample size necessary for making a reliable estimate.

The Vocabulary Knowledge Scale

I noted in Chapter 4 the relative lack of work on how to assess quality or depth of second language vocabulary knowledge. We will now review a pioneering initiative in this area undertaken by Sima Paribakht and Mari Wesche at the University of Ottawa in Canada, resulting in the development of the Vocabulary Knowledge Scale (VKS) for use in their research on incidental vocabulary acquisition. The instrument is of interest not only as a test in its own right but also as a way of exploring some issues that arise in any attempt to measure quality of vocabulary knowledge in a practical manner.

The design of the scale

The VKS is a generic instrument, which can be used with any set of words that the tester or researcher is interested in assessing. It consists in effect of two scales: one for eliciting responses from the test-takers and one for scoring the responses. The first scale (see Figure 5.1) is presented to the test-takers together with a list of words. The scale has five steps, or categories, as Paribakht and Wesche (1997: 179–180) prefer to call them. For each word on the list, the test-takers are asked to decide which category best represents how well they know the word. Category I means that the word is not recognised at all and at Category II the word is recognised but the meaning is not known. These first two categories rely on honest reporting by the test-takers, whereas at the three higher levels they are required to give some verifiable evidence for their response. The distinction between Categories III and IV also involves an element of judgement by the

Self-report categories	
I	I don't remember having seen this word before.
II	I have seen this word before, but I don't know what it means.
III	I have seen this word before, and I <u>think</u> it means ____ (synonym or translation)
IV	I <u>know</u> this word. It means ____. (synonym or translation)
V	I can use this word in a sentence: ____. (Write a sentence.) (*If you do this section, please also do Section IV.*)

Figure 5.1 The VKS elicitation scale (Paribakht and Wesche, 1997: 180)

test-takers as to how sure they are of what the word means, but in either case they have to demonstrate their understanding by means of a synonym or translation equivalent. Category V moves from receptive knowledge to production, in that the test-takers need to show that they can use the word in a sentence.

The scoring scale (see Figure 5.2) translates the test-takers' responses to each word into test scores. Category I and II responses are taken at face value and credited with scores of 1 and 2 respectively. As the arrows in the figure indicate, test-takers also receive a score of 2 if they claim some knowledge of the word at a higher category level but their response shows that they are mistaken. A score of 3 means that the test-taker has provided an acceptable synonym or translation. Scores of 4 and 5 are awarded for the sentences written in response to Category V. A score of 4 is given if the target word fits the sentence context appropriately but is used in a grammatically incorrect way (e.g. 'This famous player announced his <u>retire</u>.'). It is only when the word is used with both an appropriate meaning and the correct form that a score of 5 is awarded.

Uses of the VKS

Paribakht and Wesche have used the VKS as a tool in their research on vocabulary acquisition in an English language programme for non-native-speaking undergraduate students at the University of

Self-report categories	Possible scores	Meaning of scores
I	1	The word is not familiar at all.
II	2	The word is familiar but its meaning is not known.
III	3	A correct synonym or translation is given.
IV	4	The word is used with semantic appropriateness in a sentence.
V	5	The word is used with semantic appropriateness and grammatical accuracy in a sentence.

Figure 5.2 The VKS Scoring Categories (Paribakht and Wesche, 1997: 181)

Ottawa. The courses in the programme, which focuses on comprehension skills, use authentic spoken and written materials linked to particular themes such as media, the environment and fitness. In their first study, Paribakht and Wesche (1993) selected two themes as the basis for a study of incidental vocabulary learning, one theme being actually used in class and the other not. The researchers selected 30 content words related to each theme, together with several discourse connectives (items like *in fact* and *however*). At the beginning of the course, and again at the end, the learners' knowledge of the words was tested using the VKS. The results showed that for the whole class the average number of content words known increased significantly during the course for both the 'instructed' and the 'uninstructed' theme, although the gains were greater for the instructed one.

In the second study (Paribakht and Wesche, 1997), the researchers compared two approaches to the acquisition of theme-related vocabulary through reading. One, called Reading Plus, added to the main reading activities a series of vocabulary exercises using target content words from the themes. The other, Reading Only, supplemented the main readings with further texts and comprehension exercises. As in the earlier study, the VKS was administered as a pre-test and a post-test to measure acquisition of the target words during the course.

According to the results, the students made significant gains in vocabulary knowledge through both treatments, but the amount of acquisition was greater in Reading Plus, especially for nouns and verbs.

Another researcher who has used the VKS is Joe (1995; 1998). Her study looked at the acquisition of target words that took place when learners completed a reading task and then retold the information to someone who had not seen the source text. She found that retelling the information led to significant gains in knowledge of key content words, especially when subjects were encouraged to process the information more deeply. The VKS was one of the measures Joe used to assess how the subjects' knowledge of the target words had increased. However, she made two significant changes to the instrument. First, she used it in an interview rather than as a written procedure, to allow for more probing of what the learners knew about each word. In addition, she modified the elicitation scale by introducing a sixth category between Categories II and III, worded this way: 'I have not seen this word before, but I think . . .' This was designed to take account of the fact that learners can often make inferences about a word through recognising the prefix, stem or suffix.

Evaluation of the instrument

The VKS has thus proved to be a workable measure and seems to be sensitive to increases in vocabulary knowledge that result from reading activities. Paribakht and Wesche have been careful to make modest claims for their instrument: 'Its purpose is not to estimate general vocabulary knowledge, but rather to track the early development of specific words in an instructional or experimental situation' (Wesche and Paribakht, 1996: 33).

They have obtained various kinds of evidence in their research for its reliability and validity as a measure of incidental vocabulary acquisition (Wesche and Paribakht, 1996: 31–33). To estimate reliability, they administered the VKS to a group of students twice within two weeks and there was a high level of consistency in the students' responses to the 24 content words tested (the correlation was 0.89). They have found a strong relationship (with correlations of 0.92 to 0.97) between the way that the students rated themselves on the elicitation scale and the way that their responses were scored, which suggests that the students reported their level of knowledge of the target words reasonably accurately. The researchers also correlated students' scores in an administration of the VKS with their scores on the Eurocentres Vocabulary Size Test. In this case, the correlation was just 0.55, which was not surprising because the EVST is designed to measure breadth rather than depth of vocabulary knowledge.

In order to consider the wider value of the VKS, it is important to discuss the nature of the scale from a conceptual point of view. The instrument was not developed on the basis of any comprehensive theory of second language vocabulary acquisition because such a theory does not exist at present. The statements in the elicitation scale clearly resemble those in the one by Dale (1965), which I quoted in Chapter 2, although Paribakht and Wesche designed the VKS without being aware of Dale's work. If we look at the scale in the light of Henriksen's (1999) three dimensions of vocabulary knowledge (see Chapter 4), we can see, on the one hand, that Categories I to IV relate primarily to the 'partial–precise' dimension: how specific is the learner's knowledge of a particular meaning of the word? On the other hand, Category V brings in both of Henriksen's other dimensions. It measures 'depth of knowledge' in that the test-takers need to have grammatical knowledge about the target word and also be aware of an appropriate context for its use. The 'receptive–productive' dimension is presumably involved as well when the test-takers are asked to compose a sentence containing the word. Thus, certainly at Category V of the VKS, if not lower down, it is doubtful whether learners' developing knowledge of second language words can be meaningfully represented by a single linear scale.

One aspect of vocabulary knowledge that is not assessed by the VKS in its current form is multiple meanings of a word. Wesche and Paribakht (1996: 33) suggest that the scale could be extended to cover this aspect of word knowledge and they pass on a suggestion from John Oller that a sixth elicitation category could be worded like this: 'The following sentences show all the meanings I can think of for the word' (personal communication to the authors, cited in Wesche and Paribakht, 1996: 35, footnote 9). I did something similar in an interview I used as part of the validation procedure for my word-associates test, which I discuss in Chapter 6. However, while this may be satisfactory for elicitation purposes, it is questionable whether the test-takers' responses should be scored on a single scale. For example, one learner may have rather general Category III knowledge of two different meanings of a word, while another learner has a relatively precise

Category V knowledge of one meaning together with a vague Category II awareness of the second one. Here again we are faced with the multidimensional nature of vocabulary knowledge and the strong probability that the process of acquiring second language vocabulary does not follow a single course. It may be better to think in terms of two, three or even more scales, although of course this would detract from the practical nature of the VKS in its present form.

Another point worth noting is that asking learners to compose a sentence containing a target vocabulary item is not necessarily a good way to find out how well they understand the meaning of the word. They often produce a semantically neutral context for the word which gives little indication of its specific meaning. For example, if a learner writes, 'She said something which was profound', we can infer that the learner knows *profound* is an adjective that can be applied to what people say, but not much more than that. Paribakht and Wesche (1993) recognised this problem after their initial trial of the VKS, which is why they added an instruction to Category V of the revised elicitation scale in Figure 5.1 ('If you do this section, please also do Section IV'), so that there would be some evidence in addition to the sentence itself of the learner's understanding of the word meaning.

The problematic nature of the sentence composing task was confirmed in research by McNeill (1996), who investigated the vocabulary knowledge of Chinese trainee teachers of English in Hong Kong and Beijing. His work did not involve use of the VKS but one of his key findings is relevant here. There were numerous cases among the Hong Kong subjects of students who could produce plausible, and even quite sophisticated, sentences to illustrate the use of a target word but, when they were asked to explain the meaning in both English and Chinese, they revealed that they did not really understand it. For example, here are two examples of such sentences for the word *demographic*, with the student's explanation of the word in brackets at the end:

> Chinese immigrants are producing demographic problems in
>   Hong Kong, especially in education. ('great')
> There is a demographic difference between Hong Kong and
>   Kowloon. ('relief/contour')

As McNeill notes, this phenomenon may reflect the peculiarly bilingual character of education in Hong Kong, where teachers in officially English-medium schools switch freely between English and Cantonese in the classroom and where successful students may memorise many multi-word lexical units without really understanding what all the individual words mean. It highlights the general point that we need to be cautious about accepting a student-composed sentence as evidence of word knowledge, despite the fact that it may be grammatically correct or semantically appropriate.

Thus, the VKS represents an interesting effort to measure some aspects of quality or depth of vocabulary knowledge in a practical way. Although it has served its purpose in Paribakht and Wesche's and Joe's research studies quite effectively, close scrutiny reveals some limitations that are to be expected in any attempt to reduce the complex nature of vocabulary knowledge to a single scale. If we want to go beyond the modest range of vocabulary development covered by the VKS, we possibly need to think in terms of multiple scales. Alternatively, the whole concept of a fixed scale may not be the most appropriate way to characterise the different forms of knowledge that people have of words.

The Test of English as a Foreign Language

Our fourth case study involves one of the major language tests in the world today. The Test of English as a Foreign Language, or TOEFL, is administered in 180 countries and territories to more than 900,000 candidates. As one might expect of a test with such impressive vital statistics, this is an American invention – one of a whole range of tests, covering many spheres of education and employment in the United States, that are administered by the Educational Testing Service (ETS) of Princeton, New Jersey. Like other ETS tests, TOEFL relies on sophisticated statistical analyses and testing technology in order to ensure its quality as a measuring instrument and its efficient administration to such large numbers of test-takers. The whole edifice, though, has been built on a simple building block: the multiple-choice item. Until recently, all the items in the basic TOEFL test have been of this type. The exclusive use of the multiple-choice format has been one source of criticism of the test by language teachers, because it has limited the aspects of language proficiency that could be assessed by the test. Consequently it has been seen as having a very negative **washback** effect, in the sense that learners preparing to take it have often focused narrowly on test-taking skills at the expense of developing a wider range of academic study skills.

The primary purpose of TOEFL is to assess whether foreign students planning to study in a tertiary institution where English is the medium of instruction have a sufficient level of proficiency in the language to be able to undertake their academic studies without being hampered by language-related difficulties. Thus, students from non-English-speaking countries applying for admission to North American colleges and universities normally take the test in their own country some time in advance, and their scores help to determine whether they will be admitted and whether they will be required to take further ESL courses once they arrive on campus. Apart from university admissions officers, certain employers and professional bodies also use TOEFL scores as a basis for deciding whether foreign-trained professionals, such as doctors, are proficient enough in the language to practise their skills in an English-speaking environment. This means that the test has an important gate-keeping role, in that it can influence a person's future prospects for education and employment, and therefore intending candidates take the test very seriously. A whole industry for TOEFL preparation has grown up in many countries to provide candidates with a wide range of practice materials and intensive coaching in test-taking techniques.

From the viewpoint of vocabulary assessment, the history of the TOEFL programme represents a fascinating case study of how approaches to testing have changed in the latter part of the twentieth century. In particular, vocabulary testing has become progressively more embedded and context dependent as a result of successive revisions of the test battery during that period. Thus, we need to trace the development of the test from the early 1960s to the present to see how and why the changes occurred.

The original vocabulary items

From its beginning in 1964 until the mid-1970s, TOEFL consisted of five sections: listening comprehension, English structure, vocabulary, reading comprehension and writing ability. The inclusion of structure and vocabulary as separate sections reflected the discrete-point approach to language testing that prevailed in the US at the time the test was originally designed. At this early stage, the vocabulary section could be considered a relatively discrete test, although in practice the main focus of admissions officers and test-takers has always been on the overall score for the whole test battery rather than the individual section scores. There were two types of vocabulary-test item, which were labelled sentence completion and synonym matching. The first type provided a short definition in sentence form in the stem, with a gap in it, like this:

> A ____ is used to eat with.
>
> (A) plow
> (B) fork
> (C) hammer
> (D) needle

The other kind was more basic, presenting a word or phrase in the stem in splendid isolation:

> foolish
>
> (A) clever
> (B) mild
> (C) silly
> (D) frank

(Examples quoted in Oller and Spolsky, 1979: 93)

The 1976 revision

Obviously these were classic examples of discrete-point items. They were very effective from a psychometric perspective, as I explained in the discussion of multiple-choice items at the beginning of Chapter 4. However, as Pike (1979) reported, they were criticised by ESL teachers because they encouraged students to spend time unproductively learning lists of words and their synonyms. In addition, the words tested were often uncommon or esoteric ones that were not likely to be useful for foreign students in pursuing their academic studies. Thus, in an ETS study of alternative formats for the test, Pike included as an experimental format a 'Words in Context' item type, in which the word to be tested was presented in a whole sentence, as in these examples:

He <u>discovered</u> a new route through the mountains.

(A) wanted
(B) found
(B) traveled
(D) captured

Their success came about <u>as a result of</u> your assistance.

(A) according to
(B) before
(B) because of
(D) during

(Pike, 1979: 19)

He argued that the Words in Context items had greater face validity because they presented the words in sentences (or 'natural message units', as he called them) and they encouraged the test-takers to approach the answering of the items as being more like a reading task.

In his study involving students in Peru, Chile and Japan, Pike found that, although the existing Vocabulary section of the test correlated highly (at 0.88 to 0.95) with the Reading Comprehension section, the new Words in Context items had even higher correlations (0.94 to 0.99) with the reading section of the experimental test. These results suggested that Pike had achieved his objective of creating a new vocabulary test format that simulated more closely the experience of readers encountering words in context. However, they also raised the intriguing question of whether both vocabulary and reading comprehension items were needed in the test, and if not, which of the two could be dispensed with. There were arguments both ways:

- The vocabulary items formed a very efficient section of the test, in that they achieved a very high level of reliability within a short period of testing time.
- On the other hand, reading is such a crucial skill in university study that it would have seemed very strange to have a test of English for academic purposes that did not require the students to demonstrate their ability to understand written texts.

In the end, Pike recommended a compromise solution by which both the words in context vocabulary items and the reading comprehension items (based on short passages) were included in a new combined section of the test. Pike's recommendation was accepted and implemented in operational versions of the test from 1976 until 1995.

Towards more contextualised testing

Nevertheless, criticism of the TOEFL vocabulary-test items continued. At a conference convened by the TOEFL Program in 1984, a number of applied linguists were invited to present critical reviews of the extent to which TOEFL could be considered a measure of communicative competence. Bachman observed that the vocabulary items 'would appear to suffer from misguided attempts at contextualization' (1986: 81), because the contextual information in the stem sentence was hardly ever required to answer the item correctly. He suggested that the most effective response strategy was simply to match the underlined word with the correct option and it might be counterproductive for the test-takers to spend time figuring out what the whole sentence meant. In my terms, Bachman was arguing that, despite their label, the test items were essentially context independent.

Another way (not mentioned by Bachman) in which some of the operational items did not reflect the principle on which they were supposedly based is illustrated by this example:

> The megaphone makes the voice sound louder because it points sound waves in one direction and keeps them from <u>spreading out</u> in all directions.
>
> (A) slithering
> (B) radiating
> (B) interfering
> (D) murmuring
>
> (Hale *et al.*, 1988: 67)

In this case, all four of the options are less frequent words than the one underlined in the sentence. If the test item is intended to simulate the process of encountering a relatively 'difficult' word in context, then logically the lower-frequency word *radiating* should be in the sentence and the higher-frequency word *spreading out* should be the correct option, along with distractors of a similar frequency level. In this item the logic is reversed: the correct option is being tested rather than the underlined word.

At the 1984 conference, Oller also criticised the existing vocabulary items. He expressed the opinion that items 'embedded in useful, interesting, authentic academic contexts will yield better results on the whole. They will be easier to write, less ambiguous, and overall more valid by both norm-referencing and criterion-referencing requirements' (1986: 143). He went on to call for research on the effects of varying the amount of context in which the items were embedded. Bachman made a similar recommendation in his paper. Their views obviously reflected the results of their respective research studies on the context dependency of cloze-test items, as we saw in Chapter 4.

The call to consider more contextualised test material was taken up in two TOEFL-sponsored studies. I have already discussed the one on multiple-choice cloze items (Hale *et al.*, 1988) in Chapter 4. The other study was by Henning (1991). In order to investigate the effects of contextualisation, Henning used eight different formats, including the then-current words-in-context item type. Essentially the formats varied along three dimensions:

- the length of the stem, ranging from a single word to a whole reading passage;
- the 'inference-generating quality' of the stem sentence, i.e. the extent to which it provided clues to the meaning of the target word; and
- the inclusion or deletion of the target word: it was either included in the stem sentence or replaced by a blank.

Henning administered tests containing all eight formats to 190 ESL students in the US and analysed the results using standard psychometric criteria. He found that the existing item type performed reasonably well, but that two other formats were comparable – and even better in some respects. One of these was similar to the existing type, but its stem was reduced in length and designed to include inference-generating information:

He was guilty because he did those things <u>deliberately</u>.

(A) both
(B) noticeably
(B) intentionally
(D) absolutely

However, the best format overall was one in which numerous target words were embedded in a reading passage, with four multiple-choice options for each word, like this:

1

In a <u>democratic</u> society suspected persons are presumed

2

innocent until proven guilty. The <u>establishment</u> of guilt is

often a difficult task. One consideration is whether or not

3

there remains a <u>reasonable</u> doubt that the suspected persons

committed the acts in question. Another consideration is

4

whether or not the acts were committed <u>deliberately</u>.

Sample item: 4 (A) both
(B) noticeably
(B) intentionally
(D) absolutely

This format – the most contextualised one – had the highest reliability, the highest correlation with the total vocabulary scores, and it had items that discriminated the best on average. Thus, according to Henning's study, vocabulary-test formats that encouraged the test-takers to make use of contextual information had not only greater face validity but also very desirable psychometric qualities. It seemed, then, that Oller's faith in the value of context was justified.

Vocabulary in the 1995 version

The results of this in-house research provided support for recommendations from the TOEFL Committee of Examiners, an advisory body of scholars from outside ETS, that vocabulary knowledge should be assessed in a more integrative manner. Thus, in the 1995 revision of TOEFL, the separate set of vocabulary items was eliminated from the test. Instead, they were made an integral part of the reading comprehension section. About one word per passage was selected and used as the basis for a multiple-choice item, with the generic stem 'The word "[ ]" in line [ ] is closest in meaning to', together with four usually single-word options.

It is interesting here to revisit the issue of context dependence by looking at an item from the 1995 version of the test and considering what is involved in responding to it. Here is an excerpt from one of the sample reading passages, with the target word highlighted, followed by the test item:

> Many of the computing patterns used today in elementary arithmetic, such as those for performing long multiplications and divisions, were developed as late as the fifteenth century. Two reasons are usually advanced to account for this **tardy** development, namely, the mental difficulties and the physical difficulties encountered in such work.
>
> The word 'tardy' in line 3 is closest in meaning to
>
> (A)   historical
> (B)   basic
> (B)   unusual
> (D)   late

(ETS, 1995: 34)

There are two ways to evaluate how context dependent the item is. In one sense, it is quite independent of the context because anyone having any familiarity with the word *tardy* can readily choose option (D) as the correct answer without referring to the passage at all. It is not the kind of item I illustrated in Chapter 1, where all the options express possible meanings of the target word and the task is to pick which is the applicable meaning in this passage. On the other hand, for someone who does not know the meaning of *tardy*, there are strong clues available in the context. The correct answer *late* actually occurs in the previous sentence; in addition, the words *this* and *development* before and after the target word direct the reader's attention to the relevant part of that preceding line of the passage. In this sense, then, the item is rather more context dependent.

Not all the vocabulary items in the 1995 version of the test functioned quite like this. Their context dependence has to be individually evaluated, in much the same way that researchers have analysed what is involved in answering particular cloze-test items. However, in general the items appear to be significantly more context dependent than the sentence-based ones in the pre-1995 version, at least in the second sense I defined above.

The current situation

The latest development in the story occurred in 1998, with the introduction of a computerised version of TOEFL. In most countries candidates now take the test at an individual testing station, sitting at a computer and using the mouse to record their responses to the items presented to them on the screen. For the reading test, the passages appear in a frame on the left side of the screen and the test items are shown one by one on the right side. Vocabulary items have been retained but in a different form from before. Here is an example:

> [Excerpt from the passage, highlighted in a bold font:]
> The Southwest has always been a dry country, where water is scarce, but the Hopi and Zuni were able to bring water from streams to their fields and gardens through irrigation ditches. Because it is so rare, yet so important, water played a major role in their religion.
>
> [Item:]
> Look at the word **rare** in the passage.
> Click on the word in the **bold** text that has the same meaning.
>
> (ETS, 1998)

All the vocabulary items take this form, requiring the test-takers to locate a synonym within a sentence or so from the target word. This is context dependency of a very specific kind. Whereas with the 1995 item format the test-writers had the opportunity to exploit a range of links between the target word and its context, this type of item tends to limit them to just one. Thus, it does not really represent a further step towards context-dependent testing of vocabulary. It would be ironic if the current item type encourages students preparing for the test to learn long lists of synonyms, which is what the original 1964 item types were criticised for doing!

To sum up, the TOEFL vocabulary testing story involved a lengthy conflict during the 1970s and 1980s between the measurement specialists at ETS, with their strong institutional preference for efficient, reliable and context-independent vocabulary-test items, and the applied linguists and educationists from the wider academic community who urged that vocabulary should be assessed in a more contextualised way by applying broader criteria of test validity. It is worth noting that it was only after Henning (1991) found that vocabulary items presented in a reading text could be psychometrically virtuous that a substantial change was made to a more embedded and context-dependent test format.

Looking back over 35 years, we can see that some obvious changes in vocabulary assessment have occurred within TOEFL in that time. The vocabulary items have been successively more embedded in the reading section of the test, so that there is no question now of reporting a separate vocabulary score, as was possible in the original 1964 version. At the same time, vocabulary testing has become more contextualised, in the sense of target words being presented in sentences and later in longer texts. However, when we examine the various types of vocabulary-test item in terms of my concept of context dependence, we find that the role of context has been more limited than it may have first appeared to be. The type of item used in the 1995 version of the test had the most potential for requiring the test-takers to engage with the contextual information available in the reading text, although that potential was not fully exploited in practice. The current vocabulary items represent a step back to a more restricted, context-independent form of vocabulary assessment.

Conclusion

We have looked at four different tests in this chapter. Collectively, they illustrate some of the choices that have to be made in the design of vocabulary assessment instruments and so, in conclusion, let us review what those options are.

The first consideration is the simplicity of the assessment task. Obviously this is a major concern in tests of vocabulary size because the simpler the task, the larger the number of words that can be covered within the testing time available. Thus, the checklist format of the EVST reduces task demands to an absolute minimum by requiring the test-takers just to respond 'yes' or 'no' to a series of words appearing on the computer screen. The Vocabulary Levels Test also involves the relatively simple task of matching words and definitions, as did the early TOEFL vocabulary items. By contrast, the VKS procedure, which is designed to assess depth of vocabulary knowledge, is more demanding, in that the test-takers must not only select the appropriate category on the elicitation scale but also – if they choose Category III or above – supply a synonym, translation or sentence. Nevertheless, the VKS can be seen as a simpler and more practical alternative to an oral interview, in which the learner's knowledge of each target word is probed in greater depth.

The trade-off here, of course, is that a simpler task reduces the quality of information elicited about the test-takers' knowledge of each word. In a sense, all that we can confidently say about a 'yes' response to a word in the EVST is that the learner is familiar with the word form and can identify it as a real English word. Depending on how the test-takers interpret 'knowing the meaning of a word', the 'yes' response may mean something more than that, but clearly the information about word knowledge obtained in an individual interview is much richer. Then again, those who measure vocabulary size are not so concerned with knowledge of individual words in the test, but rather with the overall state of the learners' vocabulary, as revealed by their responses to the items as a whole. The words in the Levels Test and the EVST are merely samples of items representing their respective frequency levels, not words that are of interest in their own right.

Another factor related to the simplicity of the task is the presentation of the words. The Levels Test, EVST and VKS all present words in isolation, whereas TOEFL vocabulary items have been progressively contextualised in sentences and then whole texts. Even though TOEFL items vary in the degree to which they are context dependent, the inclusion of context adds a reading requirement which is likely to make the items more time-consuming to respond to. At the same time, though, the TOEFL items have moved from forming a discrete vocabulary subtest to being embedded in a reading comprehension task, which needs to be evaluated by different criteria. The more general issue here is whether it is valid to assess words out of context, one of the continuing themes of this book which I take up again in Chapter 6.

A third design option concerns the nature of the test-takers' responses. The EVST relies largely on self-report, with only an indirect check provided by the inclusion of the non-words. It is based on the assumption that in most cases the learners honestly and accurately report whether they know the target words or not. The VKS procedure also incorporates self-report but requires the test-takers to provide verifiable evidence of their word knowledge at the higher scoring levels. On the other hand, the Levels Test and the TOEFL items elicit only responses that can be verified as correct or incorrect. The use of self-report is a further means of simplifying the assessment task and allowing a greater number of words to be covered. However, whether or not it is feasible depends on the purpose of the assessment. Although it can be used effectively in research on vocabulary acquisition and for informal classroom purposes, self-report would be completely inappropriate in a high-stakes test like TOEFL, in which test-takers would have a strong incentive to overrate their knowledge in the interests of their future education or employment in an English-speaking country.

Thus, if we take an analytic approach to the design of vocabulary tests, it can be seen as the process of achieving a balance among several competing considerations. There is no one perfect test and it is necessary to develop a whole range of instruments to address the various purposes for vocabulary assessment. We will explore the design principles at greater length in the next chapter.

CHAPTER SIX

....

The design of discrete vocabulary tests

Introduction

In this chapter I review various considerations that influence the design of discrete vocabulary tests. As you will recall from Chapter 1, these are tests which measure vocabulary as a construct separate from other aspects of language ability. Discrete tests most commonly focus on vocabulary knowledge: whether the test-takers know the meaning or use of a selected set of content words in the target language. They may also assess particular strategies of vocabulary learning or vocabulary use. Such tests are to be distinguished from broader measures of vocabulary ability that are embedded in the assessment of learners' performance of language-use tasks. Measures which are appropriate for embedded assessment are considered in Chapter 7.

The discussion of vocabulary-test design in the first part of this chapter is based on the framework for language-test development presented in Bachman and Palmer's (1996) book *Language Testing in Practice*. Since the full framework is too complex to cover here, I have chosen certain key steps in the test-development process as the basis for a discussion of important issues in the design of discrete vocabulary tests in particular. In the second part of the chapter, I offer a practical perspective on the development of vocabulary tests by means of two examples. One looks at the preparation of classroom progress tests, and the other describes the process by which I developed the word-associates format as a measure of depth of vocabulary knowledge.

Test purpose

Following Bachman and Palmer's framework, an essential first step in language-test design is to define the purpose of the test. It is important to clarify what the test will be used for because, according to testing theory, a test is valid to the extent that we are justified in drawing conclusions from its results. For instance, we can ask whether scores on the Vocabulary Knowledge Scale really show how incidental vocabulary acquisition occurs in a theme-based reading programme, or whether results from the Eurocentres Vocabulary Size Test are a good basis for placing students in language-school classes. Thus, we evaluate the results in relation to the intended purpose of the test.

Broadly speaking, we can identify three uses for language tests: for research, making decisions about learners and making decisions about language programmes. I discussed research uses of vocabulary tests extensively in Chapter 3 and also in parts of Chapters 4 and 5. Second language vocabulary researchers have needed assessment instruments for studies on:

- how broad and deep learners' vocabulary knowledge is;
- how effective different methods of systematic vocabulary learning are;
- how incidental learning occurs through reading and listening activities;
- whether and how learners can infer the meanings of unknown words encountered in context; and
- how learners deal with gaps in their vocabulary knowledge.

In the earlier chapters I reviewed various assessment issues that need to be dealt with in undertaking research in each of these areas. In general, researchers are seeking to gain a better understanding of the nature of vocabulary knowledge and the processes of vocabulary acquisition. They do not necessarily see their assessment procedures as having practical applications in second language teaching and learning. Often they work with a small, select group of learners and they have time to refine their instruments and undertake quite elaborate analyses of their test results.

On the other hand, language teachers and testers who employ tests for making decisions about learners have a different focus. They use tests for purposes such as placement, diagnosis, measuring progress or achievement, and assessing proficiency, as in these examples:

- The vocabulary section of a **placement** test battery can be designed to estimate how many high-frequency words the learners already know. Apart from the placing of students into classes, the test scores may help the teachers to decide which vocabulary workbook to use in class or what kind of vocabulary learning programme the students need.

- A **progress** test assesses how well students have learned the words presented in the units they have recently studied in the coursebook. The purpose can be essentially a diagnostic one for the teacher, to identify words that require some further attention in class. On the other hand, the teacher may want to find out whether the learners can understand words they have learned when they encounter them in fresh contexts, with somewhat different meanings.

- In an **achievement** test, one section may be designed to assess how well the learners have mastered a vocabulary skill that they have been taught, such as the ability to figure out the meaning of unfamiliar lexical items in a text on the basis of contextual cues. Or they may be tested on their knowledge of a sample of the lexical items that they have studied during the course.

Assessment for these purposes operates under different constraints from those which apply to research. The results have to be produced in a form that will be helpful for making the relevant decision. There is typically limited time available for administering the tests to the learners and for working out the results. In addition, when the learners are enrolled in a language-teaching programme, test designers have to consider the relationship between their assessment procedures and the learning objectives of the programme. In the discussion of TOEFL in Chapter 5, I introduced the concept of washback, which refers to the impact of assessment procedures on teaching and learning. Although it may be difficult to demonstrate what the impact of a test is in practical terms (see, for example, Alderson and Wall, 1993), it is reasonable to expect that test designers will aim to select assessment tasks which reflect learning objectives rather than conflicting with them.

The third use of tests is for making decisions about language programmes, or **programme evaluation**, as it is generally known (Alderson and Beretta, 1992; Lynch, 1996). Vocabulary tests may be used discretely to judge the effectiveness of a vocabulary-learning programme, or as embedded measures in an evaluation of a language-education programme with broader objectives. Use of tests for this purpose has some of the characteristics of research, in that the study should be well designed to yield reliable and valid conclusions, but the difference is that programme evaluation is often commissioned by an external funding agency and there is usually a practical decision to be made: Should the programme continue to be funded? Does it need to be changed? Should it be adopted on a wider scale?

Construct definition

Another important foundation for test validity is the defining of the construct we are intending to measure. Bachman and Palmer (1996: 117–120) state that there are two approaches to construct definition: **syllabus-based** and **theory-based**. A syllabus-based definition is appropriate when vocabulary assessment takes place within a course of study, so that the lexical items and the vocabulary skills to be assessed can be specified in relation to the learning objectives of the course. The test covers the vocabulary learning that the students are supposed to have achieved during the course and provides feedback on areas of weakness.

For research purposes and in proficiency testing, the definition of the construct needs to be based on theory. This is where the discussion of the nature of vocabulary in Chapter 2 becomes very relevant for test design. Issues such as what we mean by a 'word', whether vocabulary includes multi-word lexical items, what it means to 'know' a word and how words are influenced by context all arise when we seek to define what any particular vocabulary test is measuring. One thing that makes construct definition rather difficult in the area of second language vocabulary is the variety of theoretical concepts and frameworks which scholars have proposed to account for vocabulary acquisition, knowledge and use. Although certain tools – such as the concept of vocabulary size and Nation's (1990) analysis of what it means to know a word – are widely known and used, there is no comprehensive, generally accepted conceptual framework for L2 vocabulary work. Chapelle's (1994) model of vocabulary ability, which I discussed extensively in Chapter 2, is one attempt to provide a broad framework. Another effort to achieve greater clarity and standardisation is represented by Henriksen's (1999) three dimensions of vocabulary development, referred to in Chapter 4. The first two of her dimensions, the 'partial–precise' and 'depth of knowledge' ones, have received considerable attention from various perspectives in earlier chapters. The third, 'the receptive–productive' dimension, has been mentioned only to a limited extent so far, but I fear I cannot put off dealing with it any longer. Since it is a widely used yet problematic distinction, with significant implications for vocabulary assessment, it is worth exploring as a case of construct definition.

Receptive and productive vocabulary

From our experience as users of both first and second languages, we can all vouch for the fact that the number of words we can recognise and understand is rather larger than the number we use in our own speech and writing. This distinction between receptive and productive vocabulary is one that is accepted by scholars working on both first and second language vocabulary development, and it is often referred to by the alternative terms passive and active. As Melka (1997) points out, though, there are still basic problems in conceptualising and measuring the two types of vocabulary, in spite of a lengthy history of research on the subject.

The difficulty at the conceptual level is to find criteria for distinguishing words that have receptive status from those which are part of a person's productive vocabulary. It is generally assumed that words are known receptively first and only later become available for productive use. Melka (1997) suggests that it is most useful to think in terms of a receptive to productive continuum, representing increasing degrees of knowledge or familiarity with a word. Thus, when they first encounter a new word, learners have limited knowledge of it and may not even remember it until they come across it again. It is only after they gain more knowledge of its pronunciation, spelling, grammar, meaning, range of use and so on that they are able to use it themselves. The problem is to locate the threshold at which the word passes from receptive to productive status. Is there a certain minimum amount of word knowledge that is required before productive use is possible? Melka acknowledges that, if there is a continuum here, it is not a simple smooth one; furthermore, there is a fluid boundary and a great deal of interaction between receptive and productive vocabulary.

The difficulty with measurement stems from the lack of an adequate conceptual definition of the difference between reception and production. Much of the research has attempted to estimate the respective sizes of receptive and productive vocabulary, both for learners and for native speakers. As with estimates of total vocabulary size (see Chapter 4), researchers have reached widely varying conclusions about relative size, from a receptive vocabulary which was much larger to receptive and productive vocabulary being of similar size. Apart from the problems I covered in the earlier discussion of vocabulary size, Melka points out that there has been no consistency in the way that the two types of vocabulary have been measured. Test formats such as checklist, multiple-choice, translation and illustration have all been used by different researchers for assessing both receptive and productive vocabulary. At the very least, we need some consensus about what counts as a receptive measure and what a productive one is.

From my own reading of the literature, I have concluded that one source of confusion about the distinction between receptive and productive measures is that many authors use two different ways of defining reception and production interchangeably. Because the difference in the two definitions is quite significant for assessment purposes, let me spell out each one by using other terms:

Recognition and recall

Recognition here means that the test-takers are presented with the target word and are asked to show that they understand its meaning, whereas in the case of **recall** they are provided with some stimulus designed to elicit the target word from their memory. The simplest example of this distinction is found in the experimental research on vocabulary learning (see Chapter 3), where recognition means that the subjects give the L1 translation of an L2 word and recall refers to the reverse process: they give the L2 word in response to the L1 translation. Takala (1984) used the same process of two-way translation to make his estimates of the receptive and productive vocabulary of Finnish learners of English (English to Finnish and Finnish to English respectively).

Another illustration of this distinction is found in Hughes's (1989: 147–150) handbook for teachers on language testing. Here is an example he gives of a 'recognition' item:

> *loathe* means A. dislike intensely
> B. become seriously ill
> C. search carefully
> D. look very angry

By contrast, his 'production' items involve the labelling of pictures or filling in a blank in a sentence, like this one:

> Because of the snow, the football match was _____ until the following week.

So the difference is between being able to recognise the word when you are presented with it and being able to recall it when prompted to do so. Recognition and recall, then, represent aspects of vocabulary knowledge which can be assessed by selective and relatively context-independent test items.

Comprehension and use

This is quite a different way of distinguishing reception and production. **Comprehension** here means that learners can understand a word when they encounter it in context while listening or reading, whereas **use** means that the word occurs in their own speech or writing. To assess these aspects of vocabulary ability adequately requires test tasks which are comprehensive and context dependent. Thus, we might test comprehension by getting the learners to listen to a talk or read a story containing numerous target words and then finding out how well they understood the words in context. Similarly, use can be tested by setting controlled tasks like retelling a story, translation or picture description, which are designed to elicit a range of target vocabulary.

From the viewpoint of vocabulary researchers investigating reception and production, such tasks may be considered unsatisfactory. Presenting the target words in a whole spoken or written text is a relatively inefficient use of testing time and the range of vocabulary which can be covered is restricted to words related to the topic of the text. Furthermore, some of the word meanings may be inferred from the context rather than already known. In the case of use tasks, the learner may not use some of the target words that the researcher is interested in assessing, as a result of deliberately or unconsciously avoiding them. Thus, the tendency in vocabulary research has been to prefer very controlled and selective tasks, with target words being presented in a limited sentence context or in isolation.

I am not arguing that only comprehension and use tasks are valid as measures of receptive and productive vocabulary. Recognition and recall tasks have their place, both in research and for making decisions about learners. The problem arises, though, when the terms reception and production are used indiscriminately to refer to both distinctions. This can lead to the assumption that, if we set a recall task such as Hughes's fill-in-the-blank item given as an example above, we can infer that learners who complete the item successfully are able to – and in fact do – use the target word correctly and appropriately in their own writing or speech. I gave an example of this in Chapter 5 (see pp. 124–126) when discussing the so-called productive (or 'active') version of the Vocabulary Levels Test (Laufer, 1998; Laufer and Nation, 1999). Although the test items simply require the learners to *recall* the target words (or at least the parts of them not already provided), the authors consider that correctly recalled words are also available for *use*. It seems to me a questionable inference, because recall items require production only in a very restricted sense.

The process of clarifying what is meant by receptive and productive vocabulary is an exercise in theory-based construct definition. My argument is that the terms reception and production are too broad and, in undertaking a vocabulary assessment project which involves making the distinction, we first need to define what specific learner ability each one refers to. This then provides a better basis for designing suitable testing tasks. My twofold distinction between the terms does not solve all the problems but it does highlight the point that, although we are dealing with degrees of vocabulary knowledge or ability here, there is not a simple continuum running from minimal receptive knowledge to advanced productive ability.

Characteristics of the test input

The design of test tasks is the next step in test development, according to Bachman and Palmer's model. In this chapter, I focus on just two aspects of task design: characteristics of the input and characteristics of the expected response.

Selection of target words

One obvious question that arises in the design of a selective vocabulary test is how to choose the target words. First, it is necessary to make a general point about the frequency distribution of words in English, and other languages for that matter. It is a well-established fact that a small proportion of the total stock of lexical items in the language occurs very frequently. For example, in their count of five million running words of English text, Carroll, Davies and Richman (1971) found that just 100 different words accounted for 49 per cent of all the running words, while 2000 words represented 81 per cent of the total. On the other hand, a huge number of words occurred only once in the whole corpus.

Based on such findings, Nation (1990: Chapter 2) proposes that, for teaching and learning purposes, a broad three-way division can be made into high-frequency, low-frequency and specialised vocabulary. The **high-frequency** category in English consists of 2000 word families, which form the foundation of the vocabulary knowledge that all proficient users of the language must have acquired. These items figure prominently in general word lists compiled for use in language teaching, because both teachers and learners at the beginning to intermediate levels can be confident that time devoted to developing a good knowledge of these words is well spent. Similarly, it is justifiable in testing learners in that proficiency range to assess whether – and how well – they can understand and use these high-frequency words.

On the other hand, **low-frequency** vocabulary as a whole is of much less value to learners. A large proportion of the items are ones that hardly anyone knows or uses, especially those words given labels like 'rare', 'obsolete' or 'dialectal' in the dictionary. The low-frequency words that learners *do* know reflect the influence of a variety of personal and social variables:

- how widely they have read and listened;
- what their personal interests are;
- how much time they have devoted to intensive vocabulary learning;
- what their educational and professional background is;
- which community or society they live in;
- what communicative purposes they use the language for; and so on.

Thus, according to Nation, with low-frequency vocabulary the focus of teaching and testing shifts to the question of whether learners have effective strategies for dealing with these lexical items when they come across them in speech and writing. The selection of specific low-frequency words for testing purposes depends on the communicative value for the learners for whom the test is designed, in relation to their shared educational, occupational or personal needs.

This is where **specialised** vocabulary comes in. It comprises technical terms and other lexical items that occur relatively frequently in particular registers of the language. It is of relevance in language courses for specific purposes and in language across the curriculum programmes. Specialised vocabulary is likely to be better acquired through content instruction by a subject teacher than through language teaching. Correspondingly, it may be more validly assessed in subject-area examinations than in general language tests.

A fourth category which is often recognised is **subtechnical** vocabulary: words which occur quite frequently across a range of registers or topic areas in academic and technical language. One of the primary functions of this vocabulary is to define and classify other more technical terms. Examples of subtechnical words in English are *analyse, context, function, interval, physical, react, transform* and *valid*. It is this kind of vocabulary which is assessed by the University word level of the Vocabulary Levels Test (see Chapter 5) and also found in Xue and Nation's University Word List (Xue and Nation, 1984; Nation, 1990: Appendix 2). This list has recently been superseded by the Academic Word List (Coxhead, 1998), a compilation of 570 word families which occurred with wide range and high frequency in a specially constructed corpus of academic texts.

Thus, these four broad categories represent different ways of specifying the vocabulary to be learned and to be assessed, depending on the learners' proficiency level and their particular learning needs.

Within the categories, there is no standard approach to the choice of target words for vocabulary testing. For some specific kinds of test, notably those measuring vocabulary size, a random selection procedure from a word list is appropriate. For most tests, though, the test-writer must exercise judgement in choosing the lexical items, having regard to the teaching/learning objectives and the purpose of the assessment. Let us look at some examples of vocabulary tests and how words might be chosen for inclusion in them.

- For a classroom progress test the teachers normally make a selection from the words that the learners have recently been studying.

Coursebooks that include word lists for each unit simplify the selection task for the teacher and at the same time specify for the learners the items that they need to learn. With more advanced learners, who have diverse lexical needs, a common practice of teachers today is to ask them to compile their own list of lexical items that seem to be useful for them to know, ones that they encounter in their daily use of the language. If the learners are required to submit their lists, the teacher can then prepare individualised tests for each person.

- For some major achievement tests, published vocabulary lists are available that specify not just the words to be tested directly but also those that are likely to be included in the reading and listening texts. The University of Cambridge Local Examinations Syndicate (UCLES) produces such lists for two examinations in the lower proficiency range of its main suite of qualifications in English as a foreign language: the Key English Test (KET) and the Preliminary English Test (PET). For example, the 1990 version of the PET vocabulary list contained 2378 items, which candidates are expected to be able to use productively as well as receptively. The list was in turn derived from the *Cambridge English Lexicon* (Hindmarsh, 1980), which was designed to perform a similar function for learners preparing for the First Certificate in English (FCE). It has 4500 items and includes a grading in terms of frequency and the level of the learners. Another feature of the lexicon is that, for words with several meanings, the individual meanings are graded as well. However, it should be noted that the selection and grading of the words depended very much on Hindmarsh's judgement as well as careful cross-checking with the contents of other vocabulary lists.

- In tests of the vocabulary size of second language learners, word-frequency lists play a significant role. The general assumption here is that the more frequently a word occurs in the language, the more likely it is that learners will know it. The venerable General Service List (West, 1953) has been used in a number of studies (for example, Quinn, 1968; Harlech-Jones, 1983; Nurweni, 1995). The Eurocentres Vocabulary Size Test (discussed in Chapter 5) draws on Thorndike and Lorge's (1944) list. To obtain a good estimate of how many words the learners know, the test developer needs to use an appropriate sampling procedure, preferably a random one.

You may wonder why these comparatively old lists continue to be used. The fact is that no one has yet produced a more recent general list of English vocabulary which matches the earlier ones in terms of their educational value. While it is true that advances in computer technology make it much easier to do some of the work, such as counting word forms in a large corpus of texts, a great deal of further processing is required, involving the application of human judgement, to create a usable list. I discuss this in more detail in Chapter 8.

- In achievement and proficiency tests where vocabulary is to be tested in context, the starting point for selection is likely to be a particular text rather than a list of words. The choice of text is influenced by whether it contains the kind of lexical items that are required for testing purposes. For example, does it include a range of the words that the learners have been studying? Are there some familiar words with an extended or metaphorical meaning that can be used to assess the learners' lexical inferencing ability? Are there low-frequency words that the test-takers can guess on the basis of contextual clues?

Presentation of words

Once target words have been selected, there is often a decision to be made as to whether they should be presented to the test-takers in isolation or in some form of context. The place of context in vocabulary assessment is an issue which has arisen frequently in earlier chapters, especially in Chapter 4 and in the discussion of the TOEFL vocabulary-test items in Chapter 5. I have noted the general trend in language testing away from discrete-point items, especially those which present words as independent units in isolation, towards test tasks where words occur within meaningful contexts. In my framework of vocabulary assessment, I have argued that the key question concerning context is not so much how target words are presented but whether the test-takers are required to draw on contextual information in responding to the test task.

Words in isolation

As with other decisions in test design, the question of how to present selected words to the test-takers needs to be related to the purpose of the assessment. We have seen various uses of vocabulary tests earlier where no context is provided at all:

- In systematic vocabulary learning, students apply memorising techniques to sets of target words and their meanings (usually expressed as L1 equivalents). They are assessed on their ability to supply the meaning when given the target word, or vice versa, whether it be for research purposes or for monitoring of progress in classroom learning. The research evidence summarised in Chapter 3 clearly shows that these techniques are effective in providing a foundation for further development of vocabulary knowledge in the second language.
- In tests of vocabulary size, such as the Vocabulary Levels Test and the Eurocentres Test (EVST), words are often presented in isolation. As I suggested in the conclusion to the previous chapter, this allows the test designer to simplify the test-takers' task and cover a large sample of words in the test, but it means that the criterion for 'knowing' a word is usually a minimal one.
- In research on incidental vocabulary learning, the learners encounter the target words in context during reading or listening activities, but in the test afterwards the words are presented separately because the researcher is interested in whether the learners can show an understanding of the words when they occur without contextual support.

Words in context

For other purposes, the presentation of target words in some context is desirable or necessary. In discrete, selective tests, the context most commonly consists of a sentence in which the target word occurs, but it can also be a paragraph or a longer text containing a whole series of target words. Although it is taken for granted these days by many language teachers that words should always be learned in context, in designing a vocabulary measure it is important to consider what role is played by the context in the assessment of vocabulary knowledge or ability. I have raised this question at various points earlier in the book by asking how context dependent particular vocabulary items are, especially those in the reading section of TOEFL (see Chapter 5). There seems to be little point in presenting words in a context unless the test-takers are required to engage with the contextual information in some meaningful way in making their response to the test task.

Let us review, then, other ways in which context can contribute to vocabulary assessment in discrete, selective tests:

- One function of a sentence context in traditional discrete-point items is to signal the particular meaning or use of a high-frequency target word which the test designer wishes to test, as in this example:

  My neighbour is a very <u>independent</u> person.

  a. never willing to give help
  b. hard-working
  c. good at repairing things
  d. not relying on other people

  In this case, the test-takers need to show that they understand what *independent* means when it is used as an adjective applied to a person. The options are all possible attributes of a neighbour and thus some knowledge of the word itself is required to answer the item correctly.

- On the other hand, if the target word is a low-frequency one that the learners are not expected to know, the ability to infer its meaning on the basis of contextual clues may be precisely what is to be assessed. In this case, stem sentences can be composed that contain a certain amount of contextual information in order to assess this skill:

  Our uncle was a <u>nomad</u>, an incurable wanderer who never could stay in one place.

  While the aunt loved Marty deeply, she absolutely <u>despised</u> his twin brother Smarty.

  Mary can be quite <u>gauche</u>; yesterday she blew her nose on the new linen tablecloth.

  (examples from Clarke and Silberstein, 1977: 145)

  The sentences used in the research study by Mondria and Wit-De Boer (1991), which I reported in Chapter 3, give another illustration of how contextual clues can be provided in a controlled way to assess whether learners are able to guess what a target word means.

- In recall-type tests of productive vocabulary knowledge, in which the test-takers are expected to supply the target word rather than being presented with it directly, a sentence context is one means of eliciting the word, as in these completion (fill-in-the-blank) items:

> The factory workers strongly s_____ the Labour Party in every election.

> Last week a flood d_____ ed the railway bridge.

The initial letter for each blank is intended to limit the range of possible answers although, as Laufer found with the active version of the Vocabulary Levels Test (see Chapter 5), it may be necessary to provide several letters if it is important to ensure that only one target word correctly fits the sentence.

- A whole passage offers greater opportunities to assess aspects of word knowledge in addition to meaning, for example, the grammar of the word, its inflectional and derivational forms, collocational possibilities, stylistic appropriateness to the context and so on. One test format that draws on these kinds of knowledge is a selective deletion cloze, in which content words are deleted from the text and the task is to write a suitable word in each blank. Here is an example from a class test for postgraduate students of agriculture and biological science:

Genetic Manipulation

> Since human beings began to raise livestock and to grow crops, they have been involved in genetic manipulation. First they simply chose to rear particular ____ or plants which had certain desirable ____. Later, as the science of genetics developed, ____ programmes were established that could produce ____ of plants and animals that had the characteristics that ____ needed. More recently, geneticists have been able to ____ individual genes and ____ them from a donor to a ____ organism. This means that ____ can be used as 'factories' to ____ particular gene products for a wide variety of ____. The gene is not transferred ____ into its host. It must first be ____ into a vector molecule that has the ____ to carry it to the host. This kind of research not only has many practical ____ but also allows us to understand much better the structure and function of the genetic code.

The test-takers must not only identify the meaning and word class (noun, verb, adverb) which is required for each blank but also recognise that most of the missing nouns should be in the plural form and all but one of the missing verbs should be in the stem form. There are also choices of style or register, as in 'It must first be [*put* / *placed* / *inserted*] into a vector molecule . . .'

Thus, my general argument is that, instead of making a blanket statement such as 'all vocabulary testing should be contextualised', we should consider what the appropriate role of context is for a particular assessment purpose, and design the test tasks accordingly.

Characteristics of the expected response

Self-report vs. verifiable response

In some testing situations, it is appropriate to ask the learners to assess their own lexical knowledge. In Chapter 5, we saw how the EVST and the VKS draw on self-report by the test-takers, although both instruments also incorporate a way of checking how valid the responses are as measures of vocabulary knowledge. As I noted in the conclusion to that chapter, the purpose of the test is a major consideration in deciding whether self-assessment is appropriate. It is not suitable in cases where significant decisions about learners are made on the basis of their test results, especially decisions which affect their future education or employment opportunities.

Even in 'low-stakes' testing situations where self-report is used, it is desirable to have a means of verifying the test-takers' judgements about their knowledge of the target words. The inclusion of non-words in a checklist test is one method. Another approach to verification is found in a test-your-own-vocabulary book for native speakers of English by Diack (1975). The book contains 50 tests, each consisting of 60 words that are listed in order from most frequent to least. To take one of the tests, you work through the list, writing down the numbers of any words that you do not know or are not sure about. When you have written 10 numbers, you stop and go back over the last five words that you *do* claim to know. For each of these words, you write some kind of definition: giving a synonym, using the word in a sentence or making a diagram or sketch. You then check your answers with a dictionary. If all or most of the five words are correct, you can assume that you know all of the preceding higher-frequency words that you claimed to know. Thus, the score is simply the number of known words (up to the point where you stopped), which

Here is a vocabulary-size test which relies mostly on self-report. Work through it and make an estimate of your vocabulary size.

Procedure

- Read through the whole list. Put a **tick** next to each word you know, i.e., you have seen the word before and can express at least one meaning of it. Put a **question mark** next to each word that you think you know but are not sure about.
- When you have been through the whole list of 50 words, go back and check the words with question marks to see whether you can change the question mark to a tick.
- Then find the last five words you ticked (the ones that are furthest down the list). Show you know the meaning of each one by giving a synonym or definition or by using it in a sentence or drawing a diagram, as appropriate.
- Check your explanations of the five words in a dictionary. If more than one of the explanations is not correct, you need to work back through the list, beginning with the sixth to last word you ticked. Write the meaning of this word and check it in the dictionary. Continue this process until you have a sequence of four ticked words that you have explained correctly.
- Estimate your vocabulary size by multiplying the total number of correctly ticked words by 500.

1 as	11 abstract	21 aviary
2 dog	12 eccentric	22 chasuble
3 editor	13 receptacle	23 ferrule
4 shake	14 armadillo	24 liven
5 pony	15 boost	25 parallelogram
6 immense	16 commissary	26 punkah
7 butler	17 gentian	27 amice
8 mare	18 lotus	28 chiton
9 denounce	19 squeamish	29 roughy
10 borough	20 waffle	30 barf

31 comeuppance	41 cupreous
32 downer	42 cutability
33 geisha	43 regurge
34 logistics	44 lifemanship
35 panache	45 atropia
36 setout	46 sporophore
37 cervicovaginal	47 hypomagnesia
38 abruption	48 cowsucker
39 kohl	49 oleaginous
40 acephalia	50 migrationist

Figure 6.1 A vocabulary size test for native speakers of English (Goulden, Nation and Read, 1990)

can be multiplied by 600 to give an estimate of vocabulary knowledge out of 36,000 words, which was the theoretical maximum size of vocabulary that the tests could measure.

Goulden, Nation and Read (1990) adopted a similar procedure for the test that we devised for measuring the vocabulary size of native speakers, based on a carefully drawn sample of words from a large unabridged dictionary. One of these tests is presented in Figure 6.1.

There is, therefore, a role for self-report in lexical assessment, particularly in estimating vocabulary size. However, for most testing purposes, we need verifiable evidence that the test-takers have the knowledge and skills that are the focus of the assessment.

Monolingual vs. bilingual testing

One last design consideration concerns the language of the test itself. Whereas in a monolingual test format only the target language is used, a bilingual one employs both the target language (L2) and the learners' own language (L1). This aspect of test design involves more than just the characteristics of the expected response, but I have chosen to deal with the choice of language in an integrated way in this section of the chapter.

I have already noted one type of bilingual test format in the previous section on receptive and productive vocabulary, where translation from L2 to L1 assesses receptive knowledge and L1 to L2 translation is the corresponding productive measure. Another example of a bilingual format is presented in Figure 6.2. Nurweni's (1995) vocabulary-size test for Indonesian learners of English had the instructions (or test rubric) in Indonesian to help ensure that the learners understood the nature of the test and how they were expected to respond to it. The input material, consisting of the target words used in short sentences, obviously needed to be in English, but the responses were in Indonesian so that the learners could express their understanding of the target word without being hampered by a lack of knowledge of synonymous English words and phrases. Vocabulary tests for native speakers of English learning foreign languages commonly have a similar kind of bilingual structure.

The question of whether a bilingual format should be used has much in common with the debate over the relative merits of monolingual and bilingual dictionaries for language learners. There are

---

Vocabulary-size test for Indonesian learners of English

Tes ini dimaksudkan untuk mengetahui banyaknya kosakata yang telah Saudara kuasai. Setiap soal terdiri atas satu kalimat yang di dalamnya ada satu kata bergaris bawah. Tuliskan makna kata yang bergaris bawah tersebut dalam bahasa Indonesia pada kolom JAWABAN yang telah disediakan.

[Translation: This test is intended to find out how much vocabulary you have mastered. Each item consists of a sentence containing an underlined word. Write the meaning of the underlined word in Indonesian in the ANSWER column provided.]

                                                        JAWABAN

1. He was born in <u>February</u>.   ――――
2. This is the <u>first</u> step in drawing a picture.   ――――
3. That was the <u>last</u> event of the day.   ――――

   · · · · · ·

Figure 6.2 Example of a bilingual vocabulary test format (Nurweni, 1995: 149–150)

both practical considerations and issues of pedagogical principle involved.

On a practical level, it obviously makes a difference whether the learners have a common first language and, if so, whether the teacher is proficient in that language. In English-speaking countries teachers of English are typically working with learners from a variety of language backgrounds, which makes it impractical for them to use bilingual test items. On the other hand, most teachers of English in secondary schools in European countries share with their students a national language, if not a mother tongue – and the same applies to foreign-language teachers in English-speaking countries. These teachers routinely use the national language as a tool in foreign-language teaching and testing.

Another practical consideration is the proficiency level of the learners. L1 is likely to play a greater role in assessing the vocabulary knowledge of lower proficiency learners than those who are more advanced. For one thing, beginning level learners lack the communicative resources in the target language to be able to express their understanding of the meaning of L2 words through that language. A related concern is that many of the words in the first 500 to 1000 frequency range are almost impossible to define or explain using words of a similar frequency, even for native speakers. Apart from function words, these include nouns and verbs like *thing, person, day, example, do, make, carry* and *understand.* They are words that are very useful for defining or qualifying other lexical items, but they may in fact lack their own clear semantic meaning.

Testing of very high-frequency words monolingually is quite a challenge. For objects and actions that can be clearly depicted, a picture identification or labelling format can be used. As an alternative way of testing very high-frequency words, Nation (1993a) has devised a format consisting of a series of true–false items. Each statement contains a target word and is written in very simple English, in such a way that the learner needs to understand the target word in order to be able to decide whether the statement is true or false. Here are some examples:

> This country is a part of the world.   ————
> When something falls, it goes up.   ————
> Milk is blue.   ————
> It is good to keep a promise.   ————
> When something is impossible, it is easy to do it.   ————

However, the format is still experimental in nature and it remains to be seen whether it can be a valid means of testing these very common words.

On a broader, more theoretical, level there is ongoing debate about the appropriate role of L1 in the teaching of English to speakers of other languages (see, for example, Harbord, 1992; Auerbach, 1993). As Phillipson (1992: 185–193) points out, native-speaking ESOL teachers (teachers of English to speakers of other languages), who are all too often ignorant of their learners' first languages, have tended to make a virtue out of their monolingualism and to assume that the most effective way of teaching the language is through the exclusive use of English in their classrooms. If teachers take this position, there is presumably no place for bilingual vocabulary tests, even in classes where the students all have the same first language. The issue of translation equivalence between languages is also relevant here. It is unwise to encourage in learners a belief that any word in L2 has a directly synonymous word or phrase in L1.

Thus, although much vocabulary testing is monolingual in L2, especially as learners advance in their proficiency, there is certainly a case for using the first language when it is practicable and when L1 provides a better means for the test-takers to express their understanding of the target vocabulary.

Practical examples

To see how these various considerations are translated into actual vocabulary tests, I now want to look at a couple of examples of test design, drawing on my own experience as a classroom teacher and test developer.

Classroom progress tests

The purpose of my class tests is generally to assess the learners' progress in vocabulary learning and, more specifically, to give them an incentive to keep studying vocabulary on a regular basis. The underlying assumption is that it is important to build their vocabulary size in the second language, which requires a systematic study of words by individual learners in addition to any class work on vocabulary. Of course, neither a single class test nor a whole series of them constitutes a vocabulary-size test in the sense that I discussed in Chapters 4 and 5; rather, class tests can be seen as monitoring the learners' progress in expanding their base knowledge of words in the second language.

In terms of construct definition, a progress test is a clear case where a syllabus-based definition is appropriate. There is an obvious tendency for teachers to choose test tasks according to how easy they are to prepare and to mark, but some consideration should be given to the relationship between the requirements of the test items and the learning objectives of the class programme. For example, does the test assess various aspects of vocabulary knowledge, or do the items just focus on word meaning?

The target words in my progress tests have usually come from a unit in the course book, or from a specialised word list, such as one of the sublists of the University Word List (Nation, 1990). A third possibility is that the learners select their own words. This is appropriate for learners who are relatively advanced in language learning and where there is a range of future language needs represented within the class. Examples of such learners are postgraduate students preparing for study or research in several different disciplines, recent migrants who are seeking employment in a range of occupations or adults proposing to travel to a foreign country to pursue a variety of social or cultural interests.

Smith (1996) outlines a vocabulary-learning programme, developed at my university – Victoria University of Wellington in New Zealand – which involves learners choosing their own words to study. The programme is based on an approach to language teaching that gives the learners a significant amount of autonomy to establish individual learning goals and work towards them in a structured way. They not only choose their own words but also, with guidance from the teacher, decide which learning strategies are going to work most effectively for them. The words may come from vocabulary lists, from reading or listening activities or from interaction with native speakers. On a record sheet the learners list each word they have selected, along with its pronunciation, part of speech, meaning, collocations and related forms (other members of the word family). The target number of words to be listed and learned each week is 30–40. Each week the learners give their lists to the teacher, who selects from them the words to be assessed. Since each learner has a different set of words, a special type of test item is needed, which I illustrate at the end of this section.

With class tests, practical considerations loom large in the choice of test items. When we have to write our own weekly tests, we need items which are easy to prepare and can be marked in a short time. However, within these constraints, other factors should play a part in the choice of test task, in keeping with the design principles I set out earlier in the chapter. Let me outline some of the considerations by looking at several item types I have used with my own English classes.

Matching items

The basic matching task requires learners to make a connection between target words and their synonyms or definitions. As such, it is a recognition rather than a recall task, focusing on basic word meaning. The standard practice is to group a number of words together with a larger number of definitions (although the reverse is also possible: more words than definitions). Here is a sample set of items:

Next to each word, write the number of its meaning.

region   —   1 position in relation to others
status   —   2 gas that we breathe
cell   —   3 part of a country
oxygen   —   4 smallest part of living things
skeleton   —   5 useful liquid
            6 set of bones in the body
            7 exciting event

There are some aspects of the design of this item type which are worth noting:

- The reason for adding one or two extra definitions is to avoid a situation where the learner knows four of the target words and can then get the fifth definition correct by process of elimination, without actually knowing what the word means.
- Assuming that the focus of the test is on knowledge of the target words, the definitions should be easy for the learners to understand. Thus, as a general principle, they should be composed of higher frequency vocabulary than the words to be tested and should not be written in an elliptical style that causes comprehension problems. In my experience, this is the most challenging aspect of writing matching test items: producing good, clear, concise definitions for all the words. One useful strategy is to look at the definitions found in learner dictionaries as a guide. The extra 'dummy' definitions for each group of items should belong to words in the vocabulary list from which the target words have been taken, or other similar words.
- If the purpose of the test is just to assess knowledge of word meaning, then all of the target items should belong to the same word class – all nouns, all adjectives, etc. – and should not include structural clues. Otherwise, the learners may be able to match up words and definitions on the basis of form as well as meaning. Look at this example:

to evaporate   —   1 to become successful
an emotion   —   2 to call for help
a vendor   —   3 very carefully
to prosper   —   4 a deep feeling
physical   —   5 to change into steam
                6 a person who sells things
                7 related to the body

The words *to* and *a/an* provide obvious clues here. Even if those words are eliminated, the word endings *-ate*, *-ion*, *-or* and *-al* can help the learners to make the correct matches.

Of course, if knowledge of word form is part of what the teacher wants to assess by means of this test format, mixing of word classes within one group of items becomes quite appropriate. However, in that case it is probably best to have a larger number of items in each group, and to avoid having a single word of a particular class, as with the adjective *physical* in the above example.

- One criticism that can be made of the standard matching task is that it presents each target word in isolation. As I noted earlier in the chapter, the decision about presenting words in isolation or context should be made by reference to the purpose of the assessment. In one test I wrote, I wanted to highlight particular meanings and uses of the target adjectives and so I devised an alternative type of matching format which looks like this:

Find the word which fits in each sentence and write it in the blank at the end.

Someone who is not worried about life is ___.	violent
A metal that is not processed is ___.	secure
An illness that never gets better is ___.	crude
Clothes that fit close to your body are ___.	hostile
Someone who hits other people hard is ___.	tight
	chronic
	parallel

The items on the left are more like definitions than authentic sentences, but they served my purpose of signalling the specific meaning of the target word that I was interested in.

This last kind of matching format is in some respects similar to the next type of item I want to discuss.

Completion items

Completion, or blank-filling, items consist of a sentence from which the target word has been deleted and replaced by a blank. As in the contextualised matching format above, the function of the sentence is to provide a context for the word and perhaps to cue a particular use of it. However, this is a recall task rather than simply a recognition one because the learners have to supply the target words from memory. Here are some sample items:

> *Write <u>one</u> suitable word in each blank. Make sure that you write the correct form of the word.*
>
> When meat and fish are not available, a_____ sources of protein must be found.
>
> Many diamond mines are l_____ in South Africa.
>
> In the tropics there is not much v_____ in temperature from one season to the next.
>
> Modern jetliners fly at an a_____ of 35,000 feet.

As you can see, my practice is to include the initial letter of the target word, which acts as a clue and usually restricts the number of possible responses to one. I have not considered it necessary to provide more than one initial letter, as Laufer and Nation (1999) did in their productive version of the Vocabulary Levels Test (see Chapter 5) to ensure that only the target word was the correct answer. In principle, in a class progress test the learners should be expected to respond with one of the words from the vocabulary list they have been studying that week. In practice, though, I have found that more advanced learners who have supplied a good alternative word consider it quite unreasonable that I should not accept it as a correct answer. After numerous (mostly good-natured) discussions on this issue, I have tended to take the line of least resistance and accept alternatives, even though strictly speaking the purpose of the test is to assess knowledge of items from the official vocabulary list.

Note that, according to the instructions for the sample items, the learners must pay attention to word form as well as to meaning. This is reflected in my marking procedure, in which I give one mark for each word that is correct in terms of meaning and subtract half a mark if it contains a structural error, for example *locate* instead of *located*, or *variations* for *variation* in the examples above. I have tended not to penalise the few minor spelling errors that occur but other teachers may consider it necessary to do so in order to encourage attention to correct spelling.

Sentence-writing items

From a test-preparation perspective, the simplest vocabulary task is the sentence-writing one:

> *Write a sentence for each of the following words to show that you know what the word means and how it is used. You may choose a different form of the word if you wish.*
>
> starve
>
> _____
>
> principal
>
> _____
>
> twist
>
> _____
>
> vegetation
>
> _____
>
> involve
>
> _____

This task can allow the learners to demonstrate several aspects of their vocabulary ability:

- whether they understand the meaning of the target word;
- whether they know how the word functions grammatically within a sentence and what its correct form is;
- whether they know how the word collocates appropriately with other words; and
- more generally, whether they can use the word 'productively' in their writing.

However, the test does not necessarily assess all of these abilities. In Chapter 5 I referred to some shortcomings of the sentence-writing component of the Vocabulary Knowledge Scale, along with McNeill's (1996) evidence that advanced learners can compose acceptable sentences without having a good understanding of what the target word means.

A second point to consider is whether it is reasonable to expect the learners to be using each of the words productively; some words that they study may be important for them to comprehend but are not so likely to be useful in their own writing. It can also be a salutary exercise to try composing one or two sentences for each word your-self. If the teacher finds it difficult to write a suitable sentence for a particular word, the learners will probably struggle even more.

Another potential problem involves cross-cultural differences in understanding what the task requires. One assumption that we tea-chers in English-speaking countries make is that the learners will compose a sentence creatively, rather than simply reproducing one which they have memorised from their course book, a learner dic-tionary or some other source. This assumption reflects the low status of memorisation as a learning technique in contemporary Western-style education. By contrast, learners in China, for instance, commit to memory large amounts of language material as an integral part of their educational experience and many of them are successful at achieving a high level of proficiency in English by means of mnemonic techniques (see, for example, Pennycook, 1996). For them, it seems quite reasonable to supply memorised sentences in response to the task. I have had Chinese students who took some convincing that I preferred their own imperfect constructions to re-productions of well-formed, native-speaker sentences. Thus, if I want the learners to approach the task creatively, I need to explain this and encourage them to see it as a composition task rather than a repro-duction one.

The validity of the test also depends on how the items are marked. My practice is to mark each sentence out of 2. To start with, no marks are awarded for a sentence which clearly shows that the learner does not understand the target word or has confused it with a similar one:

> Please keep my money thoroughly.
> The two boys walked thorough the forest.

Otherwise, I allocate one mark for the meaning of the word and another for its grammar. With regard to meaning, the key point is that the learner should write a sentence which provides an appro-priate context for the target word, including a clear indication that the meaning of the target word is known, as in this example for *thoroughly*:

> Surgeons wash themselves thoroughly before they begin an operation.

On the other hand, I would give only half a mark for 'They did it thoroughly' because the sentence is a short one which does not give specific-enough contextual information. With respect to grammar, the target word should be in the correct form and a correct grammatical structure, including appropriate collocation with adjacent words. On this basis, I would give only half a mark for these sentences:

> She is thorough person who always completes a task carefully.
> The scientists are thorough to analyse their data.

Obviously, there are other ways in which the sentence-writing task can be marked. The important thing is that the marking system is practical for a busy teacher to use and reflects the aspects of word knowledge that need to be assessed. One further point is that marks are not the only form of feedback that the learners receive on their performance in a class test. I normally also provide corrections on the test paper and oral comments when the tests are returned in class.

Generic test items

Finally let us look at the kind of items that can be used in the individualised vocabulary programme described by Smith (1996). Just before the test, the teacher returns the individual lists to each learner, having coded the words with symbols such as #, ~ and *. For example, words of more than one syllable which may cause pronunciation problems are marked with # and the learners respond to the following task in the test:

> *Copy the words marked with # on your list. Write the part of speech and underline the stressed syllable in each word.*
>
> e.g.   <u>hun</u>gry   adj
>
> a   ___   —   e   ___   —
>
> b   ___   —   f   ___   —
>
> c   ___   —   g   ___   —
>
> d   ___   —   h   ___   —

Similarly, transitive verbs on the list are coded with * and the learners have to show that they know which nouns can collocate with each one:

Copy the verbs marked with * into the middle column below. Write nouns commonly used as collocations for their subjects and objects.

e.g.	*a terrorist*	*hijacks*	*a plane*
a	——	——	——
b	——	——	——
c	——	——	——
d	——	——	——

In an individualised vocabulary programme, these generic items offer a practical alternative to having separate tests for each learner in the class. The same item types could also be used more conventionally, with target words provided by the teacher, in a class where the learners have all studied the same vocabulary.

Testing depth of vocabulary knowledge

Let us move on now to a more formal kind of test than I described in the previous section – one which can be used for achievement or proficiency purposes. Some colleagues and I wanted to find a valid and practical means of assessing how well learners knew high-frequency English words. Since we were teaching in a university department that offers intensive courses in English for academic purposes (EAP), we concentrated particularly on subtechnical vocabulary, that is, those words that occur frequently across a range of academic fields and have a crucial role in defining other more technical terms in specific disciplines. For many years our EAP courses had included a substantial vocabulary learning component, based on a series of workbooks (Barnard, 1971–75) designed to promote the acquisition of these words by the students. The question we were asking was whether the students had developed a good knowledge of the words. At that time their knowledge was assessed at the end of the course by means of a test with a matching format, which just showed whether the students could link each word with a simple definition of one of its meanings.

I did some exploratory work with methods of eliciting knowledge of particular words in greater depth. One was an interview procedure, in which students were presented with a selection of words and open-ended questions were used to elicit various aspects of their knowledge of each one. I have described this work in greater detail in Read

---

TO INTERPRET

1 Write two sentences: A and B. In each sentence, use the two words given.

    A   interpret   experiment

    B   interpret   language

2 Write three words that can fit in the blank.

       to interpret a(n) ___ .

           i ___

           ii ___

           iii ___

3 Write the correct ending for the word in each of the following sentences:

       Someone who interprets is an interpret__ .

       Something that can be interpreted is interpret__ .

       Someone who interprets gives an interpret__ .

Figure 6.3 Test sheet for the word *iterpret*

(1989). The main problem was a practical one: it is time-consuming to interview learners one by one and the number of words that can be covered in any depth, even in a 30-minute session, is quite limited.

Another approach I tried was the use of a written version of the interview procedure, divided into three stages. The first stage was a self-assessment of how well the learners knew the word, on a four-point scale. At the second stage various aspects of word knowledge were elicited. For example, for the word *interpret*, the learners were presented with the questions set out in Figure 6.3. Question 1 focused on productive use of the word. The second word supplied for each sentence (in this case, *experiment* and *language*) was chosen to cue a specific meaning of the target word. Thus, there were at least two functions for Question 1: to check the learners' awareness of different uses of the word, and to assess their knowledge of its grammar. Question 2 related to the collocational possibilities of the word, while Question 3 was to elicit other, derived forms of the word family.

At the third stage the learners were given the open-ended task of writing in their own words an explanation of the meaning of each target word. The rationale for putting this task at the end was that the more structured questions at the second stage would help to activate what knowledge the learners had of the target word, so that they would perform the third task better than if they had approached it cold. For this task, there would have been a good case for asking the learners to write the explanation in their own language if they had had one in common; as it was, their range of language backgrounds made it impractical.

When I trialled this three-stage procedure, it proved to be unsatisfactory from a number of points of view. For one thing, it was not an efficient way of testing vocabulary knowledge. The test included just ten target words and the students were allowed one hour to work on it. Even then, despite the fact that these were relatively advanced learners, a number of them did not manage to respond to all the words in that time. There were problems in evaluating the responses that the test-takers made. To what extent should the *quality* of the response be taken into account? For instance, in the case of adjectives which can collocate with *environment*, a set like *good*, *bad* and *perfect* is acceptable but you can argue that *social*, *natural* and *polluted* are better because they are more specific and give a stronger indication that the learner is familiar with different uses of the word. It was difficult, too, to be consistent in applying scoring criteria from one target word to another: some had a wider range of meanings than others; some had a larger number of derived forms or common collocations. In addition, there was not a strong relationship between the learners' self-rating and a composite score based on their responses to stages two and three of the procedure.

The word-associates test

Given all these problems, it became clear that it was impractical to attempt to elicit the full range of the learners' vocabulary knowledge; instead, I opted for the more modest goal of assessing how well they knew various meanings of the target words, using a less open test format.

The new starting point was the concept of word association. The standard word-association task involves presenting subjects with a set of stimulus words one by one and asking them to say the first related word that comes into their head. Research with native speakers of English (see, for example, Clark, 1970; Postman and Keppel, 1970) shows that they give one of a small number of responses to each stimulus. Their patterns of association are remarkably consistent from one person to another, which is taken to reflect the complex lexical networks that they have developed in their minds in acquiring native proficiency in the language. On the other hand, when they administered the same task to second language learners, Meara (1983; 1984) and his students at Birkbeck College, University of London found that the learners produced much more diverse and unstable associations. For this reason, Meara concluded that the word-association task was an unsatisfactory method of measuring the state of a learner's vocabulary knowledge.

Following a suggestion from Meara, I decided to develop a word-association task that would require the learners to *select* responses rather than supplying their own, as in the conventional approach. The basic idea was to present a stimulus word along with a group of other words, some of which were related in meaning to the stimulus word and others not. The test-taker's task would be to identify the related words (or **associates**). Here are two sample items:

edit

arithmetic	film	pole	publishing
revise	risk	surface	text

team

alternative	chalk	ear	group
orbit	scientists	sport	together

One question was how to represent the concept of depth of knowledge in some meaningful way through the selection of associates for a particular target word. After drafting a number of items, I found that there were three main types of relationship between target word and associate, as follows:

- Paradigmatic: The two words are synonyms or at least similar in meaning, perhaps with one being more general than the other: *edit – revise, abstract – summary, assent – agreement, adjust – modify*.
- Syntagmatic: The two words often occur together in a phrase, that is, they collocate: *edit – film, team – sport, abstract – concept, occur – phenomenon*.
- Analytic: The associate represents one aspect, or component, of the target word and is likely to form part of its dictionary definition: *team – together, edit – publishing, electron – tiny, export – overseas*.

The initial idea was to include at least one associate expressing each of these relationships in every test item, but this turned out to be impractical. Since the intended purpose of the test was to assess knowledge of the University Word List, it was necessary to have a representative sample of words from the list, which meant that nouns, adjectives and verbs were included as stimulus words for the items. However, I soon realised that it was not possible to follow a consistent pattern from one item to the next in selecting the associates. For instance, adjectives and verbs enter into different kinds of relationship with other words, especially in the case of collocations. Even taking just adjectives, some have a wider range of meanings and uses than others do: *physical* as compared to *military*, for example. There was also the problem that a particular word form can function as more than one part of speech. *Diffuse* as a verb and adjective, or *abstract* as a noun, verb or adjective are cases in point. The question here was whether to restrict the choice of associates to focus on just one part of speech.

Thus, in choosing associates for the test items, I had to weigh up these considerations, among others:

1 the three relationships defined above: syntagmatic, paradigmatic and analytic;
2 the various meanings of the stimulus word; and
3 the possible use of the stimulus word as more than one part of speech.

I wrote two tests, each containing 50 word-associates items based on target words selected randomly from the University Word List. Ten English teachers reviewed the items to check that they agreed as to which of the words were the associates in each item. In any case where more than one teacher could not find an associate or chose a distractor instead, the item was revised. Then the two revised tests were administered to more than 100 students taking an intensive course in English for academic purposes at my university.

In order to investigate the validity of the tests, I collected various kinds of evidence:

• I looked at the relationship between the scores in the two word-associates tests and another test of the University Word List words, which the students took a few weeks later. The other test required the learners to match the words with short definitions. The two word-associates tests correlated well with the matching test (0.76 and 0.81 respectively).

- I conducted an item analysis, using a statistical procedure known as the Rasch partial credit model. The analysis showed that the tests had a good level of reliability, which meant that they separated the learners effectively according to their level of ability. However, a number of the test-takers had patterns of responses which did not fit the general pattern established by the whole group who took the test. When I looked at the test papers of these 'misfitting' test-takers, I found that they made no response to several of the test items, apparently because they did not know the target word and were not willing just to guess which words were the associates.

- Eight learners worked through a selection of the word-associates items individually, explaining to me as they did so how they chose their responses. This 'verbal report' data provided more evidence that willingness to guess played a role in test performance. The less proficient learners preferred to skip an item when they did not know the target word. However, more proficient ones were willing to guess and were often quite successful at identifying two or three associates. Here is one example:

circulate	government	holiday	light
optional	scatter	tolerate	vague

LEARNER: I don't know what but maybe . . . 'circulate' . . . 'scatter'
. . . 'tolerate' . . . 'light' – this I don't know, it's a guess only.

RESEARCHER: So how did you guess? Before you move on, did you
have any reason for choosing those words?

LEARNER: Reasons for this? I guess this – I read on the words here
and I think something like 'circulate' and 'scatter' is – look like
the movement – something like that – and from this I decided
to guess but I am not sure . . .

Thus, when learners with a good vocabulary knowledge did not know the target word, they looked through the other eight words for ones which were related in meaning and correctly guessed that these were associates.

I concluded from these results that, while the word-associates tests were good measures of learners' overall knowledge of the University

Word List, the individual item scores were not very satisfactory measures of depth of knowledge of each target word, because of the guessing factor. A full report of this study is found in Read (1993).

Based on these research results, I decided to design a new version of the word-associates format. In order to allow for more consistency between the stimulus and the associates, only adjectives were to be used as stimulus words. In addition, the adjectives were chosen selectively rather than on a random basis. Those that had only one basic meaning or a limited range of uses were not included.

The restriction to adjectives meant that the structure of the items could be changed to one that fitted that word class specifically. Instead of being presented in a single set, the eight associates and distractors were divided into two groups of four, as in the following examples:

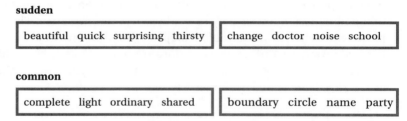

sudden

| beautiful quick surprising thirsty | change doctor noise school |

common

| complete light ordinary shared | boundary circle name party |

The words on the left are adjectival forms. The associates among them (in the first case, *quick* and *surprising*) are either synonyms of the target word or they represent one aspect of its meaning, that is, they have a paradigmatic relationship with the stimulus word. On the right side are four nouns. Among them are associates (for *sudden*: *change* and *noise*) that can collocate with the stimulus word and thus have a syntagmatic relationship with it.

Just over half of the items had this pattern of two associates on the left and two on the right. The other items had either one on the left and three on the right, or three on the left and one on the right. The main reason for varying the pattern was to reduce the potential for successful guessing by test-takers who could not identify some or any of the associates. The original word-associates items were vulnerable in this respect. Several language teachers and testers who gave me feedback on the earlier version of the test suggested that the way to reduce guessing was to have a variable number of associates for each item. The argument against this idea is that even native speakers taking the test do not necessarily find all four associates in their first pass through an item; they may have to return to the item later to find, say, the fourth associate. If they are not informed of the actual number of associates for an item, test-takers may stop at two or three responses when there are in fact further associates to be found. Therefore, the variable distribution of the associates in the revised item format represented a way of addressing the guessing problem while still maintaining a consistent number of associates in each item. However, trialling of the new version of the test has indicated that guessing still plays a role in test-taker performance (see Read, 1998).

As the preceding account shows, my quest for a workable method of assessing depth of vocabulary knowledge has led me progressively to restrict the scope of what I set out to measure, from an initial attempt to elicit by various means quite a range of information about the meaning and form of content words to the development of a carefully structured type of item that focuses specifically on the meanings and collocational possibilities of adjectives. Let us review the resulting test format in relation to the design considerations discussed in the first part of this chapter.

- It focuses on high-frequency words that the learners are expected to have acquired to some extent and ones that they need to know well because of the frequency and usefulness of the words in the language. This is the guiding principle for the selection of the target words in particular.
- It is designed to produce verifiable evidence of how well the test-takers know the target words.
- It is monolingual in nature, primarily because of the range of language backgrounds among the learners for whom it was designed. However, given that it involves making linkages between words in the target language, the logic of the test-takers' task requires a monolingual format. A bilingual version is conceivable, with L2 stimulus words and L1 associates, but that would presumably be restricted to testing meanings of the stimulus word and it would require some careful thinking about the nature of associations between words across languages.
- It treats words as independent lexical units and thus presents them in isolation from any context. A major reason for this is to allow for coverage of a reasonable number of words, and of different meanings of those words, using the simplest possible test task. The

format relies on the associates to trigger in the test-taker's mind knowledge of particular semantic aspects of the stimulus words. However, the fact that native speakers sometimes have difficulty finding a third or fourth associate for a particular item suggests that the word-associates task does not necessarily simulate the way that proficient users gain access to the lexical knowledge stored in their brain.

- It involves a recognition task, certainly in the sense that the test-takers select responses rather than recalling them from memory. This avoids the problem of interpreting responses that applies to the standard open-ended word-association task. It also reduces the demands of the task, by comparison with, say, a format that requires the test-takers to compose a sentence or one that involves a significant amount of reading by presenting words in context.

Conclusion

We have looked at a number of design considerations in this chapter. These are not intended as an exhaustive list, but they seem to be some of the most significant factors to take into account in developing vocabulary tests. It is crucial to keep in mind the *purpose* of the assessment as a guide to the selection of the appropriate features for the design of test formats. In the field of language testing, the prevailing views tend to be strongly influenced by the requirements of proficiency testing. Since vocabulary as such tends not to be assessed in current proficiency tests, language testers have not given much attention in recent years to the question of how to design tests of vocabulary knowledge, let alone measuring the broader concept of lexical ability. However, the content and objectives of classroom tests and other measures of learner achievement are somewhat different from those of proficiency tests, and the assessment of vocabulary learning often has a significant place in such tests. In this context, the design features discussed earlier in the chapter are very relevant.

The other point to emphasise, as I noted at the end of Chapter 5, is that various kinds of trade-off are necessary in vocabulary-test design. This is particularly clear in the case of vocabulary-size tests where a large sample of words needs to be covered within the testing time available in order to obtain a satisfactory estimate of the total number of words known. This means that the test-takers' task needs to be a simple one, the words are normally presented in isolation, or in a very limited context, and it may be necessary to rely on self-report to a great extent. Something similar happened during my efforts to develop a measure of depth of vocabulary knowledge, as I recounted earlier in the chapter. The various practical constraints resulted in the change from a test procedure that sought to elicit a range of knowledge about each word, both receptively and productively, to a much more limited selected-response format that focuses on the meaning and collocations of adjectives. On the other hand, if you opt for a contextualised approach to vocabulary testing, the question may be: how much context is really needed? There must be a point where context (in the form of the stimulus text) becomes too extensive for efficient assessment, if the main purpose is primarily to test certain lexical items within it. Thus, having regard for the purpose of the assessment and the definition of the construct, the different variables discussed in this chapter need to be weighed up in order to reach the most suitable design for a discrete vocabulary test.

....

CHAPTER SEVEN

Comprehensive measures of vocabulary

Introduction

In this chapter we move to a broader concept of vocabulary assessment than the kinds of tests that were covered in Chapter 6. Instead of a selective focus on particular words, the measures to be discussed here look more comprehensively at the vocabulary content of a spoken or written text. In a language test, we are most frequently interested in what learners produce in response to writing or speaking tasks; however, we can also use similar procedures to evaluate the suitability of a text to function as the input for a reading or listening task.

Comprehensive measures are particularly suitable for assessment procedures in which vocabulary is embedded as one component of the measurement of a larger construct, such as communicative competence in speaking, academic writing ability or listening comprehension. However, we cannot simply say that all comprehensive measures are embedded ones, because they can also be used on a discrete basis. For example, a number of the studies which have applied lexical statistics to learner compositions have been conducted by L2 vocabulary researchers who were not interested in an overall assessment of writing ability but just in making inferences about the learners' productive vocabulary knowledge. These researchers are clearly treating vocabulary as a separate construct and not making any more general assessment of the quality of the learners' writing.

In this chapter, we look first at measures related to test input and then at those applied to test-taker responses. However, I do not attempt to cover all the test design issues that I addressed in relation to the development of discrete vocabulary tests in Chapter 6. The reason is that, since these comprehensive measures are very often embedded in a test to measure some larger construct, their design cannot be considered in isolation from that of the whole test. And it goes beyond the scope of this book to discuss in any detail the range of language-test tasks in which vocabulary measures might be embedded.

Another point I should emphasise at the outset is that most of the statistical measures presented in this chapter are more likely to be used by researchers investigating aspects of second language vocabulary development than by teachers or educationists making decisions about learners. The time-consuming work involved in calculating the statistics limits their practical value, especially when they represent just one component of the test-takers' performance and must be interpreted in conjunction with other measures. In addition, there is limited research evidence as yet for the validity of the statistics as measures of the quality of learner performance. The goal of this chapter, then, is to present the research results and consider the possible contribution of the statistics in vocabulary assessment.

By far the longest section of the chapter is on quantitative measures of learners' writing. This is not to suggest that these are the most important comprehensive measures of vocabulary. Rather, it reflects the fact that more research has been undertaken on these measures than the others by scholars interested in second language vocabulary and also that the statistical analyses require a significant amount of explanation in order to be comprehensible.

Measures of test input

In reading and listening tests we have to be concerned about the nature of the input text. At least two questions can be asked:

1 Is it at a suitable level of difficulty that matches the ability range of the test-takers?
2 Does it have the characteristics of an authentic text, especially if it has been produced or modified for use in the test?

Here we are specifically interested in the extent to which information about the vocabulary of the text can help to provide answers to these questions.

As I reported in Chapter 4, it is a well-established finding in research on the reading comprehension of native speakers that vocabulary is the most important contributing factor. The same applies to second language readers. For example, Laufer and Sim (1985a) set out to define a threshold level of language competence that represented the minimum needed by Israeli students to be able to gain an adequate understanding of academic texts in English, a foreign language for them. The threshold was identified by interviewing students in their first language about their comprehension of selected texts. The researchers found that vocabulary knowledge was what the students needed most in order to make sense of what they were reading. Those below the threshold not only understood fewer of the words in the text but also had more limited contextual information provided by known words to allow them to guess the meaning of unfamiliar ones. Knowledge of the subject matter was also an important factor, whereas the interpretation of grammatical structures and discourse markers seem to play a much more limited role in the students' comprehension of the texts. Laufer (1997a) marshals a range of other evidence in support of the threshold vocabulary concept for second language reading comprehension, although the actual level of the threshold in terms of number of words is still a matter for debate.

Similarly, with respect to listening comprehension, Kelly (1991) analysed the errors made by advanced foreign-language learners in Belgium when they were asked to transcribe and translate excerpts from British radio broadcasts. The errors were classified into three categories:

- perceptual, where particular sounds were inaudible or not correctly heard;
- lexical, where the meaning was not understood; and
- syntactic, where the sentence structure was misinterpreted.

The results showed that more than 60 per cent of the errors were lexical in nature. Moreover, when the errors were considered in terms of their effect on comprehension, lexical errors accounted for nearly three-quarters of the cases in which part of the text was completely misunderstood. Thus, Kelly argues that lack of vocabulary knowledge is the main impediment to successful listening comprehension for advanced language learners.

If we accept research findings such as these, it seems reasonable to think that appropriate measures of the lexical characteristics of texts will contribute to an evaluation of how suitable they are for use in an assessment instrument. It is important, of course, to keep these factors in perspective. Even though vocabulary knowledge plays an important role in comprehension, there are obviously other factors that influence learners' level of understanding of written and spoken texts. With this in mind, let us review the limited amount of work that has been done in this area.

Readability of written texts

In L1 reading research, the basic concept used in the analysis of texts is **readability**, which refers to the various aspects of a text that are likely to make it easy or difficult for a reader to understand and enjoy. During the twentieth century a whole educational enterprise grew up in the United States devoted to devising and applying formulas to predict the readability of English texts for native-speaker readers in terms of school grade or age levels (for a comprehensive review, see Klare, 1984). Although many of the formulas are complex, the most popular ones are reasonably simple, especially those that are designed for use by classroom teachers. Simple readability formulas focus on just two variables: the frequency of the vocabulary and the length of the sentences in the text. As Harrison (1980: 19) notes, '[s]urveys of readers' opinions going back to the 1930s . . . support the view that vocabulary plays a large part in whether a book is readable or not, and . . . research studies consistently find vocabulary to be the surest single predictor of text difficulty'.

Let us look at one of the most commonly used measures, Gunning's FOG formula, and see how it is calculated.

$$\text{US grade} = 0.4 \times (\text{WDS/SEN} + \%\text{PSW})$$

The formula calculates the reading level in terms of grade levels in the school system of the US and uses just two variables. The first one (WDS/SEN) is the average number of words per sentence, which is a measure of how complex the grammatical structures are in the passage. The other (% PSW) is the percentage of polysyllabic words (that is, words of three or more syllables) (Harrison, 1980: 79). This and other formulas operate on the principle that longer words are less frequent in the language and thus less familiar to readers. As a result, the more of these words there are in a text, the less readable it will be.

When teachers, testers and researchers have needed to evaluate the difficulty of texts for L2 readers, they have typically turned to the L1 formulas because so little work has been done on readability in the context of English as a second language. However, as Carrell (1987) points out, there are numerous reasons for being cautious about applying the formulas to L2 reading. Second language readers may be hampered by their lack of relevant cultural knowledge and by differences in the way that texts are organised in the two languages – what the researchers call content and formal schemata, respectively. On the other hand, mature L2 readers may have compensating advantages over younger native speakers, such as wider experience of the world or specialised knowledge in their professional field.

Another important lexical variable highlighted by Brown (1997: 90) is the fact that for L2 readers, especially those who are native speakers of Western European languages, their L1 vocabulary knowledge may play a role in understanding English texts. We have already seen in Chapter 5 how knowledge of cognate words can affect performance in the Vocabulary Levels Test and the Eurocentres Vocabulary Size Test. The effect is likely to vary according to the relationship of the other language to English. Speakers of Greek and of Romance languages like French or Spanish find many low-frequency words in English that have been borrowed from their languages. Of course, these may turn out to be *faux amis* ('false friends'), in that they have a different meaning or range of use in English as compared to the source language. However, for certain kinds of reading in English, especially academic and technical texts, it is reasonable to expect that speakers of those European languages would find many recognisable words that would assist their comprehension of the text. Something similar might apply to speakers of languages that have borrowed heavily from English, such as Japanese.

Japanese learners of English were the subjects of a recent study by Brown (1997) to see if he could develop a readability index that would work more effectively for EFL learners than the L1 formulas. This is the procedure that he followed:

- First, he randomly selected a set of 50 passages from books in the public library of a US city and converted each one into a cloze test by deleting every 12th word.
- Each cloze test was taken by about 45 Japanese university students, who were also randomly chosen. The mean score for each test was

taken as a direct measure of how difficult the passage was for Japanese students to read.

- He calculated the predicted readability of each passage by applying six widely used first language readability formulas.
- In addition, he used statistical analyses to investigate a large number of textual variables that might possibly affect the readability of the passages for the Japanese learners and selected the four most useful ones:
  - The average number of syllables found in the sentences in each passage.
  - The average frequency with which the correct answers in the 30 blanks appeared elsewhere in the passage.
  - The percentage of words that contained seven or more letters in the passages.
  - The percentage of function (grammatical) words among the 30 deleted words in each passage.

(from Brown, 1997: 97)

All of these measures (except perhaps the first one) can be seen as reflecting the length and frequency of the vocabulary items in the passages to varying degrees.

- He employed correlational procedures to compare the relative effectiveness of the L1 formulas and his combination of four variables in predicting the readability of the passages, as measured by the cloze scores.

The results showed that the six first language formulas accounted for 23 to 30 per cent of the **variance** (or the pattern of distribution) in the cloze-test scores. By contrast, Brown's four variables collectively predicted 55 per cent of the variance in the scores. Thus, he demonstrated that it was possible to compose a readability index that made a better prediction than the standard formulas did of the difficulty that foreign language learners experienced in reading a range of texts in English.

However, Brown readily acknowledges the limitations of his findings. First, they apply only to university students in Japan. It is likely that a somewhat different index would be required for learners from other language and educational backgrounds. Secondly, the index is difficult to calculate. One of the attractions of the popular L1 readability formulas is that they combine reasonable predictive accuracy for their intended purpose with simplicity of application, and Brown's index lacks this virtue. A further limitation of the index is that, while it performed substantially better than the L1 formulas did, it still accounted for just 55 per cent of the variance in the cloze scores. In other words, there are clearly other factors influencing the readability of the passages in addition to the text features represented by Brown's four variables. This lends support to Carrell's (1987) argument that readability measures which focus just on aspects of the text are inherently limited in what they can tell us about the difficulty that particular groups of learners have in understanding reading passages.

Brown's study is a pioneering effort to develop a readability formula that is suitable for learners of English as a foreign language. As in the case of the L1 formulas, vocabulary measures are prominent among the variables that make up his index. It is reasonable to expect that, if similar research were undertaken with learners from other language backgrounds, different lexical variables would have more predictive power. Such variables might include the percentage of words in the text that are derived from Greek and Latin, or the percentage that have cognates in the learners' first language.

That research, though, is yet to be carried out. In the meantime, it seems that readability formulas based on vocabulary measures have a limited role to play in the selection of suitable texts for the assessment of second language reading comprehension. Text selection must continue to rely primarily on the judgements of test developers and teachers who have experience of working with the population of learners for whom the test is intended. In fact, pooled teacher judgements have been shown to be reliable measures of the difficulty level of reading material for native-speaking students (Harrison, 1980: 11) and they are often used as the criterion for evaluating the accuracy of readability formulas. Once texts have been chosen on the basis of their overall suitability for testing purposes, it is common practice to deal with difficult words and phrases by replacing them with more familiar synonyms or paraphrases. Alternatively, glosses may be provided for such items within or beside the text.

Listenability of spoken texts

Much more work has been done on the comprehensibility of written texts than of spoken language. Whereas the term readability is now very well established, its oral equivalent, **listenability**, has had only limited currency. However, it seems reasonable to expect that spoken texts used for the assessment of listening comprehension vary in the demands that they place on listeners in comparable ways to the demands made of readers by different kinds of written language. One way to evaluate the input of a listening test, then, would be simply to treat it as a written text and apply a readability formula to determine its suitability for the target population of test-takers. There is a certain logic in doing so, because input for a listening test often consists of a written text that is read aloud.

However, this strategy does not take into account the fundamental differences between speech and writing. In fact, even within spoken forms of language, there is a continuum that runs from the very 'oral', like a conversation between friends, to the highly 'literate', such as a scripted lecture delivered on a formal occasion. A number of linguists (for example, Tannen, 1982; Chafe, 1982; Biber, 1988) have noted features of language that make a particular text 'oral' in nature to a greater or lesser extent. These include:

- whether it is planned in advance;
- whether there is a listener who interacts with the speaker;
- to what extent speaker and audience share knowledge of each other and of the world;
- whether or not the audience can see the speaker, so as to be able to observe facial expressions, gestures and other non-verbal aspects of communication; and
- whether information is presented in a concentrated and precise form or in a more diffuse and general way.

It is this last feature in particular that can be measured by analysing the vocabulary content of the text, as I explain below.

There is one published study that has investigated the listenability of texts in a listening-comprehension test. Shohamy and Inbar (1991) devised a test that presented the same factual information through three distinct types of oral text:

- a scripted monologue simulating a news broadcast;
- a semi-scripted lecturette based on written notes, involving some interaction between the speaker and an addressee;
- an unscripted dialogue in the form of a consultation between an expert and an enquirer, with constant interaction.

The texts were designed to be progressively more oral in nature and the researchers expected that this would make the more oral ones easier to understand. The mean scores for the three versions of the test confirmed this trend, although only the difference between the monologue and the others was statistically significant.

The three texts differed according to several of the features of oral language that I previously listed, but one key one is what Shohamy and Inbar (1991: 34) describe as the relative density of the propositions. The news broadcast presented information in a dense and concise form, which required intensive concentration on the part of the test-takers, whereas the redundancies, pauses and repetitions in the lecturette and the dialogue meant that new ideas came at a slower pace, so that they were easier for the listeners to process. This variable can be measured lexically by calculating the percentage of content words in the text, a measure known as **lexical density**. The higher the lexical density of a text, the more literate it is. Although Shohamy and Inbar do not explicitly state that they calculated lexical density as part of their analysis, it would undoubtedly show that the monologue had the highest percentage of content words, with progressively lower figures for the other two texts. I discuss lexical density again in more detail later in this chapter.

Thus, as with the readability of written texts, a vocabulary measure may provide an indication of how easy it will be for the test-takers to understand a spoken text when it is used for assessment purposes. In the case of listening, it is not just the relative frequency of the content words that affects comprehension but also how concentrated they are in the text. Thus, a text that is quite readable for learners when presented to them in a written form may pose a much greater challenge if they have to listen to it being read aloud. The issue is not simply one of level of difficulty but also one of authenticity and content validity. Bachman and Palmer (1996) emphasise that the design of language-test tasks should be based on an analysis of the way that the test-takers are expected to use the language outside the learning context. There may be some situations in which learners need to listen to lexically dense scripted monologues, but in most listening situations – whether it be a university postgraduate seminar, a marketing presentation at the office or a phone call to an insurance company – the speech will be much more oral in nature and the input to the corresponding listening test task should reflect that.

Measures of learner production

We move on now to consider ways of measuring the vocabulary content of the writing and speech that learners produce in response to tasks set for assessment or research purposes. Most of this section is concerned with statistical measures of writing, because there is more published research on that topic, but I also consider measures of spoken production, as well as the more qualitative approach to assessment represented by the use of rating scales to judge performance.

Statistical measures of writing

One way in which we can assess the written production of learners is by calculating various statistics that reflect their use of vocabulary. Some of these measurements were originally developed by literary scholars to analyse the stylistic features of major authors and to date they have been applied to second language writing only to a limited extent. Researchers in second language acquisition have certainly been interested in quantitative, or 'objective', measures of learner production but, in keeping with the general orientation of their work, they have mostly counted grammatical units, such as the length of sentences or of clauses. Those scholars who have worked with lexical measures have used them for research purposes rather than for assessment of learners. The relative complexity of the procedures involved in calculating the statistics makes it difficult to apply them in an operational writing test, although the results of such studies may provide valuable input into the design of the rating scales that are most commonly used for the assessment of learner production in a less time-consuming, qualitative manner.

The researchers have used the lexical statistics to investigate a variety of research questions:

1 Do these measures give consistent results when they are applied to two compositions written by the same learners, with only a short time interval in between? (Arnaud, 1992; Laufer and Nation, 1995).
2 How do the compositions of second language learners compare with those of native speakers of a similar age and/or educational level? (Arnaud, 1984; Linnarud, 1986; Waller, 1993).

3 What is the relationship between the lexical statistics and holistic ratings of the quality of the learners' compositions? (Nihalani, 1981; Linnarud, 1986; Engber, 1995).
4 What is the relationship between the lexical quality of learners' writing and their vocabulary knowledge, as measured by a discrete-point vocabulary test? (Arnaud, 1984; 1992; Laufer and Nation, 1995).
5 Does the lexical quality of advanced learners' writing increase after one or two semesters of English study? (Laufer, 1991; 1994).

The first question is one way of addressing the reliability of the statistics, which according to traditional testing theory comes logically before any consideration of the kind of validity issues raised by the other four questions. I report what answers the researchers have found to these questions later, but before that it is necessary to discuss the role of the writing task and then see how the statistics are calculated.

The effects of the writing task

An important aspect of the validity of any writing measure is the nature of the task that the learners are given. It is only since the late 1980s that the significance of task design has been properly recognised in writing assessment (see, for example, Ruth and Murphy, 1988; Read, 1991; Kroll and Reid, 1994). It is reasonable to expect that tasks vary in the demands that they make on the learners' vocabulary resources. If the task is intended to elicit a fluent sample of writing under test conditions without advance preparation, it makes sense to set a familiar topic that is related to the learners' experience. Thus, one of the topics that Arnaud's (1992) French university students wrote about was 'What is wrong with French secondary education? What improvements do you suggest?', while the foreign students at a university in the US who participated in Engber's (1995) study responded to the following prompt: 'How will studying in the US help your country?' On the other hand, if the focus of the research was on the application of communication strategies to writing, along the lines discussed in Chapter 3, the researcher might deliberately choose a task that poses lexical challenges for the learners to see how well they can express information or ideas without knowing the appropriate terms. Of course, even familiar topics create such challenges for second language writers, but the point is that the choice of task has an effect on the kind of vocabulary that is elicited.

Linnarud's experience is interesting in this regard. In her pioneering pilot study (1975), she set the writing task for her Swedish university students by simply giving them this opening fragment: 'Sir, I protest . . .' However, she found that such an unspecific prompt produced very divergent responses and the kind of vocabulary used varied a great deal from one student to another. Thus, in her subsequent research (1986) with Swedish and British secondary school students, she gave them a series of six cartoon-type pictures that outlined an amusing story without any captions. She set the task in this way for two reasons:

1 to ensure as much uniformity as possible in the content of the compositions, so that a comparison could be made within and between the Swedish and native-speaker groups;
2 to stimulate the imagination of writers with a low creative ability.

(Linnarud, 1986: 40)

It should be noted here that Linnarud's pictures specified not only the content but also the rhetorical style of the students' compositions. That is to say, the students were being asked to write a narrative rather than the kind of expository or argumentative essays that were elicited by Arnaud's and Engber's prompts which I quoted above. Although the writing of an imaginative story was clearly appropriate in terms of the goals of the secondary-school English curriculum, we would expect it to have different vocabulary content from other types of writing. Some evidence on this point comes from a quantitative study by Reid (1990) analysing essays written for the TOEFL Test of Written English (Educational Testing Service, 1996) in response to two different tasks. One was 'Comparison/Contrast and Take a Position' (for example, on the advantages and disadvantages of exploring outer space) and the other was 'Describe and Interpret a Chart or Graph' (for example, depicting changes in farming in the US from 1940 to 1980). Reid found that the two types of essay were significantly different on three lexical variables: the average length of the words, the percentage of content words (lexical density) and the percentage of pronouns. Thus, in this kind of research, it is important to consider the suitability of the writing task in relation to the research questions and to be very cautious about the interpretation of the results if

comparisons are being made between compositions written in response to different topics or tasks.

Components of lexical richness

Once the writing task has been set and the learners have written their
compositions, the analysis can begin. Before we look at some of the
statistics and how they are calculated, it may be helpful to consider
what assumptions they make about effective vocabulary use. The
general term that is used for the characteristics measured by these
statistics is **lexical richness** and it is assumed that good writing has
the following lexical features:

- A variety of different words rather than a limited number of words
  used repetitively. In writing assessment, this is part of what is often
  referred to as 'range of expression'. It is reasonable to expect that
  more proficient writers have a larger vocabulary knowledge that
  allows them to avoid repetition by using synonyms, superordinates
  and other kinds of related words. The measures applied in this case
  are the **type–token ratio** or **lexical variation**.
- A selection of low-frequency words that are appropriate to the topic
  and style of the writing, rather than just general, everyday vocabulary. This is another aspect of range of expression, which includes
  the use of technical terms and jargon as well as the kind of uncommon words that allow writers to express their meanings in a
  precise and sophisticated manner. In fact, this characteristic can be
  called **lexical sophistication**.
- A relatively high percentage of lexical (or content) words, as compared to grammatical (or function) words. This is known as **lexical
  density** and is one characteristic that distinguishes written from
  spoken language. The author who originated this measure, Ure
  (1971), found that usually more than 40 per cent of the words in
  written texts are lexical, whereas in spoken texts the percentage is
  generally below 40 per cent. This reflects the fact that information
  and ideas are presented in a more concentrated way in written
  language than is typical of speech.
- Few if any errors in the use of words. One obvious feature of the
  writing of second language learners is that it contains vocabulary
  errors of various kinds. For example, they choose the wrong word to

express an intended meaning, the word has the right meaning but is in the wrong form or is stylistically inappropriate, the word does not fit grammatically into the sentence in which it occurs and so on. Thus, another possible measure of writing quality is the **number of errors** found in the text.

Calculating the statistics

It may seem quite a straightforward – though tedious – matter to work out these various statistics; however, none is as simple as it appears. For a start, it is necessary to identify the units of analysis, which involves adopting practical answers to some of the questions that we looked at in Chapter 2:

- What is a word?
- How do we classify word forms into word families?
- How do we distinguish content words from grammatical ones?
- What counts as a low-frequency word?
- Should multi-word items be counted as single units?

Specific rules are needed for putting words into the appropriate categories and, in order to obtain reliable statistics, they have to be followed consistently. This means that a significant amount of processing of the written texts is required before the calculations can be done. Some of the work can be performed by a computer running a concordance or word-count program, which lists all the word forms in the texts and counts how frequently each one occurs. It is also possible to enter into the computer a comprehensive list of grammatical words, for example, or a list of the 2000 most frequent words in the language, so that any word form not on the list is classified as a lexical word or low-frequency one, respectively. However, the computer classifications need to be checked manually and there are certain decisions that require human judgement, such as whether two different word forms belong to the same word family, or whether a word has been used incorrectly.

Another complicating factor is that the figure obtained for some of the statistics varies according to the length of the text. For example, it is well known that the type–token ratio of, say, a 500-word text is lower than that for a 300-word one. This reflects the fact that, as authors write more, they use fewer and fewer words that they have not already used earlier in the text. Various attempts have been made to use mathematical transformations to adjust for the effects of text length, but Richards and Malvern (1997) argue that all of them are problematic. A group of learners inevitably produce compositions of different lengths, even if the required number of words is specified in the instructions and they write within a strict time limit. Thus, in order to make meaningful comparisons between them, some sort of adjustment needs to be made, especially when length varies greatly. In her study, Laufer (1991) obtained a set of essays that were all at least 250 words long; therefore, she simply took the first 250 words of every one to make her calculations. A different solution was adopted by Arnaud (1984). Since the shortest of his essays was 180 words, he programmed his computer to take a random selection of 180 words (tokens) from each of the other essays. Arnaud's method had the advantage of giving all of the words written by the students an equal chance of being selected for the analysis, including those towards the end of the longer essays.

Currently Richards and Malvern (1997) are developing a new measure of lexical diversity based on the type–token ratio, which they believe overcomes the problem of variable text length. Their procedure uses mathematical modelling to plot the way that the ratio changes as the number of tokens increases. It is not dependent on the total number of words in the text and it makes use of all the words in the calculation. Richards and Malvern work in the area of child language research, but their index may also be applicable to second language writers if it proves to be a reliable and practical measure.

A third problem in calculating the statistics is how to treat vocabulary errors made by the learner. Since Laufer (1991) wanted to use her measures to assess her students' active vocabulary use, she excluded words containing errors from the analysis, on the basis that an error demonstrated that the learner had not yet fully acquired the word. However, other researchers have used error counts for at least one of their measures. Whether erroneous words are counted or not, there is the additional difficulty of distinguishing vocabulary errors from grammatical ones.

All these problems need to be addressed before the various statistics can be properly calculated. Let us now look at each of the statistics in turn.

- Lexical density: This is the proportion of lexical (or content) words – basically nouns, full verbs, adjectives and adverbs derived from adjectives – in the text. We can write it this way:

$$LD = \frac{\text{total number of lexical words}}{\text{total number of words in the composition}}$$

Although lexical density is calculated for written texts, it plays more of a role in the analysis of spoken texts and we therefore consider it in more detail later in this chapter.

- Lexical variation: This is the type–token ratio of the lexical (as distinct from grammatical) words in the text. The 'types' here are the different lexical words used in the text, while the 'tokens' are all the lexical words in the text, including the repetitions of words that are used more than once. A high figure means that the text contains a wide range of different words; a low one indicates that the writer has relied on a small stock of words that are frequently repeated. To make the calculation, the lexical words must first be classified into the appropriate units of analysis. For example, Laufer (1991) took the **lexeme** as her unit. A lexeme is a single lexical item which may consist of more than one word form. Thus, when she entered student texts into her computer program, Laufer followed these guidelines to identify the lexemes: 'all inflected forms of verbs were entered in the base form; homonyms were distinguished as separate entries; an idiom was entered as one item; derivatives of base words were counted as separate words (e.g. tolerate, tolerance, tolerable).' (p. 442) Then the calculation was done as follows:

$$LV = \frac{\text{the number of different lexemes in the text}}{\text{the total number of lexemes in the text}}$$

- Lexical sophistication: Also referred to as 'rareness', this is a measure of the proportion of relatively unusual or advanced words in the learner's text. Arnaud (1984) and Linnarud (1986) defined sophistication by reference to official vocabulary lists for English teaching in secondary schools in their respective countries. Sophisticated words were ones that the students were not expected to know well at their level in the education system. On the other hand, Laufer (1991) took any word in the University Word List (Nation, 1990: 235–239) as being advanced for her Israeli university students.

$$LS = \frac{\text{the number of sophisticated word families in the text}}{\text{the total number of word families in the text}}$$

A related measure is **lexical individuality** (Linnarud, 1986) or **originality** (Laufer, 1991), which involves a count of the number of words (if any) in one learner's text that were not used by any of the other learners in the study. Obviously, this is a less stable measure than the others, depending as it does on the range of ability among the learners in the comparison group. However, it may have some value when used with a relatively homogeneous student population.

- The Lexical Frequency Profile (LFP): Laufer and Nation (1995) devised a new measure which they claim overcomes various shortcomings of the conventional lexical statistics. The Lexical Frequency Profile is based on the relative frequency of words in the language and involves simply calculating the percentage of word families in the learner's composition that belong to each of three or four frequency bands. In their original study, Laufer and Nation used a profile that comprised four levels: first 1000 most frequent words, second 1000 most frequent words, words in the University Word List, and any other (less frequent) words. Thus, if a learner wrote an essay containing 200 word families in total and these consisted of 150 from the first 1000 list, 20 from the second 1000 list, 20 from the University Word List, and 10 other words, the profile would be 75%–10%–10%–5%. The authors' argument is that the LFP provides a more objective and differentiated measure of the learners' vocabulary use than the other statistics, because it draws on a range of established word lists to classify the words into categories.

  However, like earlier statistics, the LFP is affected by the variable amount that different learners write, unless samples of a standard length are used. In addition, the profile is a little unwieldy to compare with other, single measures and, in subsequent research, Laufer (1994, 1995) found that simply taking the percentage of words that were not within the first 2000 words gave a clearer indication of progress in vocabulary use over one or two semesters of university study than the full profile did. The 'beyond 2000' percentage is in fact an alternative way of calculating lexical sophistication. Since the profile always adds up to 100 per cent, more words beyond the 2000-word level inevitably means a smaller proportion of the high-frequency words.

- Occurrence of errors: Several of the studies have included a measure of the number or percentage of lexical errors in each composition. In a sense, this is the converse of the notion of lexical richness. As noted above, the major challenge here is to identify the errors and to distinguish them from non-lexical ones. Arnaud gives this list of typical errors in his 1984 study:

– minor spelling mistakes: *personnal, teatcher*
– major spelling mistakes: *scholl*
– derivation mistakes: *to comparate, he successed*
– *faux-amis* (deceptive cognates): *They should be prevented that it is difficult*
– interference from another language on the curriculum: *to spare money*
– confusion between two lexemes: *The teachers learn them maths.*

(Arnaud, 1984: 19)

The more elaborate classification scheme developed by Engber (1995) for her research is presented in Table 7.1. No matter how detailed such a scheme is, subjective judgements are required and it is highly desirable to have the errors in a set of compositions classified independently by the researcher and one other person, to see whether they are able to achieve a high level of agreement (or inter-rater reliability) in their identification of the lexical errors. Another limitation of this kind of measure is that it does not take into account the relative seriousness of different errors. Minor spelling errors (if they are counted) have the same weight as word choices which make a sentence difficult to interpret.

Research findings

Having reviewed the various measures in some detail, let us return to the research questions to see what substantive findings the studies have produced.

1 Only two studies looked at the reliability of lexical statistics, in the sense of how consistent they are when applied to two compositions written by the same learners within a limited period of time. Using a composite index of lexical quality, Arnaud (1992) obtained just a moderate correlation of 0.64 between two essays with a six to eight week gap between them. With that kind of interval it is likely that a variable amount of learning took place in the meantime, which would have reduced the size of the correlation. On the other hand, Laufer and Nation (1995) found little significant difference in the Lexical Frequency Profiles of two compositions written in the same week.

Table 7.1 *Classification of lexical errors (Engber, 1995: 146)*

I. Lexical choice

A. Individual lexical items
    1. Incorrect – semantically unrelated
        a. It has some *meanings* to study in the US.
        b. We can help ourselves with *doing* as international students.
    2. Incorrect – semantically close
        a. They have to *come back* to Indonesia. (*go back*)
        b. We can study some *strange* subjects. (*unusual*)

B. Combinations
    1. Two lexical items
        a. Young people can *say* their *ideas*.
        b. I will *bring to go* the development of my country.
    2. Phrases
        a. We have *a lot common*. (*a lot in common*)
        b. They can discuss their ideas *from the bottom of mind*.
    3. Multiple errors involving core lexical items
        a. Who would want to have more exactly their major.
        b. It is being popular year and year.
        c. I will get English comprehension perfectly.

II. Lexical form

    1. Derivational errors
        a. There are a lot of *confliction* between these two countries.
        b. It keeps the class more *activity*. (*active*)
    2. Verb forms
        a. It isn't a good way for *looking* a job. (*looking for*)
        b. I want to *make business* with foreign companies. (*do business*)
    3. Phonetically similar – semantically unrelated
        a. It is difficult to think in the *wild* horizon. (*wide*)
        b. I *thing* that English will help my country. (*think*)
    4. Word distorted – major spelling error
        a. We have learned how to produce a *munifactual* machine.
            (*manufactured*)
        b. We can see the road shows *stimulously*. (*simultaneously*)

2 In terms of the comparison with native-speaker performance, both Arnaud (1984) and Linnarud (1986) found that on average the second language learners used vocabulary that was substantially less varied and sophisticated than that of their native-speaking

peers. A few of the best learners were comparable to the native speakers on the lexical measures but most of them fell well below that level. The one clear-cut difference that came from Waller's (1993) comparison was that texts with a lexical density above 50 per cent were either actually written by native speakers or were perceived that way by native-speaker readers.

3 The correlation of quantitative statistics and qualitative ratings has yielded inconsistent findings. In Nihalani's (1981) study, there was a trend towards more varied vocabulary and a higher percentage of lexical words in the better essays, but the differences were not statistically significant. Similarly, Linnarud (1986) found that only one of her lexical statistics – lexical individuality – was significantly correlated (at 0.47) with the holistic ratings of the Swedish students' compositions. To put it another way, a highly rated essay was likely to contain some words that were not used in any of the other students' writing. Her results also showed that there was quite a strong relationship (–0.77) between highly rated writing and a low percentage of errors, but it was *grammatical* rather than lexical errors that accounted for the strength of the correlation. Errors in vocabulary did not seem to influence the raters very much at all. On the other hand, Engber (1995) did find a significant correlation (–0.43) between percentage of lexical errors and the quality of the compositions written by her foreign students in the US. Furthermore, there was a moderate relationship between the holistic ratings and two measures of lexical variation, one including lexical errors (0.45) and the other without them (0.57).

4 The fourth research question concerns the relationship between lexical statistics and vocabulary-test scores. Arnaud found a modest correlation of 0.36 between lexical variation in his students' compositions and the vocabulary translation test in his 1984 study. In the later research (1992), there was a higher but still moderate relationship of 0.51 between a composite measure of the lexical quality of the essays and a multiple-choice vocabulary test. Laufer and Nation (1995) compared the Lexical Frequency Profile with performance in the 'active' version of the Vocabulary Levels Test (see Chapter 5). They reported correlations of 0.6–0.8 between the test scores and the percentages of low-frequency words and, conversely, a strong inverse relationship (–0.77) between the scores and the percentage of high-frequency words.

5 Finally, there is the matter of monitoring vocabulary development over time. In Laufer's (1991) study, there was no evidence that the Israeli university students' use of vocabulary significantly changed overall after a semester of English study. After two semesters, lexical sophistication was the one statistic that had a significant increase. The students who showed the most signs of lexical development in their writing were those whose language proficiency was quite low at the beginning of the academic year. The later study (Laufer, 1994), using the LFP, confirmed that it was the less frequent vocabulary, especially the words from the University Word List, that gave a clearer indication of lexical development during the academic year.

Interpreting the results

Overall, it is hard to draw any firm conclusions from these findings. First of all, there have been relatively few studies addressing a range of research questions in diverse international settings. Secondly, the researchers have used various combinations of statistics and often calculated each one slightly differently. The several decisions that have to be made about how to classify words and identify errors add further variability to the analysis.

Nevertheless, there are some points that can be made. As one might expect, the writing of learners shows less variation and sophistication in vocabulary use than that of their native-speaking peers. It is only at a very advanced level that it becomes difficult to distinguish non-native from native writing, as Waller (1993) found in a comparison of essays by Finnish and American university students. Among learners themselves, there is some evidence from Laufer and Nation's (1995) work with the Lexical Frequency Profile that different levels of proficiency can be identified on the basis of lexical statistics and that some increase in the lexical quality of students' writing can be measured after an extended period of study.

The other general issue is how large a role vocabulary ability plays in determining the overall quality of learner writing. The researchers have attempted to address this issue by correlating lexical statistics with holistic ratings of the writing and with the scores of vocabulary tests. In both cases, the relationships are moderate at best, with the possible exception of those obtained by Laufer and Nation (1995) with the active form of the Vocabulary Levels Test. Correlations in this range (0.40 to 0.80) are notoriously difficult to interpret. It is hard to know what the contribution of vocabulary ability is, compared to other aspects of language knowledge and ability, unless learners are given a whole battery of tests and the relationships among them are systematically investigated. Linnarud's (1986) results indicate that grammatical errors are much more salient for raters than lexical errors are, while Engber (1995) found that her ratings did reflect the frequency of lexical errors as well as variation in vocabulary use. In many respects, the problem is similar to the one discussed in Chapter 4 of establishing to what extent vocabulary knowledge or ability plays a role in cloze-test performance.

Statistical measures of speaking

Quantitative statistics have been applied much less to learner speech than to learner writing. The one measure that has played a significant role is lexical density. As noted above, Ure (1971) was the first scholar to show that the percentage of lexical words was a useful way of distinguishing written from spoken texts. Her research demonstrated that written texts generally had a lexical density of 40 per cent or more, whereas for spoken texts it was usually less than 40 per cent. She also noted two other variables that seemed to influence this statistic when it was calculated for spoken texts. One was whether the speaker obtained feedback while speaking (as in a conversation) or not (as in a formal speech). An interactive situation produced a lower lexical density than a monologue. The second variable was the degree to which speakers were able to plan what they were going to say in advance. Spontaneous talk had a lower density than a prepared speech. Other scholars such as Stubbs (1986) and Halliday (1989) have also found lexical density a useful indicator of the characteristics of different types of text.

In language testing, lexical density has been used to evaluate learner performance in a semi-direct as compared to a direct test of speaking ability. An essential feature of a direct test is that the test-takers interact face to face with at least one examiner, who acts as an interlocutor as well as assessing each test-taker's performance. The most influential model for direct tests in the United States is the Oral Proficiency Interview (OPI), which was originally developed for use in American government agencies and has since been widely adopted for the assessment of language students in universities and high schools. An OPI is an expensive form of testing, not only because it is administered individually to each test-taker but also because it requires well-trained, skilled examiners to elicit good samples of speech and assess them consistently. Therefore, the Simulated Oral Proficiency Interview (SOPI) has been developed as an alternative (Stansfield, 1991; Stansfield and Kenyon, 1992). A SOPI is a 'semi-direct' speaking test, in the sense that the test-takers perform a variety of speaking tasks but without any live interaction with an examiner. Instead, they take the test in a listening laboratory and respond to stimulus material that is presented to them on a pre-recorded tape and in a booklet. Their responses are recorded for later assessment.

Although a SOPI is designed to simulate the live interview as closely as possible, and research has shown that the ratings that learners obtain in a SOPI are highly correlated with those from an OPI, there is still a question as to whether a semi-direct test elicits the same kind of speech as a direct one. Perhaps the artificiality of the test setting causes learners to speak significantly differently from the way they would perform in a more natural setting. Supporting evidence for this point of view comes from a study by Shohamy (1994) of recordings made of Hebrew learners taking both an OPI and a SOPI. Lexical density was one of a whole battery of measures she used to compare the discourse features of the speech elicited in the two types of test. She reported that the lexical density of OPI speech was about 40 per cent, whereas it rose to around 60 per cent in the SOPI recordings. As you might expect, SOPI speech was relatively formal and concise. Sitting at their places in the language lab, the test-takers responded to the task requirements without much elaboration or personal involvement. It was much more like written language than the free-flowing conversational speech obtained from the OPI.

The testing researcher who has done the most work on lexical density is O'Loughlin (1995), who also applied it to the comparison of direct and semi-direct speaking tests. In his case, it was the oral interaction component of *access* (The Australian Assessment of Communicative English Skills), a proficiency test for people planning to migrate to Australia. The intention was to have a speaking test that could be administered either face to face with a live interlocutor or on tape in a language laboratory, depending on the availability of personnel and resources in the cities outside Australia where immigration applicants would take the test. The two versions were designed to be as similar as possible in terms of the type of tasks and the range of speech functions that the test-takers were asked to perform. The issue, though, as in Shohamy's study, was whether the two versions actually elicited comparable speech from the test-takers.

O'Loughlin (1995) made two modifications to Ure's original method of calculating lexical density.

1 The first one, which was proposed by Halliday (1989: 64–65), was to distinguish between high- and low-frequency lexical items. Halliday pointed out that words like *thing, people, way, do, make, get, have* and *good* are not only very common in English but they often function in a similar fashion to grammatical words. They have little specific meaning of their own and so, according to Halliday, they should have half the value of less frequent lexical words in the calculation of density. In his study, O'Loughlin calculated it both ways – with and without the distinction between the frequency of lexical items – and found that the results were similar. This suggests that for practical purposes the extra effort involved in distinguishing between high- and low-frequency items is not worthwhile. However, O'Loughlin argues, on the basis of his analysis, that the calculation which makes the distinction is more accurate and should be used in formal research studies.

2 O'Loughlin produced a much more refined system than either Ure or Halliday for classifying lexical and grammatical items. He uses the term *item* rather than *word* because the units of analysis include phrasal verbs (e.g. *pick up*), idioms (e.g. *kick the bucket*) and discourse markers (e.g. *the point is*), as well as word families. The full system is set out in Table 7.2.

Obviously, as with other lexical statistics that we have reviewed, it is a time-consuming process to work through a set of transcripts manually, identifying and classifying each item before the overall calculation of lexical density can be made. A less exact but still usable measure can be obtained by computer by entering a list of grammatical words and obtaining a count of the number of words not on the list.

The results of O'Loughlin's analysis showed that the lexical density of the semi-direct (taped) version of the *access* oral-interaction test was consistently higher than that for the direct (live) version across four different tasks: description, narration, discussion and role play. Although the differences were statistically significant, they were not

Table 7.2 *Classification of items for analysis of lexical density (O'Loughlin, 1995: 228)*

A. *Grammatical items*
- **Verbs** 'to be' and 'to have'. All **modals** and **auxiliaries**.
- All **determiners** including articles, demonstrative and possessive adjectives, quantifiers (e.g. *some, any*) and numerals (cardinal and ordinal).
- All **proforms** including pronouns (e.g. *she, they, it, someone, something*), proverbs (e.g. A: Are you coming with us? B: Yes, I *am*), proclauses (e.g. *this, that* when used to replace whole clauses).
- **Interrogative adverbs** (e.g. *what, when, how*) and **negative adverbs** (e.g. *not, never*).
- All **contractions**. These were counted as two items (*they're* = they are) since not all NESB [non-English-speaking background] speakers regularly or consistently use contractions.
- All **prepositions and conjunctions**.
- All **discourse markers** including conjunctions (e.g. *and, but, so*), sequencers (e.g. *next, finally*), particles (e.g. *oh, well*), lexicalized clauses (e.g. *y'know, I mean*), metatalk (e.g. *what I mean, the point is*), temporal deictics (e.g. *now, then*), spatial deictics (e.g. *here, there*) and quantifier phrases (e.g. *anyway, anyhow, whatever*).
- All **lexical filled pauses** (e.g. *well, I mean, so*).
- All **interjections** (e.g. *gosh, really, oh*).
- All **reactive tokens** (e.g. *yes, no, OK, right, mm*).

B. *High-frequency lexical items*
- Very common lexical items as per the list of the 700 most frequently used words in English (accounting for 70% of English text) identified in the COBUILD dictionary project. This list is included in the *Collins COBUILD English course, level 1, student's book* (Willis and Willis, 1988: 111–12). It includes **nouns** (e.g. *thing, people*), **adjectives** (e.g. *good, right*), **verbs** (e.g. *do, make, get*), **adverbs of time, manner and place** (e.g. *soon, late, very, so, maybe, also, too, here, there*). No items consisting of more than one word are included in this category as the COBUILD list consists of words, not items.
- **Repetition of low-frequency lexical items** (see below) including alternative forms of the same item (e.g. *student/study*).

C. *Low-frequency lexical items*
Lexical items not featuring in the list of 700 most frequently used English words cited above including less commonly used **nouns**, **adjectives**, **verbs** including participle and infinitive forms (all multi-word and phrasal verbs count as one item), **adverbs of time, place** and **manner** and all **idioms** (also counted as one item).

---

large, except in the case of the role play. This was the only task which involved a substantial amount of interaction between the test-taker and the interlocutor in the live version. Whereas in the other three tasks the interlocutor said very little, the live role play required her or his active participation in the conversation. Thus, O'Loughlin concluded that the degree of interaction was the most important variable that lowered the lexical density of spoken texts.

Lexical density, then, is a statistic that has a useful role in the evaluation of the kind of speech elicited by different tasks and modes of test delivery. However, as with the statistics applied to learner writing, the time and effort needed to calculate it limits its widespread operational use.

Ratings of writing and speech

It should be clear from the previous section that quantitative statistics are useful mainly for research purposes. In the case of speaking tests, a full transcript needs to be produced before the analysis can begin. The analysis itself is time consuming and cannot be fully automated, because subjective judgements are required to identify the lexical units and classify them into the appropriate categories. And once the calculating is done, there is still the question of what the statistics mean. The limited amount of research in this area has not established norms for interpreting the learners' performance in any absolute way. In each particular context, the learners' statistics have to be compared with some appropriate point of reference, which may be the performance of a similar group of native speakers or the performance of the learners themselves at the beginning vs. the end of their course of study.

Of course, another kind of reference point is a judgement of the overall quality of each learner's performance using a rating scale. When learners are taking a test for some practical purpose, it is qualitative measures of this kind that will be used to assess their vocabulary use along with other aspects of their spoken or written performance. So let us turn now to the use of rating scales for the assessment of the lexical dimension of learners' speech and writing. As with the quantitative statistics, I will refer primarily to the testing of writing in the following discussion, but the basic principles apply equally to oral testing.

There are two main approaches to the qualitative assessment of writing or speaking. The first one, called **global** or holistic, employs a single rating scale that provides descriptions of several levels of performance. The scale for the TOEFL Test of Spoken English (TSE) (Table 7.3) is a good example of this kind of instrument. It consists of five levels, but other scales range from three to nine levels or more. The raters listen on tape to the test-taker's performance of 12 short tasks and decide which description matches each one most closely. The ratings for each task are then averaged to produce a single overall score on the same five-level scale. The level descriptions incorporate a number of different features. In the TSE case, these include effectiveness of communication, appropriateness to the situation, coherence and accuracy, with vocabulary getting a mention as part of this last category. Other scales include different elements, depending on the nature of the task and the aspects of writing that the test designers value the most.

One of the problems with global assessment, though, is that the writing or speech of many learners has what Hamp-Lyons (1991: 254) calls a 'marked profile', with varying strengths and weaknesses. For example, in the case of writing, the sentences may have few errors in grammar and vocabulary but there is no clear paragraph structure and the ideas are difficult to follow. Or the learner may write fluently and engage the reader's interest but in an inappropriately colloquial style and with numerous spelling mistakes. In such cases, a global score represents a compromise between competing considerations. This means that, if we are specifically interested in vocabulary, we cannot make any direct inferences about the lexical quality of the learner's writing from the result of a global assessment. Even though the descriptions may refer to vocabulary use, we cannot be sure how salient it was in the rater's mind when deciding on the rating. The lexical aspect of the learner's writing may be better or worse than the overall rating suggests.

Thus, the second main qualitative approach has more to offer for vocabulary assessment. This is **analytic** rating, which involves the use of several scales, each focusing on one aspect of the writing or speech. After the raters have assessed the learner on each of the scales, the result can be reported as a profile consisting of the separate ratings, which provide diagnostic information on the strengths and weaknesses of the learner's performance. This is one reason why leading scholars such as Hamp-Lyons (1991: 247–261) and Bachman

Table 7.3 *Rating Scale for the TOEFL Test of Spoken English (Educational Testing Service, 1995: 21)*

TSE RATING SCALE

60 Communication almost always effective: task performed very competently; speech almost never marked by nonnative characteristics

Functions performed clearly and effectively
Appropriate response to audience/situation
Coherent, with effective use of cohesive devices
Almost always accurate pronunciation, grammar, fluency, and vocabulary

50 Communication generally effective: task performed competently, successful use of compensatory strategies; speech sometimes marked by nonnative characteristics

Functions generally performed clearly and effectively
Generally appropriate response to audience/situation
Coherent, with some effective use of cohesive devices
Generally accurate pronunciation, grammar, fluency, and vocabulary

40 Communication somewhat effective: task performed somewhat competently, some successful use of compensatory strategies; speech regularly marked by nonnative characteristics

Functions performed somewhat clearly and effectively
Somewhat appropriate response to audience/situation
Somewhat coherent, with some use of cohesive devices
Somewhat accurate pronunciation, grammar, fluency, and vocabulary

30 Communication generally not effective: task generally performed poorly, ineffective use of compensatory strategies; speech very frequently marked by nonnative characteristics

Functions generally performed unclearly and ineffectively
Generally inappropriate response to audience/situation
Generally incoherent, with little use of cohesive devices
Generally inaccurate pronunciation, grammar, fluency, and vocabulary

20 No effective communication: no evidence of ability to perform task, no effective use of compensatory strategies; speech almost always marked by nonnative characteristics

No evidence that functions were performed
Incoherent, with no use of cohesive devices
No evidence of ability to respond appropriately to audience/situation
Almost always inaccurate pronunciation, grammar, fluency, and vocabulary

and Palmer (1996: 211–222) strongly advocate the use of analytic scales for the assessment of learner production. They note other advantages in this approach as well. Analytic rating allows for more reliable assessment because it is based on multiple measures and it reflects what raters actually do when they read a script or listen to a tape. Research on rater behaviour in writing tests shows that, even when working with a global scale, they weigh up different aspects of the learner's performance before arriving at their rating. Therefore, analytic scales direct their attention in a systematic way to certain dimensions of writing and allow them to record their judgements on each one. In addition, Hamp-Lyons (1991) argues that it is feasible for a group of teachers at a particular institution to develop their own analytic rating system, one that is grounded in their educational context and focuses on facets of writing that they consider to be important.

Let us look at one particular analytic system, the ESL Composition Profile developed by Holly Jacobs and her colleagues at Texas A&M University (Jacobs, Zingraf, Wormuth, Hartfiel and Hughey, 1981). This was the first instrument of its kind and has been widely used in university ESL programmes in the US for the scoring of timed essay tests. The full profile is reproduced in Figure 7.1. If we look specifically at the Vocabulary scale, we can see that the descriptors are quite elaborate. They incorporate several aspects of vocabulary use: a suitable range of different items to express the writer's ideas, effective choice and usage of particular items within the writing context, accuracy of word forms, and register.

Vocabulary is one of five scales that make up the profile. Although the term profile implies that each rating is reported separately, there is also a score out of 100 calculated by combining marks awarded for each of the rating criteria. For this purpose, the scales are unevenly weighted because the authors wanted to encourage raters to focus on the communicative quality of the writing rather than the grammatical and mechanical errors. Thus, they saw Vocabulary as clustering with Content and Organization as measures of communicative effectiveness, together worth 70 per cent of the total, with correspondingly lower scores for Language Use and Mechanics (30 per cent) (Jacobs *et al.* 1980: 34–37).

However, the whole notion of calculating a total score is somewhat at odds with the idea of a *profile* of the learners' writing performance. The trend in more recent analytic rating systems is either to report

ESL COMPOSITION PROFILE

STUDENT   DATE   TOPIC

SCORE	LEVEL	CRITERIA	COMMENTS
CONTENT	30–27	EXCELLENT TO VERY GOOD: knowledgeable ● substantive ● thorough development of thesis ● relevant to assigned topic	
	26–22	GOOD TO AVERAGE: some knowledge of subject ● adequate range ● limited development of thesis ● mostly relevant to topic, but lacks detail	
	21–17	FAIR TO POOR: limited knowledge of subject ● little substance ● inadequate development of topic	
	16–13	VERY POOR: does not show knowledge of subject ● non-substantive ● not pertinent ● OR not enough to evaluate	
ORGANIZATION	20–18	EXCELLENT TO VERY GOOD: fluent expression ● ideas clearly stated/supported ● succinct ● well-organized ● logical sequencing ● cohesive	
	17–14	GOOD TO AVERAGE: somewhat choppy ● loosely organized but main ideas stand out ● limited support ● logical but incomplete sequencing	
	13–10	FAIR TO POOR: non-fluent ● ideas confused or disconnected ● lacks logical sequencing and development	
	9–7	VERY POOR: does not communicate ● no organization ● OR not enough to evaluate	
VOCABULARY	20–18	EXCELLENT TO VERY GOOD: sophisticated range ● effective word/idiom choice and usage ● word form mastery ● appropriate register	
	17–14	GOOD TO AVERAGE: adequate range ● occasional errors or word/idiom form, choice, *usage but meaning not obscured*	
	13–10	FAIR TO POOR: limited range ● frequent errors of word/idiom form, choice, usage ● *meaning confused or obscured*	
	9–7	VERY POOR: essentially translation ● little knowledge of English vocabulary, idioms, word form ● OR not enough to evaluate	
LANGUAGE USE	25–22	EXCELLENT TO VERY GOOD: effective complex constructions ● few errors of agreement, tense, number, word order/function, articles, pronouns, propositions	
	21–18	GOOD TO AVERAGE: effective but simple constructions ● minor problems in complex constructions ● several errors of agreement, tense, number, word order/function, articles, pronouns, prepositions *but meaning seldom obscured*	
	17–11	FAIR TO POOR: major problems in simple/complex constructions ● frequent errors of negation, agreement, tense, number, word order/function, articles, pronouns, prepositions and/or fragments, run-ons, deletions ● *meaning confused or obscured*	
	10–5	VERY POOR: virtually no mastery of sentence construction rules ● dominated by errors ● does not communicate ● OR not enough to evaluate	
MECHANICS	5	EXCELLENT TO VERY GOOD: demonstrates mastery of conventions ● few errors of spelling, punctuation, capitalization, paragraphing	
	4	GOOD TO AVERAGE: occasional errors of spelling, punctuation, capitalization, paragraphing *but meaning not obscured*	
	3	FAIR TO POOR: frequent errors of spelling, punctuation, capitalization, paragraphing ● poor handwriting ● *meaning confused or obscured*	
	2	VERY POOR: no mastery of conventions ● dominated by errors of spelling, punctuation, capitalization, paragraphing ● handwriting illegible ● OR not enough to evaluate	

TOTAL SCORE   READER   COMMENTS

Figure 7.1 ESL composition profile (Jacobs *et al.*, 1981: 30)

each rating separately or to give each one equal weight when they are combined. Hamp-Lyons (1991: 249) argues that we do not know enough about how the different components of writing are inter-related to make valid judgements concerning their relative contribu-tions. Therefore, she recommends that each component should be weighted equally if it is necessary to combine the ratings into a single score for reporting purposes.

Analytic scales are not intended to cover all possible aspects of the test-takers' performance. For one thing, the more scales there are, the more difficult it is to define each one distinctly and the more de-manding the raters' task becomes. Hamp-Lyons and Henning (1991) undertook a study of writing assessment in which seven scales were used, each having nine steps. As they noted, 'Essay scoring is a complex cognitive task and the combination of multiple traits with a very long scale puts a heavy cognitive burden on raters' (p. 364). Thus, there needs to be a trade-off between having a rating system which is comprehensive and one that can be applied effectively in practice.

The designers of analytic rating systems typically select three to five aspects of learner performance to provide the basis for the develop-ment of the scales. Published analytic rating systems for the assess-ment of L2 writing often include a scale that focuses on vocabulary use. However, in some cases vocabulary is seen as forming part of a larger dimension of learner production. For example, one of Brown and Bailey's (1984) scales for the assessment of academic writing is labelled 'Style and Quality of Expression'. The scale descriptors are as follows:

- Excellent to Good: 20–18   Precise vocabulary usage; use of parallel structures; concise; register good
- Good to Adequate: 17–15   Attempts variety; good vocabulary; not wordy; register OK; style fairly concise
- Adequate to Fair: 14–12   Some vocabulary misused; lacks aware-ness of register; may be too wordy
- Unacceptable – not college-level work: 11–6   Poor expression of ideas, problems in vocabulary, lacks variety of structure;
- Inappropriate use of vocabulary: 5–1   No concept of register or sentence variety

(from Brown and Bailey, 1984: 41)

Thus, the raters are asked to consider how appropriately the writer has used vocabulary, with appropriateness being judged in terms of both register and concise expression. In addition, there is some reference to the way in which sentence structures contribute to the style of the writing, although it is not consistently maintained in all five descriptors. It seems, then, that Brown and Bailey saw vocabulary as the primary means through which ideas are expressed in writing. This suggests in turn that the construct of vocabulary here is not defined simply in terms of single words but includes larger lexical units as well.

Another example of a rating system in which vocabulary is embedded in a broader dimension is the experimental communicative writing profile used by Hamp-Lyons and Henning (1991). As noted above, the profile consists of seven scales, two of which are Linguistic Accuracy and Linguistic Appropriacy. For Linguistic Accuracy, the raters are asked to judge the extent to which they are conscious of errors in vocabulary as well as punctuation, spelling and grammar. For example, Level 6 on the nine-point scale is defined like this: 'The reader is aware of errors of vocabulary, spelling, or grammar – but only occasionally' (p. 371). In this case, vocabulary has quite a different role from what it had in Brown and Bailey's Style and Quality of Expression scale above, where it was central to the way in which that dimension of writing was defined. Here it is one *possible* source of error, and the one that is mentioned first, but it may well be that grammatical or spelling errors have much more influence on the rating that is given. The Linguistic Appropriacy scale refers even more generally to 'linguistic systems'. Here is the descriptor for Level 6: 'There is limited ability to manipulate the linguistic systems appropriately, but this intrudes only occasionally' (p. 371). Elsewhere in the article, Linguistic Appropriacy is defined as 'Strength of grammatical and lexical features chosen' (p. 344) and the authors also indicate that the concept of register is relevant here in cases where the task requires the test-takers to write in a particular register (p. 363). Thus, although the scale descriptors for Linguistic Appropriacy do not refer explicitly to vocabulary, it is apparently seen by the researchers as an important aspect of it.

In contrast to the scales in which vocabulary is part of a larger dimension of learner production, there are others with a very specific focus on vocabulary use. For example, Weir's (1990) Test in English for Educational Purposes (TEEP) has scales for the assessment of both writing and speaking tasks that are labelled 'Adequacy of vocabulary for purpose'. Here is the one for speaking:

0 Vocabulary inadequate even for the most basic parts of the intended communication.
1 Vocabulary limited to that necessary to express simple needs; inadequacy of vocabulary restricts topics of interaction to the most basic; perhaps frequent lexical inaccuracies and/or excessive repetition.
2 Some misunderstandings may arise through lexical inadequacy or inaccuracy; hesitation and circumlocution are frequent, though there are signs of a developing active vocabulary.
3 Almost no inadequacies or inaccuracies in vocabulary for the task. Only rare circumlocution.

(Weir, 1990: 147)

The scale measures range and accuracy of vocabulary use, judged in relation to the performance of several tasks that are intended to simulate the experience of studying in an English-medium university. The tasks include participating in a small group discussion, asking questions about a chart or graph, and making a short prepared oral presentation.

Whether there is a separate analytic scale for vocabulary use or vocabulary is incorporated into the definition of a broader scale depends on how test designers define the construct which they are setting out to measure. Bachman and Palmer's (1996: 117–120) distinction between syllabus-based and theory-based approaches to construct definition, which I introduced in Chapter 6, is relevant here. A syllabus-based definition is appropriate in an instructional setting, where the purpose is to measure the learners' progress towards specific learning goals and, if these include aspects of vocabulary knowledge and use, it makes sense to use an analytic scale to provide information on how well those goals have been achieved. On the other hand, a theory-based definition draws on a model of language ability together with an analysis of the situations in which the learners need to use the target language. The latter approach is necessary for proficiency purposes, without reference to a particular teaching syllabus. My distinction between discrete and embedded vocabulary assessment also applies here. The more that vocabulary is embedded in a larger construct of language ability, the less likely it is that there will be a scale that focuses just on vocabulary.

Conclusion

In this chapter we have looked at measures which can be used to assess the vocabulary content of writing and speech. They can be applied both to the evaluation of texts as input for reading or listening tests and the assessment of what learners produce in response to writing or speaking tasks. Although the lexical statistics are often described as 'objective' measures, it should be clear from the description of how they are calculated that subjective judgement plays an important role. The listing and counting of word forms is made easy by computer analysis, but a considerable amount of human work is required to define the relevant lexical categories and then classify the individual lexical items. This tends to restrict the statistics to use for research purposes.

There has only been a limited amount of research to explore the relationships between the lexical statistics and subjective ratings. I mentioned in the discussion of lexical statistics for writing that some researchers have correlated them with qualitative ratings of the same compositions. However, the ratings employed in these studies have been global rather than analytic ones. There appears to be no published research that compares individual lexical statistics with specific analytic scales, for example the statistic of lexical variation with a rating for range of vocabulary use, or a count of lexical errors with raters' subjective judgements of the amount of error in learners' writing or speech. The statistical measures could provide one kind of evidence for the validity of analytic ratings. Of course this does not necessarily mean that the statistical calculations can capture all the relevant aspects of language use or that the subjective ratings are invalid if they turn out to be inconsistent with the statistical measures. Both kinds of evidence are needed for validating the assessment of learner performance in speaking and writing tasks.

CHAPTER EIGHT

....

Further developments in vocabulary assessment

Introduction

In earlier chapters, I have surveyed a diverse range of work on second language vocabulary assessment and proposed three dimensions which allow us to locate the different types of measure within a common framework. Conventional vocabulary tests – which I would describe as predominantly discrete, selective and context independent – are effective research tools for certain purposes and are routinely administered in second language teaching programmes around the world. Existing tests of this kind will continue to be used and new ones devised. They work best in assessment situations where it makes sense to focus on vocabulary as a discrete form of language knowledge and to treat lexical items as individual units of meaning. At a time when the pendulum in language-teaching methodology is moving back to a greater emphasis on form-focused instruction, there is renewed interest in giving explicit attention to learners' mastery of the structural features of the language, including its lexical forms.

However, I have also set out to show that conventional tests cannot meet all of our contemporary needs for vocabulary assessment. We need to broaden our thinking about the topic to incorporate a larger range of measures, ones that are embedded, comprehensive and/or context dependent. In the main body of this chapter, I want to review some current areas of work on second language vocabulary, which will provide additional evidence for my view that a wider perspective is required, and then explore the implications for further developments in vocabulary assessment for the future. My comments on the assessment implications may seem rather limited when compared to the extensive coverage of various theoretical concepts and research findings in the chapter. This reflects the fact that very few scholars have been investigating how to apply a broader view to the design of vocabulary measures. I present my ideas on how to do it below, and I also hope that the following discussion will stimulate your thinking about ways in which vocabulary assessment might develop in the future.

There are two interwoven themes running through the discussion. The first is the potential of computers to contribute to vocabulary analysis and assessment. One increasing trend will undoubtedly be the administration of language tests by computer, as in two of the cases I reviewed in Chapter 5: the Eurocentres Vocabulary Size Test (EVST) and the most recent version of the Test of English as a Foreign Language (TOEFL). The basic item types for discrete vocabulary testing – checklist, multiple-choice, matching, labelling, blank-filling – are suitable for computerised presentation, and context-independent items in particular lend themselves well to **computer adaptive testing**, in which individual test-takers respond to a set of items selected successively by the computer from an established item bank on the basis of the individual's developing pattern of responses. In addition, if learners write compositions on the computer, formal features of the text can more readily be analysed by means of the statistics discussed in Chapter 7. It is important, though, that test tasks be chosen according to the purpose of the assessment, rather than simply because they can be computerised. The convenience of automated administration and scoring has to be weighed up against our judgement as to what represents valid ways of eliciting samples of learners' vocabulary knowledge and use.

In this chapter, I do not comment further on computer-based test administration, but instead focus on how computer analysis can contribute to the second general theme: the need to develop a richer understanding of vocabulary in the context of normal language use. In Chapter 2, I showed how there is a lot more to vocabulary than just an inventory of word forms and their associated meanings. If you reflect on the various vocabulary assessment procedures covered in the following chapters, you will realise that they embody a limited view of the subject matter in at least three respects. One is that they still focus on individual words rather than longer lexical items. Secondly, they are predominantly based on the use of vocabulary in written language; the distinct characteristics of spoken vocabulary have not received much attention by comparison. And the third limitation is the lack of a strong sociolinguistic perspective on vocabulary use. For assessment purposes, lexical items tend to be treated as structural and semantic units, with less emphasis on the wider social or pragmatic dimensions of their use.

In all three of these areas, computer analysis offers opportunities to gain fresh insights, especially through the emerging field of corpus linguistics (for up-to-date introductions, see Kennedy, 1998; Biber, Conrad and Reppen, 1998). However, the same proviso as I stated above applies here: we need a clear sense of how the computer output can help us achieve our assessment goals. The quantitative data which the computer provides has to be classified and interpreted using sound qualitative judgements.

The identification of lexical units

One basic requirement for any work on vocabulary is good quality information about the units that we are dealing with. In this section of the chapter, I first review the current state of word-frequency lists and then take up the question of how we might deal with multi-word lexical items in vocabulary assessment.

New word lists

It is clear from earlier chapters that vocabulary size is an important concept in vocabulary testing. This means in turn that we need to have good data on how frequently words occur in the language, preferably in the form of a standard list to refer to, and sample from, in creating vocabulary-size tests. In the case of English, generations of vocabulary teachers and researchers have used West's (1953) *General Service List* as an inventory of the high-frequency words which all learners need to know, and Thorndike and Lorge's (1944) *Teacher's Word Book* as a more extended guide to word frequency in the language. These were based on counts of words in written texts, undertaken laboriously by hand in the period from the 1920s to the 1940s. Since that time, although computers have made it much easier and faster to assemble large corpora and to count the occurrences of word forms in them, no single list has emerged to replace either of these long-established ones.

The earliest major computerised counts were carried out in the United States in the 1960s. Kučera and Francis (1967) counted the words in the one-million-word Brown University corpus of American English texts for adults, while Carroll, Davies and Richman (1971) used a five-million word corpus of published materials for American elementary and junior high-school students. However, the two lists have a number of limitations as general references on word frequency.

- They are strictly counts of word forms as they appeared in the texts, so that for example *hammer, Hammer, HAMMER, hammered, hammering* and *hammers* were counted as separate items in the list compiled by Carroll, Davies and Richman (1971). That is to say, the original lists were not lemmatised, although Francis and Kučera (1982) subsequently produced a lemmatised version, including a ranked list of the 6000 most frequent lemmas.
- Similarly, it is just single word forms that are counted. For instance, familiar place names like *Santa Fe* and *New York* are counted as two separate words.
- The lists do not cluster the word forms into word families, either by distinguishing the various meanings and grammatical functions of homographs, or by bringing together base words and their derived forms.
- They represent vocabulary use only in written texts published in the United States. However, comparable data on British word frequencies is found in Hofland and Johansson (1982), a parallel volume to Francis and Kučera (1982) based on the Lancaster–Oslo–Bergen (LOB) corpus of British English, which has the same structure as the Brown corpus.
- The corpora on which the lists are based are limited in scope. The Brown corpus is small by the standards of the 1990s, even though it includes texts from a wide range of genres. The American Heritage corpus used by Carroll, Davies and Richman is larger and covers many subject areas but it is restricted to educational texts for school children.

In the 1990s a number of much larger corpora have been constructed. The British National Corpus and the Cambridge International Corpus both total 100 million words, while the COBUILD Bank of English stood at 329 million words in July 1998. Although their contents are still dominated by written texts, they include substantial samples of spoken language as well. Advances in software make it easier than ever to count word forms, identify recurring combinations of words and inspect the contexts in which particular words occur. Nevertheless, no definitive, stand-alone word-frequency list has been published from any of the current corpus projects. One reason is that the big corpora are joint ventures between leading universities and publishers of learner dictionaries, who employ them primarily for their own purposes: linguistic research and lexicography. This means that word-frequency data is used selectively to address specific questions in these areas rather than on a more general basis. In addition, commercial considerations restrict open access to the corpora for those outside the participating organisations.

The generally accessible vocabulary lists from these corpus projects are limited in scope. Sinclair and Renouf (1988: 149) give the 200 most frequent word forms in the COBUILD (Birmingham) corpus at that time, in their article advocating a lexical syllabus for language teaching. The principles of this approach were put into practice by Willis and Willis (1988–89) in the *COBUILD English Course*, and the teacher's books accompanying the series include the cumulative list of 2500 words on which the three levels of the course were based. More recently, McCarthy and Carter (1997: 23–24) presented (copyrighted) lists of the 50 commonest words in written and spoken corpora sponsored by Cambridge University Press.

Another way in which frequency data from the corpora has become available is through learner dictionaries. The 1995 editions of the *Collins COBUILD English Dictionary* and the *Longman Dictionary of Contemporary English* use coding systems to identify higher-frequency words. The Longman dictionary has a simple 1–2–3 code for the first, second and third thousand words in both speaking and writing, whereas the COBUILD volume has a more elaborate system of five frequency bands, plus in effect a sixth band consisting of all the other words which are not coded. The first band covers the 700 most frequent words and the other four include the next 1200, 1500, 3200 and 8100 words respectively, giving a total of 14,700 words. Thus, one method of constructing corpus-based vocabulary lists for the purpose of measuring vocabulary size would be to comb through one of the dictionaries and collate words according to their frequency band.

It is important to note, though, that the dictionary editors do not state explicitly how they defined what a word was for the purposes of the frequency count. Although some inferences can be made about this from analysing the way that the dictionary entries are structured, a general word-frequency list needs to have associated with it a clear statement of how the word forms were classified: are the items in the list the actual word forms appearing in the source texts, or are they lemmas, or perhaps word families? Another question which should be addressed is whether frequency was the only criterion used in selecting and ordering the items in the list. In this sense, 'word *frequency* list' is often a misnomer because other considerations are brought to bear as well.

Let us take the General Service List (West, 1953) as a case in point. The list was compiled as a foundation vocabulary of 2000 high-frequency word families, which every learner of English as a foreign language should know. Since the work was done so long ago, it has frequently been criticised for being out of date (see, for example, Richards, 1974). In addition, Engels (1968) argued that the second 1000 words of the list were much less 'general' – in the sense of occurring frequently across a wide range of texts – than the first 1000 words. If you browse through the list, it is not difficult to find words like *applaud, carriage, empire, noble* and *rake*, which are not likely to be useful for contemporary learners in the early stages of acquiring the vocabulary of English.

It might seem a straightforward matter to produce a new list of high-frequency vocabulary, taking advantage of modern computer technology. However, a number of different processing procedures and selection criteria would need to be applied if the list is to have widespread value for teaching and assessment purposes (cf. Nation and Waring, 1997: 18–19).

- It should be based on at least one of the large multi-million-word corpora, which is as representative as possible of current English in terms of mode (spoken vs. written), major varieties (British vs. American) and registers.
- The word forms initially need to be listed in descending order of frequency and lemmatised. Although this process can now be automated to a large extent, the output still needs to be checked manually for errors in classifying the lemmas.
- The selection of words for a general high-frequency list must take account of *range* as well as frequency. Separate frequency counts are needed for each of the varieties represented in the corpus, in order to identify words used in a wide variety of contexts.

- A decision has to be made as to whether the list will consist just of individual words or whether certain fixed phrases occur with sufficient frequency and range to be included as items in their own right.
- Other selection criteria need to be considered as well. For instance, the General Service List contains words like *behave, berry, fry, left, polite, sew* and *spoon*, which are doubtful candidates on frequency alone but they represent everyday objects, activities or concepts not easily expressed in another way. Conversely, a word or phrase may be excluded because its meaning can readily be covered by higher frequency items.
- There should be a thorough semantic analysis of the lemmas chosen, so that they can be grouped into word families. One of the strengths of West's (1953) list is that it includes information about the relative frequency of different forms and meanings within a word family, along with recommendations as to which meanings should be taught to learners just acquiring knowledge of the vocabulary for the first time. The skills required are those of lexicographers composing entries for learner dictionaries.

Thus, although there are certainly ways in which computer analysis can make the development of a truly representative, high-frequency word list much less time-consuming than it was for the pioneering scholars in the early years of this century, it would require a substantial amount of skilled analysis and judgement to produce a good quality list, and so far no one has taken up the challenge.

Going beyond the first 2000 words, vocabulary researchers and teachers have a continuing interest in estimating the vocabulary size of learners who have advanced past the beginning level of learning (see Chapter 4). This means that there is a demand for a general word-frequency list, based on the principles I have just outlined, extending at least to the 5000-word level and possibly as far as 10,000 words. It would be useful to have a standard reference work which reported the frequencies of word families in contemporary English as a whole up to this level. However, the further we move from the first 2000 or so, the less significant frequency becomes in an absolute sense. That is to say, the selection of lower-frequency words depends increasingly on the learners' specific needs and interests. Therefore, to complement a general list, a range of more specialised ones is also required.

One group of words which has often been identified as important for students in secondary school and university is subtechnical or academic vocabulary. I have referred in earlier chapters to the University Word List (Nation, 1990: 235–239), which, in the late 1990s, has been replaced by the Academic Word List (Coxhead, 1998). To develop the list, Coxhead assembled a corpus of academic reading material totalling about 3,500,000 running words. The corpus was made up of journal articles, book chapters, course workbooks, laboratory manuals and course notes covering 28 subject areas from the Arts, Commerce, Law and Science faculties of a New Zealand university. Initially, the word forms were lemmatised and classified into word families, using the structural criteria presented by Bauer and Nation (1993). This means that the word families were identified according to the kinds of prefixes and suffixes that the stem form could take, rather than by the sort of semantic analysis used by Nagy and Anderson (1984) (see Chapter 4). Certain types of word were excluded from consideration: high-frequency words (the General Service List), proper nouns and Latin abbreviations (*et al.*, *i.e.*, *etc.*). The remaining word families had to occur at least 100 times in the corpus and they also needed to meet a range criterion, which was that members of the family were found fairly uniformly in all four faculty sections of the corpus and in more than half of the subject areas. The resulting list comprises 570 word families. Thus, the compilation of the Academic Word List followed the basic principles which I outlined above for a general high-frequency list, except that in this case a more specific corpus was used and particular emphasis was given to range of occurrence across subject areas.

The Academic Word List is designed primarily for use in English for Academic Purposes programmes, where students are preparing for study in a variety of disciplines. Obviously, there is also a role for specific lists which present the key vocabulary of particular disciplines or subject areas. This applies not just to the academic context but also the learning of second language vocabulary for occupational, technical and social purposes. In Chapter 2, I quoted Chapelle's (1994) argument that a logical outcome of adopting a communicative approach to vocabulary ability is that vocabulary size should be assessed in relation to contexts of use, rather than in absolute terms. Later in this chapter I take up the issue of defining a context of use but, assuming that can be done, the question is how to identify and select lexical items for a context-specific vocabulary list. Our first thought is that it should include technical terms, which tend to be used only in that specific context and may be completely foreign to anyone who is not familiar with it. Thus, we can refer to specialised dictionaries of psychology, law, botany, automotive engineering, philately and so on as one source of information as to what are considered technical terms in particular fields. A more empirical strategy was adopted by Yang (1986), who applied statistical analyses to a corpus of texts from nine scientific fields. The statistics were essentially the converse of the measures used by Coxhead (1998) for the Academic Word List, in that they were designed to identify words of high frequency in one field and low to zero frequency in the others. Yang also presented a procedure for identifying possible multi-word technical terms by programming the computer to search for frequent collocations of two or more words. In this case, the word forms in the corpus needed to be grammatically tagged, so that the program could locate word combinations which had the formal features of complex noun phrases.

However, technical terms as just defined are not the only kind of words to be considered for inclusion in a specific vocabulary list. According to two recent studies of vocabulary in particular academic disciplines, another important group of items are relatively familiar words that occur with high frequency in that discipline. In the first study, Flowerdew (1993) analysed a corpus consisting mostly of transcripts of undergraduate lectures in biology and found that the most frequent nouns included words such as *cell, water, food, plant, root, wall, energy, concentration, animal, stem, structure* and *body,* as well as more distinctively biological terms like *membrane, molecule* and *cytoplasm.* Similarly, in their analysis of the lexical content of an economics textbook, Sutarsyah, Nation and Kennedy (1994) showed that these were the most frequent lexical words in the book: *price, cost, demand, curve, firm, supply, quantity, margin, economy, income* and *produce.* This suggests that the vocabulary which is characteristic of a particular context of use cannot be identified just by looking for unusual or distinctive items, because words from a general or a subtechnical list may have technical meanings that justify including them in a specific list as well. Flowerdew (1993: 236) observed that the distinction between technical and subtechnical vocabulary is applicable even within an academic subject and learners of English for specific purposes need to acquire the particular meanings of subtechnical terms in their fields of study.

There is therefore certainly a role for specific word lists in vocabulary learning and assessment; however, compiling one is not a straightforward process. First, the scope of the specific field has to be defined and a representative selection of textual material obtained. Decisions have to be made about what constitutes the specific vocabulary of the field, both conceptually and in terms of selection criteria. Then the same kind of principles of vocabulary selection should be applied as I listed above for a general list. Again, in this case, computer analysis can facilitate the process in some respects but it does not eliminate the need for a thoughtful analysis of the word forms and their associated meanings.

Multi-word lexical items

In Chapter 2, I noted the growing recognition among language scholars of the significance of multi-word items in vocabulary knowledge and use, and yet in subsequent chapters the discussion of vocabulary testing has focused almost entirely on individual words. This reflects the reality of current second language vocabulary assessment. Very little thought has been given to ways in which larger lexical items might play a role in assessment.

In research on both first and second language writing, a widely used measure of *grammatical* quality is the T-unit, which consists of a main clause plus any subordinate clauses associated with it. The assumption is that more sophisticated writing has T-units which are longer and, in the case of second language writers, mostly free of errors. The T-unit is relatively easy to identify – in written if not in spoken texts – and in principle all the sentences in the text can be classified in this way. It would be nice if we could have a similar unit for the *lexical* analysis of texts, but unfortunately none exists. There is no straightforward way of taking a text and analysing all of the multi-word lexical items in it. We saw in Chapter 2 that these items form an open set with fuzzy boundaries, especially since they vary in the extent to which their internal structure is fixed.

There are two approaches to identifying multi-word items. The traditional one is to rely on native-speaker judgement as to what represents a recurring combination of words, especially an idiomatic phrase where the meaning of the whole is quite different from those of the individual words. In the past this method has been supplemented by a manual analysis of the occurrence of multi-word items in texts. The recent development of corpus linguistics, using large computerised collections of texts, offers an alternative, more objective approach. Corpus researchers have produced software to search the corpora for **collocations**, words that tend to cluster together in the same textual environment. The words do not necessarily have to occur sequentially; there may be other words in between. In addition, statistics have been devised to measure collocation strength: how frequently and how consistently words appear in close proximity to each other. Oakes (1998: 158–193) surveys a range of statistical measures which can help researchers identify meaningful multi-word items by taking into account:

- their absolute frequency in the corpus;
- their relative frequency, as compared to the probability that the words would occur together by chance;
- the number of words occurring in a fixed sequence, on the basis that longer collocations are more distinctive than shorter ones;
- the consistency with which the items occur in different texts or genres within the corpus.

Thus, these statistics provide objective criteria for the identification of multi-word items, but human judgement is still required to select those that fit the objectives of the research. Or, in our case, the objectives of the assessment. Even if we are able to obtain much better information about the occurrence of multi-word items in the language, how do we make use of it in the design of tests and the assessment of learner performance? There are a number of possibilities.

- One straightforward application would be to choose appropriate target items for a discrete selective test of learners' knowledge of multi-word phrases. However, we need to recall Moon's (1997) observation (reported in Chapter 2) that, while there are large numbers of them, individual items do not necessarily occur frequently in the language as a whole. There may be more of a case for assessing selectively in a test which focuses on vocabulary use in a particular genre or field of study.
- A suitable collocational measure may help to refine estimates of the readability and listenability of input texts, as discussed in Chapter 7, especially if one can be found to reflect the occurrence of idio-

matic phrases, where the meaning of the whole is quite different from what the individual words suggest. Such multi-word items cause obvious difficulty for learners in a comprehension task.

- In spoken and written production, one significant aspect of performance is the extent to which the learners have achieved what Pawley and Syder (1983) called 'native-like selection'. In other words, do they produce multi-word items that are the natural form of expression by native speakers, or do they create odd collocations of the kind illustrated by McCarthy (1990)?:

    His books commanded criticism from many people.

    I am doing this exam because I want to achieve a step in my career.

    She won many competitions, forming fame in the process.

- The other component of native-like production, according to Pawley and Syder (1983), is fluency. Fluent performance is made easier if the learner has command of a range of multi-word items which can be readily accessed as the occasion demands. However, the mere occurrence of these items may not form a satisfactory basis for assessment of the quality of the learner's production. For instance, many of the most recognisable multi-word items are overused expressions or cliches, which may be regarded as inappropriate in the context in which they are used.

With all of these possibilities, it is still an open question whether there is a valid quantitative measure which can be devised, or whether continuing research on multi-word items will provide the foundation for better informed qualitative judgements instead. One difficulty in applying statistical analyses to individual student texts is that the text may not be long enough or contain sufficient examples of particular lexical items to allow for reliable measurement.

Peter Skehan and his associates Pauline Foster and Uta Mehnert at Thames Valley University, London have conducted a series of research studies which have a bearing on the issue of the role of multi-word items in learner production (Foster and Skehan, 1996; Skehan and Foster, 1997; Mehnert, 1998). In order to gain a better understanding of task-based language teaching, they have investigated how different ways of designing a task affect the quality of the speech learners produce in response to it. The two main task variables are the type of task (personal, narrative, decision-making) and the amount of time the learners have for planning how to do it (from no time up to

10 minutes). To evaluate the learners' oral production, three criteria have been used: accuracy, complexity and fluency. None of these was measured lexically in the first two studies, but Mehnert (1998) added a fourth criterion, density, measured by O'Loughlin's (1995) modified lexical density statistic, which was described in Chapter 7. Mehnert found that density tended to increase as the learners were given more time to plan. Her results also showed that lexical density was associated with fluency. In other words, subjects who were more fluent used a larger percentage of content words, especially when they had about ten minutes beforehand to plan what they were going to say. Thus, although the density measure was based on counting individual words, it seemed to reflect the learners' ability to produce the multi-word chunks that are an essential feature of fluent speech.

As a theoretical foundation for their research, Skehan (1996; 1998) proposes that there are two modes of processing available to language users, reflecting Sinclair's (1991) distinction between the open-choice and the idiom principles (see Chapter 2). The first mode is based on grammatical rules and involves generating novel utterances, more or less word by word. This rule-based system is required when meanings need to be expressed precisely or creatively. The other mode draws on memorised multi-word items, which can be retrieved quickly as whole units to allow the user to communicate fluently under normal time constraints. Adult native speakers have both processing modes available to them and can apply them flexibly according to the demands of different communication situations. This adult capability can be seen as developing from early childhood in three stages.

- Lexicalisation: At the first stage children communicate by means of lexical phrases which have meaning within their immediate environment.
- Syntacticisation: Then they move into a second stage when their language knowledge becomes 'syntacticised'. Implicitly they are able to analyse linguistic structures into individual elements and generate new structures on the basis of grammatical rules.
- Relexicalisation: However, effective language use requires a third stage whereby language structures which can be analysed grammatically are stored as whole lexical units.

According to Skehan, progress through these stages is not as automatic for older second language learners as it is for children acquiring their first language. Thus, language teachers and course designers need to develop balanced programmes incorporating tasks which allow opportunities for both syntacticisation and relexicalisation to occur.

From an assessment viewpoint, if embedded vocabulary measures are to be used, Skehan's work highlights the point that the conditions under which the task is performed will affect the outcome of the measure. Learners are limited in their ability to operate the dual modes of processing and whether they produce rule-based or lexicalised language depends on the nature of the task and the kind of preparation they have to perform it. In addition, two other points grow out of Skehan's analysis that are relevant to assessment.

- In analysing samples of the speech produced by learners in performing a task, it may be possible to identify multi-word items that they use, but then the question arises as to whether they are lexicalised or relexicalised. The same multi-word item may represent a lower or higher level of lexical development, depending on whether the learner is able to analyse the internal structure of the item.
- Following from the previous point, the lexical nature of learners' production may be best measured not by directly counting or classifying multi-word items, but by a more indirect measure. One possibility (perhaps ironically) is a quantitative measure based on counting individual word forms, such as modified lexical density – which Skehan and his associates have already used – or the type–token ratio (lexical variation). Another indirect lexical index may be Skehan's measure of fluency: the number of pauses and hesitations in the learner's speech.

In short, Skehan's conceptual framework and the research studies based on it offer some intriguing ideas about the role of multi-word lexical items in learners' performance of language tasks. Although he and his associates have made little use of vocabulary measures so far, there is plenty of scope for further investigation of how the lexical dimension of the performance can be captured, both for research purposes and for making decisions about learners' ability.

The vocabulary of informal speech

In the preceding section, I have made reference to the lexical features of spoken English in discussing Skehan's work. The vocabulary of speech is the second area of vocabulary study that has received less attention than it should have, as indicated by the fact that perhaps the most frequently cited research study is the one conducted by Schonell *et al.* (1956) in the 1950s on the spoken vocabulary of Australian workers. I mention this not to cast aspersions on research coming from Australia (tempting though it may be for a New Zealander to do so) but simply to highlight the limited number of more recent studies from anywhere else. There are several reasons for this (see also McCarthy and Carter, 1997: 20):

- As I have frequently noted, in Chapter 4 and elsewhere, a large proportion of the research on vocabulary has been undertaken by reading researchers, who obviously focus on words in written texts. There is no equivalent research tradition on the vocabulary of spoken language, especially in informal settings.
- Almost all the established word-frequency lists have been compiled by counting words in corpora of written texts. Although spoken corpora are becoming more common now, they are usually much smaller than the corresponding written ones because samples of spoken language are difficult both to collect and to store. Making recordings of natural speech is quite a challenge: people tend to be self-conscious when they know they are being recorded, and there are legal and ethical constraints on recording speakers without their knowledge or consent. Once the speech has been recorded, it then has to be painstakingly transcribed before being entered into the computer for analysis.
- Spoken language also creates problems of analysis. Speech is not 'grammatical', at least according to the rules for the sentences of written language, and McCarthy and Carter (1997: 28–29) point out various difficulties in the identification of vocabulary items as well. For instance, are vocalisations like *mm*, *er* and *um* to be considered as lexical items? Should contracted forms like *don't, it's* and *gonna* be counted as one word form or two? O'Loughlin (1995) faced such problems when he applied the lexical density statistic to speaking test data and I showed in Chapter 7 (Table 7.2) how he had to develop quite an elaborate set of rules for distinguishing lexical and grammatical items.

The neglect of speech is significant, because we know there are characteristics of spoken vocabulary which are different from those in the written language. For example, people typically use a smaller vocabulary for speech than they do for writing. McCarthy and Carter (1997: 27) compared the CANCODE corpus of British conversational English and a similar-sized sub-section of the Cambridge International Corpus containing newspaper and magazine texts. They found that the 50 most frequent word forms accounted for over 48 per cent of the words in the spoken corpus, whereas the corresponding figure for the written corpus was about 38 per cent. This suggests that, if we apply the concept of vocabulary size to spoken language, it needs to be interpreted differently from the way it has been used in reading research. While there has been some work done to determine what the threshold level of vocabulary knowledge may be for reading comprehension (Laufer, 1997a), we lack a similar basis for estimating the minimum vocabulary required for spoken language use.

Part of the explanation for the smaller amount of spoken vocabulary is that, at least in informal conversational interaction, speakers use less explicit language because they are talking about objects, persons and activities which can be seen at the time or are familiar to the participants in the conversation. Thus, they can rely on the non-linguistic context to make it clear what they are referring to. In place of noun phrases, pronoun forms like *it, she, they, these, here* and *there* commonly occur. In addition, a considerable percentage of the high-frequency lexical items in speech are words and phrases which have communicative functions rather than semantic meaning, like *well, OK, right, you know, sort of, is that so?, don't worry* and *sorry about that*. The research on communication strategies, which I reviewed in Chapter 3, is also relevant here. A learner who has mastered effective strategies is able to compensate in a variety of ways for not knowing key vocabulary items and can thus carry on an adequate conversation with a more proficient speaker.

One distinctive feature of conversation noted by McCarthy (1990) is the way that native speakers of English negotiate meaning by the use of synonyms, as in these examples (with McCarthy's interpretation in parentheses):

> 1 JIM: I love those Spanish ones.
> BRIAN: I *like* them . . . wouldn't say I *love* them.
> JIM: Oh I *think they're great!*
> (Brian downtones 'love' to 'like'; Jim offers an *equivalent* phrase.)

2 MADGE: I'm surprised you don't have a *cat*.

ANNIE: We never did like *pets*.

(Annie *broadens* the meaning by using a superordinate.)

3 NICK: He's *shy*, really *timid*, you know.

LYNDA: Like a *little mouse*.

(Lynda fixes the meaning by offering equivalents.)

(McCarthy, 1990: 53; italics in original)

Thus, the second speaker does not repeat a word exactly but uses an equivalent lexical item, which can be seen as performing a particular function in the conversation. It would be interesting to explore whether a lexical variation statistic can validly reflect this feature of speech or, from a more qualitative perspective, whether rater judgements in speaking test tasks are significantly influenced by the learners' ability to exploit their vocabulary knowledge in this way, rather than simply repeating what their interlocutor has said.

In the discussion of spoken vocabulary so far, I have been mostly referring to informal face-to-face interaction, but of course this is only one form of speech. An important corpus-based study by Biber (1988) showed that there were several dimensions of variation that serve to distinguish spoken from written genres. The most important dimension, which Biber labels 'Informational vs. Involved Production', separates language production which is carefully planned and precisely expressed (like official documents, academic prose and prepared speeches) from that which is more interactional and created in real time (like telephone conversations, personal letters and spontaneous speeches). In informational language, nouns and relatively long words occur with high frequency, and there is also a high type–token ratio. Conversely, 'involved' production is characterised by low values for these variables as well as frequent occurrence of verbs referring to mental acts and states (for example *believe, decide, fear, remember*), discourse particles (*well, now, anyway*), hedges (*at about, something like, almost*) and amplifiers (*absolutely, extremely, perfectly*).

Some of the other dimensions are as follows:

- 'Narrative vs. Non-narrative Concerns': The distinction here is between genres (like fiction, biography and oral story-telling) which report a series of past events and those that do not.
- 'Explicit vs. Situation-dependent Reference': I referred above to the fact that conversational language typically depends highly on the immediate context and, in this regard, it contrasts with genres in

which people, objects and places are explicitly identified (official documents, professional letters, academic prose), particularly by the use of complex noun phrases.

- 'Abstract vs. Non-abstract Information': This dimension distinguishes writing which is abstract, technical and impersonal from other forms of language production. One characteristic of abstract language use is relatively low lexical variation because precise technical terms tend to be repeated numerous times.

Overall, vocabulary features play a less significant role in defining these dimensions than they do for the first one.

Biber's analysis highlights the fact that speech and writing vary in several respects; more is involved than just the aural vs. visual channel of communication. Therefore, McCarthy and Carter's (1997) recent survey of research on 'spoken vocabulary' is misleading in the sense that it focuses entirely on informal conversation. This is the form of speech that is the most unlike the written texts which have been the traditional foundation of vocabulary studies, and we certainly need to have a better understanding of its lexical features, but there is a whole range of other spoken varieties of language as well. One way to measure this range is by calculating the lexical density of different texts. We saw in Chapter 7 how this statistic has been used in language testing research to distinguish different varieties of learner speech. However, the research by Biber reinforces the point I made there that variation in lexical density may represent a number of different characteristics of the language-test task. It is not just whether the test-takers respond in speech or writing, but also whether they are communicating face to face with someone else, whether they have time to plan what they are going to say, how technical the subject matter is, and so on.

The social dimension of vocabulary use

The third limitation of current work on vocabulary assessment is the relative lack of attention to social and cultural factors in second language vocabulary acquisition. For example, as we saw in Chapters 4 and 5, it is generally assumed in measures of vocabulary size that simple frequency in the language is a good guide to the likelihood that a word will be known. In addition, vocabulary knowledge and use are typically thought of in psycholinguistic terms, which minimises the existence of social variation among learners, apart from the fact that they undertake various courses of study, pursue different careers and have a range of personal interests. Although these assumptions may be true for learners in the educational mainstream, they are questionable when applied to learners from working class, ethnic minority and/or bilingual backgrounds.

Researchers on bilingualism have long used vocabulary measures as evidence of patterns of language acquisition and use. For instance, as part of a classic study (Fishman, Cooper and Ma, 1971) of a Puerto Rican neighbourhood in Jersey City, USA, Cooper (1971) reports on the use of a word naming task to investigate the subjects' use of Spanish and English in various social contexts, or **domains**: family, neighbourhood, religion, education and work. For each domain the subjects were asked to name within one minute as many words as they could which were associated with that context. They performed the task separately in each language. The directions took the form (for the family domain in this case): 'Tell me as many English (Spanish) words as you can that name things you can see or find in a kitchen – your kitchen or any other kitchen. Words like *salt* (*sal*), *spoon* (*cuchara*), *rice* (*arroz*).' The results showed that the subjects could produce significantly more words in the language they characteristically used in each domain, which in turn reflected how old they were and how recently they had migrated to the US.

For assessment purposes, the education domain is obviously an area of major concern, especially when there is evidence that learners from particular social backgrounds lack the opportunity to acquire the vocabulary they need for academic study. In Chapter 4, I referred to the research in the Netherlands by Verhallen and Schoonen (1993), which showed that Turkish–Dutch bilingual children did not have the depth of Dutch vocabulary knowledge of their monolingual Dutch-speaking peers.

The Graeco-Latin vocabulary of English

In the case of English, Corson (1985; 1997) has drawn attention to the significance of words derived from Greek and Latin for educational achievement at the secondary and tertiary levels. His work is based on a series of research studies involving secondary school students in

England and Australia who were monolingual in English and had low socioeconomic status. He employed two measures of their knowledge and use of Graeco-Latin words:

- A 'passive' selective test (Corson, 1983), in which the students were asked to compose orally sentences containing each target word, along with a 'key word' selected to cue the particular use of the target word which the researcher wanted to elicit. Examples (with the key words in brackets) are: *define* (*problem*), *composition* (*substance*), *product* (*market*), *harmony* (*music*), *observe* (*rituals*) and *reason* (*mind*).
- An 'active' comprehensive measure (Corson, 1982), which was simply the percentage of Graeco-Latin words that each student used in performing two speaking tasks: a description of their former primary school, and an explanation of their ideas on several common moral issues.

The results showed that, although these students had a reasonable passive knowledge of the words, they used few of them in their own speech. By the age of 15, a highly significant gap had opened up in the percentages on the active measure between them and a comparison group of upper-middle-class students, who greatly increased their use of Graeco-Latin words in their early teenage years.

Corson (1997) points out a number of ways in which Graeco-Latin words are difficult to learn, both for native speakers and for L2 learners (unless they happen to be speakers of languages like French or Spanish).

- The words occur very infrequently, especially in everyday speech.
- They are often long, polysyllabic words which are difficult to pronounce unless you have heard people using them. I myself am not sure of the pronunciation of some words I want to use occasionally, such as *chimerical*, *genus* and *polysemous*.
- They typically refer to abstract concepts and do not have strong visual images associated with them.
- They are semantically opaque, in the sense that they tend to be made up of morphemes like *de-*, *meta-*, *-fect*, *-duct*, *-cord*, *lexi-*, *-ic* and *-cy*, which are not independent words or meaningful in themselves to most native speakers. Thus, the words have to be memorised as whole units rather than being analysable into parts.
- They are difficult to acquire for active use simply by reading them

in books, without having the opportunity to discuss the concepts they represent with other people, especially peers.

This last point is the core of Corson's explanation for the socioeconomic differences revealed in his research studies. The advantage of middle-class students lies not just in their greater exposure to written language away from school but also in the way they are encouraged in their home environment to talk about what they have read and to discuss abstract ideas. For most students of low socioeconomic status, on the other hand, the culture of literacy associated with formal education has little connection with their experience of spoken and written language outside the classroom. It is unusual for them to encounter Graeco-Latin words in conversation, printed material or the electronic media. The words are perceived as 'hard' and even alien. Thus, according to Corson (1985: 28), there exists 'a lexical bar in the English lexicon which hinders the members of some social groups from lexical access to knowledge categories of the school curriculum in their oral and written language and perhaps in their thinking as well.'

To put it another way, although secondary school students from such groups have some familiarity with Graeco-Latin words, it is 'unmotivated' vocabulary for them. In this regard, Corson's work gives a new perspective on the receptive–productive distinction, which I discussed in Chapter 6. Melka (1997: 95) observes that speakers may avoid words they know receptively which are considered distasteful or offensive. However, Corson's analysis points to a deeper inhibition rooted in sociocultural factors that can have quite a serious impact on the student's prospects for educational achievement. Corson's research subjects were native speakers of English, but large numbers of second language learners grow up in a similar socioeconomic environment in English-speaking countries and so his analysis is equally applicable to them.

The concept of register

I observed several times in earlier chapters that in vocabulary assessment context has generally been defined *linguistically* as the sentence, paragraph or text in which a lexical item occurs. Taking a broader social perspective requires us to investigate the notion of

Table 8.1 *Rating scale for knowledge of register in writing (Bachman and Palmer, 1996: 288)*

Levels of ability/ mastery	Description
0 Zero	*No evidence of knowledge* of register Range: zero Accuracy: not relevant
1 Limited	*Limited knowledge* of register Range: limited distinctions between formal and informal register Accuracy: frequent errors
2 Moderate	*Moderate knowledge* of register Range: moderate distinction between formal and informal registers Accuracy: good, few errors
3 Complete	*Evidence of complete knowledge* of register Range: complete distinction between formal and informal registers Accuracy: no errors

Note: This scale is defined in terms of range and accuracy with four levels.

context beyond the text. One way to do so is through the concept of register. As noted in Chapter 1, Bachman and Palmer (1996) included knowledge of registers as one component of sociolinguistic knowledge of a language and I also quoted McCarthy (1990) as suggesting that vocabulary choice is the major feature of a register.

In language testing, the term register is used in defining rating scales for speaking and writing tasks. For instance, in the specifications for a selection/placement test designed to assess the writing ability of telephone company employees, Bachman and Palmer have knowledge of register as one of six assessment criteria, as defined in the scale in Table 8.1. Apart from the reference to formulaic expressions and discourse in the construct definition, it is not very clear from the scale what particular features of the writing the raters should focus on in making their assessment. Of course, in an actual testing project the raters do not rely just on the written scale. They analyse the nature of the task, study exemplars of test-taker performance at different levels, discuss the rating criteria among themselves and seek to resolve discrepancies in their ratings of individual scripts. Nevertheless, if register is a significant concept for the embedded assessment of vocabulary in use, it is important to try to clarify what it means.

As part of their definition of the knowledge of register scale, Bachman and Palmer distinguish between formal and informal registers. This may cause some confusion because level of formality is often associated in the linguistic literature with the concept of style rather than register. Indeed, as Biber and Finegan (1994a: 4) point out, the terms register and style, along with genre and text type, have been used in inconsistent and overlapping ways by many different authors to refer to varieties of language defined in relation to their context of use. In the anthology they edited on the topic (Biber and Finegan, 1994b), they adopt register as the cover term for all such varieties and the volume includes analyses of sports reporting, coaching language, dinner table narratives and personal ads in a newspaper. Another contributor to the book, Ferguson (1994: 20), elaborates on the concept of register with this statement of the assumption on which it is based:

> A communication situation that recurs regularly in a society (in terms of participants, setting, communicative functions, and so forth) will tend over time to develop identifying markers of language structure and language use, different from the language of other communication situations.
>
> (Ferguson, 1994: 20 italics in original)

Some of the salient markers for Ferguson are obviously lexical in nature: 'special terms for recurrent objects and events, and formulaic sequences or "routines"' (p. 20). However, Biber (1994: 34–35) argues that it is not particular words or phrases which make a register distinct lexically so much as the kind of lexical features that he used in his 1988 study, referred to above in the section on spoken vocabulary. I return to this point in a moment.

Adopting register as the general term does not solve the whole of the problem with terminology because this means that the term includes language varieties which exist 'at very different levels of generality' (Biber, 1994: 34, 37):

- At a high level, we can distinguish formal vs. informal and spoken vs. written varieties.
- Another high level classification is represented by the four modes of classical rhetoric: narration, description, exposition and argument.

- Varieties at several intermediate levels include conversations, narratives, essays, fiction, novels, science articles and editorials.
- At a low level come specific varieties such as methodology sections in psychology articles and newspaper headlines.

Clearly, if all of these varieties are to be called registers, at least there need to be criteria for analysing them and classifying them into subcategories. Since the identification of the distinctive features of a register involves comparing it with others, it is important that the varieties being compared should be comparable in terms of their level of generality.

We saw in Chapter 2 how Chapelle (1994) advocated the use of Halliday's (Halliday and Hasan, 1989) framework for analysing the context of language use, comprising the three elements of field, tenor and mode. Biber (1994: 40–41) proposes a more elaborate system, which includes the following major categories:

I   Communicative Characteristics of Participants
II   Relations Between Addressor and Addressee
III   Setting
IV   Channel
V   Relation of Participants to the Text
VI   Purposes, Intents and Goals
VII   Topic/Subject

The details of Biber's framework need not concern us here. It is sufficient to note two points. The first is that the proper specification of a register may involve quite a complex description. The other point is that Biber's framework has much in common with Bachman and Palmer's (1996: 49–50) list of the characteristics of language-test tasks. In other words, we can say that a test task is **authentic** (Bachman and Palmer's term) to the extent that it incorporates the key features of the relevant register, which is in turn determined by the learners' needs and the objectives of the assessment.

Conversely, there is reason to doubt the validity of a test task if it elicits from the learners speech or writing that lacks those authentic elements. For example, Grabe and Biber (1987, cited in Biber, 1988: 203–204) analysed the linguistic features of essays written by both native and non-native student writers and found that in effect the essays were written in a distinctive register, different from any of those that Biber had previously analysed. Similarly, van Lier (1989) has questioned whether it is possible to elicit speech in a genuinely conversational register in an oral interview test. The research on oral interviews by Ross and Berwick (1992) among others, which I referred to at the end of Chapter 2, is also relevant here. These researchers are using the techniques of discourse analysis to identify what we could call the features of the register of interview talk.

Let us return now to the role of vocabulary as a distinguishing feature of various registers. Earlier in this section, I noted Biber's (1994: 34–35) position that clusters of lexical and grammatical features are more significant than particular words or phrases. This suggests that lexical statistics, like the type–token ratio, lexical density, the average length of words and the frequency of particular classes of words, have a significant role to play. However, it seems unlikely that any simple quantitative measure will serve to identify the lexical characteristics of a register for assessment purposes. One practical difficulty is that individual learners' production in a speaking or writing task is usually too short to allow reliable measures to be calculated. This leaves us with qualitative judgements using scales like the one from Bachman and Palmer (1996) quoted above. More sociolinguistic research is needed to provide a better foundation for defining the expected response to language-test tasks in lexical terms. What sort of vocabulary use does a particular task require? What are some key indicators that the test-taker lacks the ability to use lexical items which are appropriate to the register of the task?

These indicators have to be features that not only can be revealed by research but also are salient to the raters of the test-takers' performance. They are likely to include the use of: colloquial or slang expressions in a formal task, general terms and circumlocutions in situations where a more specific word would be appropriate, and technical terms in a context where more everyday language is called for. Of course, this assumes that the raters are competent to make such judgements. The teachers who usually act as raters in language tests are generally able to assess appropriate vocabulary use in relation to some registers better than others. In the context of testing language for specific purposes, their judgements may not be well founded in areas outside their educational background or direct experience.

Conclusion

In this chapter, I have identified ways in which most current vocabulary assessment is based on a limited view of the nature of vocabulary and then explored recent work in applied linguistics which can help us to broaden our perspective in various ways. Although I have given particular emphasis to corpus linguistics, there are numerous other fields which have valuable contributions to make. Let me now pull together various ideas from earlier parts of the book and suggest some future directions.

Discrete, selective vocabulary testing has traditionally been concerned with assessing whether learners know the lexical items they need to meet their learning objectives. Identifying and selecting those items on a principled basis is still a significant issue. Computer corpus software allows us to calculate the frequency and range of particular lexical items in large sets of texts more efficiently than was possible in the past. Concordance programs can rapidly assemble multiple examples of a particular word or phrase, each in its linguistic context, so that we can see its typical meaning(s), its grammatical function(s), the other words it collocates with and so on. Of course, these kinds of analyses have already been carried out by the professional lexicographers who have produced the current generation of learner dictionaries of English. However, more work of a similar kind is required to compile specific vocabulary lists that are relevant to the occupational, technical, cultural and recreational needs of particular groups of learners. These lists do not necessarily have to be the work of lexicographers or academics, because commercially published corpus programs such as *WordSmith Tools* (Scott, 1997) now give teachers and advanced learners the opportunity to create their own vocabulary lists for learning and assessment purposes from a set of relevant texts.

Once the target vocabulary has been identified, the question is what to assess. I presented the well-known vocabulary knowledge frameworks of Richards (1976) and Nation (1990) in Chapter 2. While they outline how much is involved in knowing individual words well, these frameworks do not show how the various components are related to each other, and nor is it clear how some individual components can be satisfactorily measured. Schmitt and Meara (1997) took a step in this direction with their investigation of how learners' knowledge of word parts (in this case verb suffixes) was related to their familiarity with word associations. In a succession of more recent studies, Schmitt has developed measures of collocational knowledge (1998a) and word-association responses (1998b), as well as exploring what sort of knowledge of the target word can be assumed when a learner responds correctly to a TOEFL vocabulary item (1999). Further work in this area has value for research purposes, in helping us to understand better the complex nature of vocabulary knowledge at the microlevel of individual items. It is not so clear what the role of such measures is in making decisions about learners. If a whole set of them is created, there is a danger of finding out more and more about the test-takers' knowledge of fewer and fewer words, unless we have a definite assessment purpose in mind. I outlined various reasons for testing depth of vocabulary knowledge in Chapter 4, and my own word-associates format (see Chapter 6) represents one effort to go beyond conventional tests of word meaning while still employing a simple item type. Maybe other measures will emerge from the research which are both practical to use and valid indicators of how well particular lexical items are known.

This focus on individual words should be complemented by a more macrolevel perspective on the overall state of the learners' vocabulary knowledge. According to Meara (1996a), vocabulary size is the best measure of this kind up to a level of 5000–6000 words in the case of English. You will recall that vocabulary-size tests were discussed extensively in Chapters 4 and 5. In such tests, the target words are selected as a sample of the relevant frequency range, rather than as items of interest in their own right, and thus a good sampling frame is required in the form of an up-to-date standard word-frequency list, as I noted earlier in this chapter. Beyond the 5000-word level, Meara (1996a) proposes that vocabulary size is less important than some measure of the way in which vocabulary is organised in the learner's mind. The general hypothesis is that those with a more developed vocabulary knowledge have a more complex and highly structured network of associations among the words they know. Meara has tentatively explored this idea in various ways, such as asking test-takers to connect pairs of randomly selected words by a chain of associations:

> sea . . . sand . . . sandwich . . . **butterfly**
> sea . . . green . . . cabbage . . . caterpillar . . . **butterfly**

However, it remains to be seen whether it is possible to devise valid measures of mental organisation which can serve practical assessment needs.

Another aspect of vocabulary assessment which would benefit from some re-thinking is the distinction between receptive and productive vocabulary. I highlighted its problematic nature in Chapter 6 and suggested that one way to reduce the conceptual confusion was to look separately at recognition vs. recall and understanding vs. use. The former distinction applies more to discrete vocabulary tests, whereas the latter one is appropriate for embedded, comprehensive and context-dependent measures. We also need to take a critical view of the whole notion of a receptive–productive *continuum*, the commonly held idea that vocabulary items typically move along a path from receptive to productive status as the learner acquires more knowledge of them. The Vocabulary Knowledge Scale (VKS – discussed in Chapter 5) is based on a similar concept of a regular progression from one stage to another towards a high level of knowledge. Although the use of a scale – with or without a linked series of test tasks representing degrees of lexical knowledge – is certainly attractive for assessment purposes, the validity of the underlying construct is a matter for debate. The reality of second language vocabulary development seems more complex and untidy than this.

Meara (1996b) has advocated using a discrete state model of vocabulary acquisition in which words can be in one of several states of knowledge in the learner's mind, and they are free to move from one state to any other state. Thus, a useful word for the learner can go quite quickly from being unknown to being readily available for use; on the other hand, a low-frequency word that is known to a limited extent at one point may be forgotten over time. In order to obtain data for the analysis, learners are asked to report on the state of their knowledge of a large set of words, in terms of a small number of categories. The data-gathering is repeated at least once, in order to provide a basis for calculating the probability of words moving from one state to another over time. The model offers a method of tracking the overall development of a learner's vocabulary without assuming a process of regular, staged expansion of word knowledge. Vocabulary researchers certainly need to explore such models in order to overcome the well-recognised deficiency of the receptive–productive continuum.

In Chapter 4, I identified the role of context as a major issue in the history of vocabulary assessment, and it has figured prominently in all the other chapters of the book. We can approach context from a variety of viewpoints. At one level, it refers to the immediate linguistic environment of a target word. This was the sense in which I used it in discussing contextual influences on cloze-test items in Chapter 4 and the context dependence of TOEFL vocabulary items in Chapter 5. As their language proficiency grows, learners must be able to exploit contextual information to recognise the specific meaning of a high-frequency word or infer the sense of an unfamiliar lexical item when they encounter them in use. It is one thing to recognise these as assessment objectives, though, and quite another to design suitable test tasks. There is a tension between presenting words in natural environments, which may be either too lean or too rich in contextual clues, and manipulating the context by means of editing or specially composing sentences. A richer context also creates difficulty in determining to what extent vocabulary knowledge, as distinct from other forms of language knowledge, accounts for the learners' success or otherwise in performing the task.

At another level, context is created through whole texts (both spoken and written) which test-takers are required to interpret or produce. Here we move into the realm of comprehensive and embedded vocabulary assessment, where we look at the lexical items in a text collectively, in relation to the demands of the assessment task, which may not have a primary focus on vocabulary. The question then is not simply whether the learners know a range of vocabulary items related to the context but whether they can use vocabulary appropriately to achieve communicative goals. At a broader level again, appropriateness is determined by features of the social situation in which language use occurs. I am surely not the first person to observe that context is an inherently complex phenomenon.

The concept of register offers a way through the complexity if it allows us to identify the lexical items or features which are associated with particular contexts of use. There is work to be done, though, in defining just what a register is and how different types of register can be classified. Fields such as corpus linguistics and discourse analysis can offer conceptual tools, as well as descriptions of particular registers but, as I tried to show earlier in the chapter, we also have to think in practical terms what contributions register analysis can make to language-test design. For instance, we need to know a lot more about how raters judge the lexical aspects of learner performance of speaking and writing tasks. Do they focus on register-specific features when they are asked to evaluate the appropriateness of a test-taker's vocabulary use? How do their judgements compare with quantitative analyses of what the test-taker said or wrote? Such research could lead to rating procedures that make contextualised vocabulary use a more salient component of language assessment.

In this discussion of context, the perspective has shifted from the conventional view of vocabulary assessment as being concerned with knowledge of discrete lexical items to looking at how an analysis of lexical features can be embedded in an integrative assessment of language ability. Both perspectives are important, but the notion of an embedded measure is the one I want to highlight here, if only because it has received so little systematic attention. Although individual measures – like the vocabulary component of readability formulas, the lexical density statistic and the vocabulary scale of the ESL Composition Profile (all discussed in Chapter 7) – are quite familiar, we are not used to thinking of them as forms of vocabulary assessment. Accepting them as such provides a way to bring vocabulary back more into the mainstream of the field of language testing and stimulate fresh thinking about measures to capture the lexical dimension of language performance. Lexical statistics are attractive as measures because word forms are so easy to count, if not to classify. However, as I have written more than once already in this chapter, the statistics need to be complemented by soundly based qualitative measures.

In the 1990s study of vocabulary is a booming area in linguistic research and language teaching practice. Some scholars go so far as to suggest that language acquisition is essentially a matter of developing lexical competence in the target language. Certainly there is a wealth of evidence of how important the lexical dimension is in second language learning as well as in fluent language use. Nevertheless, the field of language testing has tended to lag behind in recognising and taking account of the current resurgence of interest in vocabulary, with the result that language testers have shown limited interest in vocabulary assessment. On the other hand, second language vocabulary researchers have continued to develop instruments for their purposes, without necessarily applying contemporary standards of test design and validation to them. It is time to bridge the gap between the two fields and so I hope that this volume will not only help to give lexical measures a more prominent place in language assessment but also encourage a more integrated approach to evaluating them in relation to their various purposes.

References

Abraham, R. G. and C. A. Chapelle. (1992). The meaning of cloze test scores: an item difficulty perspective. *Modern Language Journal* 76, 468–479.

Ahmed, M. O. (1989). Vocabulary learning strategies. In P. Meara (ed.), *Beyond Words* (pp. 3–14). London: CILT.

Aitchison, J. (1994). *Words in the Mind: An Introduction to the Mental Lexicon*. Second edition. Oxford: Blackwell.

Alderson, J. C. (1979). The cloze procedure and proficiency in English as a foreign language. *TESOL Quarterly* 13, 219–227.

Alderson, J. C. (2000) *Assessing Reading*. Cambridge: Cambridge University Press.

Alderson, J. C. and A. Beretta (eds.). (1992). *Evaluating Second Language Education*. Cambridge: Cambridge University Press.

Alderson, J. C. and D. Wall. (1993). Does washback exist? *Applied Linguistics* 14, 115–129.

American Council on the Teaching of Foreign Languages. (1986). *ACTFL Proficiency Guidelines*. Yonkers, NY: ACTFL.

Ames, W. S. (1966). The development of a classification scheme of contextual aids. *Reading Research Quarterly* 2, 57–82.

Anderson, R. C. and P. Freebody. (1981). Vocabulary knowledge. In J. T. Guthrie (ed.), *Comprehension and Teaching: Research Reviews* (pp. 77–117). Newark, DE: International Reading Association.

Anderson, R. C. and P. Freebody. (1983). Reading comprehension and the assessment and acquisition of word knowledge. In B. Huston (ed.), *Advances in Reading/Language Research*. Volume 2 (pp. 231–256). Greenwich, CT: JAI Press.

Anivan, S. (ed.). (1991). *Current Developments in Language Testing*. Singapore: SEAMEO Regional Language Centre.

Arnaud, P. J. L. (1984). The lexical richness of L2 written productions and the validity of vocabulary tests. In T. Culhane, C. Klein-Braley and D. K. Stevenson (eds.), *Practice and Problems in Language Testing* (pp. 14–28).

Occasional Papers, No. 29. Department of Language and Linguistics, University of Essex.

Arnaud, P. (1989). Vocabulary and grammar: a multitrait–multimethod investigation. *AILA Review* 6, 56–65.

Arnaud, P. J. L. (1992). Objective lexical and grammatical characteristics of L2 written compositions and the validity of separate-component tests. In Arnaud and Béjoint (eds.), 1992, pp. 133–145.

Arnaud, P. J. L. and H. Béjoint (eds.). (1992). *Vocabulary and Applied Linguistics*. London: Macmillan.

Auerbach, E. R. (1993). Reexamining English only in the ESL classroom. *TESOL Quarterly* 27, 9–32.

Bachman, L. F. (1982). The trait structure of cloze test scores. *TESOL Quarterly* 16, 61–70.

Bachman, L. F. (1985). Performance on cloze tests with fixed-ratio and rational deletions. *TESOL Quarterly* 19, 535–556.

Bachman, L. F. (1986). The Test of English as a Foreign Language as a measure of communicative competence. In Stansfield (ed.), 1986, pp. 69–88.

Bachman, L. F. (1990). *Fundamental Considerations in Language Testing*. Oxford: Oxford University Press.

Bachman, L. F. and A. S. Palmer. (1996). *Language Testing in Practice*. Oxford: Oxford University Press.

Baker, E. L., H. F. O'Neil, Jr. and R. L. Linn. (1993). Policy and validity prospects for performance-based assessment. *American Psychologist* 48, 1210–1218.

Barnard, H. (1971–75). *Advanced English Vocabulary. Workbooks 1–3B*. Rowley, MA: Newbury House.

Bauer, L. and I. S. P. Nation. (1993). Word families. *International Journal of Lexicography* 6, 253–279.

Beglar, D. and A. Hunt. (1999). Revising and validating the 2000 Word Level and University Word Level Vocabulary Tests. *Language Testing* 16, 131–162.

Bensoussan, M. (1983). Multiple-choice modifications of the cloze procedure using word-length and sentence-length blanks. *Foreign Language Annals* 16, 189–198.

Bensoussan, M. and B. Laufer. (1984). Lexical guessing in context in EFL reading comprehension. *Journal of Research in Reading* 7, 15–32.

Bensoussan, M. and R. Ramraz. (1984). Testing EFL reading comprehension using a multiple-choice rational cloze. *Modern Language Journal* 68, 230–239.

Bialystok, E. (1990). *Communication Strategies*. Oxford: Basil Blackwell.

Biber, D. (1988). *Variation Across Speech and Writing*. Cambridge: Cambridge University Press.

Biber, D. (1994). An analytical framework for register studies. In Biber and Finegan, 1994b, pp. 31–56.

Biber, D., S. Conrad and R. Reppen. (1998). *Corpus Linguistics: Investigating Language Structure and Use*. Cambridge: Cambridge University Press.

Biber, D. and E. Finegan. (1994a). Situating register in sociolinguistics. In Biber and Finegan, 1994b, pp. 3–12.

Biber, D. and E. Finegan (eds.). (1994b). *Sociolinguistic Perspectives on Register*. New York: Oxford University Press.

Blum-Kulka, S. and E. A. Levenston. (1983). Universals of lexical simplification. In Faerch and Kasper (eds.), 1983a, pp. 119–139.

Brown, C. (1993). Factors affecting the acquisition of vocabulary: frequency and saliency of words. In T. Huckin, M. Haynes and J. Coady (eds.), *Second Language Reading and Vocabulary Learning* (pp. 263–286). Norwood, NJ: Ablex.

Brown, J. D. (1983). A closer look at cloze: validity and reliability. In J. W. Oller, Jr. (ed.), *Issues in Language Testing Research* (pp. 237–250). Rowley, MA: Newbury House.

Brown, J. D. (1997). An EFL readability index. *University of Hawaii Working Papers in English as a Second Language* 15, 85–119.

Brown, J. D. and K. Bailey. (1984). A categorical instrument for scoring second language writing skills. *Language Learning* 34, 21–42.

Bruton, A. and V. Samuda. (1981). Guessing words. *Modern English Teacher* 8, 18–21.

Campbell, D. T. and D. W. Fiske. (1959). Convergent and discriminant validation by the multitrait–multimethod matrix. *Psychological Bulletin* 56, 81–105.

Campion, M. E. and W. B. Elley. (1971). *An Academic Vocabulary List*. Wellington: New Zealand Council for Educational Research.

Carrell, P. L. (1987). Readability in ESL. *Reading in a Foreign Language* 4, 21–40.

Carroll, J. B., P. Davies and B. Richman. (1971). *The American Heritage Word Frequency Book*. Boston, MA: Houghton Mifflin.

Carter, R. A. (1987). *Vocabulary: Applied Linguistic Perspectives*. London: Allen and Unwin. 2nd edition: Routledge, 1999.

Carter, R. and M. McCarthy. (1988). *Vocabulary and Language Teaching*. London: Longman.

Carton, A. S. (1971). Inferencing: a process in using and learning language. In P. Pimsleur and T. Quinn (eds.), *The Psychology of Second Language Learning* (pp. 45–58). Cambridge: Cambridge University Press.

Chafe, W. L. (1982). Integration and involvement in speaking, writing, and oral literature. In Tannen (ed.), 1982a, pp. 35–53.

Chandrasegaran, A. (1980). Teaching the context clue approach to meaning. *Guidelines* 3, 61–68.

Chapelle, C. A. (1994). Are C-tests valid measures for L2 vocabulary research? *Second Language Research* 10, 157–187.

Chapelle, C. A. and R. G. Abraham. (1990). Cloze method: what difference does it make? *Language Testing* 7, 121–146.

Chihara, T., J. W. Oller, Jr., K. A. Weaver and M. A. Chávez-Oller. (1977). Are cloze items sensitive to constraints across sentences? *Language Learning* 27, 63–73.

Chun, D. M. and J. L. Plass. (1996). Effects of multimedia annotations on vocabulary acquisition. *Modern Language Journal* 80, 183–198.

Clark, H. H. (1970). Word associations and linguistic theory. In J. Lyons (ed.), *New Horizons in Linguistics*. Harmondsworth: Penguin.

Clark, J. L. D. (1972). *Foreign Language Testing: Theory and Practice*. Philadelphia: Center for Curriculum Development.

Clarke, D. F. and I. S. P. Nation. (1980). Guessing the meanings of words from context: Strategy and techniques. *System* 8, 211–220.

Clarke, M. and S. Silberstein. (1977). Toward a realization of the psycholinguistic principles in the ESL reading class. *Language Learning* 27, 135–154.

Coady, J. and T. Huckin (eds.). (1997). *Second Language Vocabulary Acquisition*. Cambridge: Cambridge University Press.

Cohen, A. D. (1987). The use of verbal and imagery mnemonics in second language vocabulary learning. *Studies in Second Language Acquisition* 9, 43–62.

Cohen, A. D. and E. Aphek. (1981). Easifying second language learning. *Studies in Second Language Acquisition* 3, 221–236.

Collins COBUILD English Language Dictionary. (1995). New edition. London: HarperCollins.

Cooper, R. L. (1971). Degree of bilingualism. In Fishman, Cooper and Ma, (1971), pp. 273–309.

Corrigan, A. and J. A. Upshur. (1982). Test method and linguistic factors in foreign language tests. *IRAL* 20, 313–321.

Corson, D. J. (1982). The Graeco-Latin (G-L) Instrument: a new measure of semantic complexity in oral and written English. *Language and Speech* 25, 1–10.

Corson, D. J. (1983). The Corson Measure of Passive Vocabulary. *Language and Speech* 26, 3–20.

Corson, D. (1985). *The Lexical Bar*. Oxford: Pergamon.

Corson, D. (1997). The learning and use of academic English words. *Language Learning* 47, 671–718.

Coxhead, A. (1998). *An Academic Word List*. English Language Institute Occasional Publication, No. 18. Wellington: School of Linguistics and Applied Language Studies, Victoria University of Wellington.

Cronbach, L. J. (1942). An analysis of techniques for diagnostic vocabulary testing. *Journal of Educational Research* 36, 206–217.

Cummins, J. (1981). Age on arrival and immigrant second language learning in Canada: a reassessment. *Applied Linguistics* 2, 132–149.

Cziko, G. A. (1983). Another response to Shanahan, Kamil, and Tobin: further reasons to keep the cloze case open. *Reading Research Quarterly* 18, 361–365.

Dale, E. (1965). Vocabulary measurement: techniques and major findings. *Elementary English* 42, 895–901, 948.

Day, R. R., C. Omura and M. Hiramatsu. (1991). Incidental EFL vocabulary learning and reading. *Reading in a Foreign Language* 7, 541–551.

Diack, H. (1975). *Wordpower: Your Vocabulary and its Measurement*. St Albans: Paladin.

Dieterich, T. G., C. Freeman and J. A. Crandall. (1979). A linguistic analysis of some English proficiency tests. *TESOL Quarterly* 13, 535–550.

Dolch, E. W. and D. Leeds. (1953). Vocabulary tests and depth of meaning. *Journal of Educational Research* 4, 181–189.

Dörnyei, Z. (1995). On the teachability of communication strategies. *TESOL Quarterly* 29, 55–85.

Dörnyei, Z. and L. Katona. (1992). Validation of the C-test amongst Hungarian EFL learners. *Language Testing* 9, 187–206.

Dörnyei, Z. and M. L. Scott. (1997). Communication strategies in a second language: definitions and taxonomies. *Language Learning* 47, 173–210.

Dupuy, B. and S. D. Krashen. (1993). Incidental vocabulary acquisition in French as a foreign language. *Applied Language Learning* 4, 55–63.

Educational Testing Service (ETS). (1995). *TOEFL Sample Test*. Fifth edition. Princeton, NJ: Educational Testing Service.

Educational Testing Service (ETS). (1996). *The TOEFL Test of Spoken English Guide*. Princeton, NJ: Educational Testing Service.

Educational Testing Service (ETS). (1998). *TOEFL Sampler*. [CD-ROM]. Princeton, NJ: Educational Testing Service.

Elley, W. B. (1989). Vocabulary acquisition from listening to stories. *Reading Research Quarterly* 24, 174–187.

Ellis, N. C. (1997). Vocabulary acquisition: word structure, collocation, word-class, and meaning. In Schmitt and McCarthy (eds.), (1997), pp. 122–139.

Ellis, N. C. and A. Beaton. (1993a). Factors affecting the learning of foreign language vocabulary: imagery keyword mediators and phonological short-term memory. *Quarterly Journal of Experimental Psychology* 46A, 533–558.

Ellis, N. C. and A. Beaton. (1993b). Psycholinguistic determinants of foreign language vocabulary learning. *Language Learning* 43, 559–617.

Ellis, R. (1995). Modified oral input and the acquisition of word meanings. *Applied Linguistics*, 16, 409–441.

Ellis, R., Y. Tanaka and A. Yamazaki. (1994). Classroom interaction, comprehension, and the acquisition of L2 word meanings. *Language Learning* 44, 449–491.

Engber, C. A. (1995). The relationship of lexical proficiency to the quality of ESL compositions. *Journal of Second Language Writing* 4, 139–155.

Engels, L. (1968). The fallacy of word counts. *IRAL* 6, 213–231.

ETS see Educational Testing Service.

Faerch, K. and G. Kasper (eds.). (1983a). *Strategies in Interlanguage Communication*. London: Longman.

Faerch, K. and G. Kasper. (1983b). Plans and strategies in foreign language communication. In Faerch and Kasper (eds.), 1983a, pp. 20–60.

Farr, R. (1969). *Reading: What can be Measured?* Newark, DE: International Reading Association.

Farr, R. and R. F. Carey. (1986). *Reading: What can be Measured?* Second edition. Newark, DE: International Reading Association.

Feldmann, U. and B. Stemmer. (1987). Thin__ aloud a__ retrospective da__ in C-te__ taking: diffe__ languages – diff__ learners – sa__ approaches? In C. Faerch and G. Kasper (eds.), *Introspection in Second Language Research* (pp. 251–267). Clevedon: Multilingual Matters.

Ferguson, C. A. (1994). Dialect, register, and genre: working assumptions about conventionalization. In Biber and Finegan, 1994b, pp. 15–30.

Fishman, J. A., R. L. Cooper, R. Ma. (1971). *Bilingualism in the Barrio*. Bloomington, IN: Research Center for the Language Sciences, Indiana University.

Flowerdew, J. (1993). Concordancing as a tool in course design. *System* 21, 231–244.

Foster, P. and P. Skehan. (1996). The influence of planning and task-type on second language performance. *Studies in Second Language Acquisition* 18, 299–323.

Francis, W. N. and H. Kučera. (1982). *Frequency Analysis of English Usage: Lexicon and Grammar*. Boston: Houghton Mifflin.

Goodrich, H. C. (1977). Distractor efficiency in foreign language testing. *TESOL Quarterly* 11, 69–78.

Goulden, R., P. Nation and J. Read. (1990). How large can a receptive vocabulary be? *Applied Linguistics* 11, 341–363.

Haastrup, K. (1987). Using thinking aloud and retrospection to uncover learners' lexical inferencing procedures. In C. Faerch and G. Kasper (eds.), *Introspection in Second Language Research* (pp. 197–212). Clevedon: Multilingual Matters.

Haastrup, K. (1991). *Lexical Inferencing Procedures, or, Talking about Words*. Tübingen: Gunter Narr.

Hale, G. A., C. W. Stansfield, D. A. Rock, M. M. Hicks, F. A. Butler and J. W. Oller, Jr. (1988). *Multiple-Choice Cloze Items and the Test of English as a*

Foreign Language. TOEFL Research Reports, 26. Princeton, NJ: Educational Testing Service.

Hale, G. A., C. W. Stansfield, D. A. Rock, M. M. Hicks, F. A. Butler and J. W. Oller, Jr. (1989). The relation of multiple-choice cloze items to the Test of English as a Foreign Language. *Language Testing* 6, 47–76.

Halliday, M. A. K. (1989). *Spoken and Written Language.* Oxford: Oxford University Press.

Halliday, M. A. K. and R. Hasan. (1989). *Language, Context and Text: Aspects of Language in a Social-Semiotic Perspective.* Oxford: Oxford University Press.

Hamp-Lyons, L. (1991). Scoring procedures for ESL contexts. In L. Hamp-Lyons (ed.), *Assessing Second Language Writing in Academic Contexts.* (pp. 241–276). Norwood, NJ: Ablex.

Hamp-Lyons, L. and G. Henning. (1991). Communicative writing profiles: an investigation of the transferability of a multiple-trait scoring instrument across ESL writing assessment contexts. *Language Learning* 41, 337–373.

Harbord, J. (1992). The use of the mother tongue in the classroom. *English Language Teaching Journal* 46, 350–355.

Harklau, L. (1994). ESL vs. mainstream classes: contrasting L2 learning environments. *TESOL Quarterly* 28, 241–272.

Harlech-Jones, B. (1983). ESL proficiency and a word-frequency count. *English Language Teaching Journal* 37, 62–70.

Harley, B. (1995). Introduction: the lexicon in second language research. In B. Harley (ed.), *Lexical Issues in Language Learning* (pp. 1–28). Amsterdam: John Benjamins.

Harris, D. P. (1969). *Testing English as a Second Language.* New York: McGraw-Hill.

Harrison, C. (1980). *Readability in the Classroom.* Cambridge: Cambridge University Press.

Hatch, E. and H. Farhady. (1982). *Research Design and Statistics for Applied Linguistics.* Rowley, MA: Newbury House.

Haynes, M. (1984). Patterns and perils of guessing in second language reading. In J. Handscombe, R. A. Orem and B. P. Taylor (eds.), *On TESOL '83: The Question of Control* (pp. 163–176). Washington, DC: TESOL.

Hazenberg, S. and J. H. Hulstijn. (1996). Defining a minimal receptive second-language vocabulary for non-native university students: an empirical investigation. *Applied Linguistics* 17, 145–163.

Heaton, J. B. (1975). *Writing English Language Tests.* London: Longman.

Heaton, J. B. (1988). *Writing English Language Tests.* Second edition. London: Longman.

Henning, G. H. (1973). Remembering foreign language vocabulary: acoustic and semantic parameters. *Language Learning* 23, 185–196.

Henning, G. (1991). *A Study of the Effects of Contextualization and Familiar-*

ization on Responses to the TOEFL Vocabulary Test Items. TOEFL Research Reports, 35. Princeton, NJ: Educational Testing Service.

Henriksen, B. (1999). Three dimensions of vocabulary development. *Studies in Second Language Acquisition* 21, 303–317.

Higa, M. (1963). Interference effects of interlist word relationships in verbal learning. *Journal of Verbal Learning and Verbal Behavior* 2, 170–175.

Higa, M. (1965). The psycholinguistic concept of 'difficulty' and the teaching of foreign language vocabulary. *Language Learning* 15, 167–179.

Hindmarsh, R. (1980). *Cambridge English Lexicon*. Cambridge: Cambridge University Press.

Hofland, K. and S. Johansson. (1982). *Word Frequencies in British and American English*. Bergen: Norwegian Computing Centre for the Humanities.

Holmes, J. (1995). A quite interesting article about linguistics. *Campus Review* 5, 13.

Honeyfield, J. (1977). Word frequency and the importance of context in vocabulary learning. *RELC Journal* 8, 35–42.

Horst, M., T. Cobb and P. Meara. (1998). Beyond a Clockwork Orange: acquiring second language vocabulary through reading. *Reading in a Foreign Language* 11, 207–223.

Hughes, A. (1989). *Testing for Language Teachers*. Cambridge: Cambridge University Press.

Hulstijn, J. H. (1992). Retention of inferred and given word meanings: experiments in incidental vocabulary learning. In Arnaud and Béjoint (eds.), (1992), pp. 113–125.

Hulstijn, J. H. (1993). When do foreign-language learners look up the meanings of unfamiliar words? The influence of task and learner variables. *Modern Language Journal* 77, 139–147.

Hulstijn, J. H. (1997). Mnemonic methods in foreign language vocabulary learning: theoretical considerations and pedagogical implications. In Coady and Huckin (eds.), (1997), pp. 203–224.

Hurlburt, D. (1954). The relative value of recall and recognition techniques for measuring precise knowledge of word meaning: nouns, verbs, adjectives. *Journal of Educational Research* 47, 561–576.

Jacobs, H. L., S. A. Zingraf, D. R. Wormuth, V. F. Hartfiel and J. B. Hughey. (1981). *Testing ESL Composition: A Practical Approach*. Rowley, MA: Newbury House.

Jenkins, J. R., M. Stein and K. Wysocki. (1984). Learning vocabulary through reading. *American Educational Research Journal* 21, 767–787.

Joe, A. (1995). Text-based tasks and incidental vocabulary learning. *Second Language Research* 11, 149–158.

Joe, A. (1998). What effects do text-based tasks promoting generation have on incidental vocabulary acquisition? *Applied Linguistics* 19, 357–377.

Johnson, R. K. (1981). Questioning some assumptions about cloze testing. In

J. A. S. Read (ed.), *Directions in Language Testing* (pp. 177–206). Singapore: Singapore University Press.

Jonz, J. (1976). Improving on the basic egg: the m-c cloze. *Language Learning* 26, 255–265.

Jonz, J. (1987). Textual cohesion and second language comprehension. *Language Learning* 37, 409–438.

Jonz, J. (1990). Another turn in the conversation: what does cloze measure? *TESOL Quarterly* 24, 61–83.

Jonz, J. and J. W. Oller, Jr. (1994). A critical appraisal of related cloze research. In Oller and Jonz, (1994), pp. 371–407.

Kasper, G. and E. Kellerman (eds.). (1997a). *Communication Strategies: Psycholinguistic and Sociolinguistic Perspectives*. London: Longman.

Kasper, G. and E. Kellerman. (1997b). Introduction: approaches to communication strategies. In Kasper and Kellerman (eds.), 1997a, pp. 1–13.

Kellerman, E. (1991). Compensatory strategies in second language research: a critique, a revision, and some (non-)implications for the classroom. In R. Phillipson, E. Kellerman, L. Selinker, M. Sharwood Smith and M. Swain (eds.), *Foreign/Second Language Pedagogy Research* (pp. 142–161). Clevedon: Multilingual Matters.

Kelley, T. L. and A. C. Krey. (1934). *Tests and measurements in the social sciences*. New York: Scribner.

Kelley, V. H. (1933). An experimental study of certain techniques for testing word meanings. *Journal of Educational Research* 27, 277–282.

Kelly, P. (1991). Lexical ignorance: the main obstacle to listening comprehension with advanced foreign language learners. *IRAL* 24, 135–149.

Kennedy, G. (1998). *An Introduction to Corpus Linguistics*. London: Addison Wesley Longman.

Klare, G. R. (1984). Readability. In P. D. Pearson (ed.), *Handbook of Reading Research*. New York: Longman.

Klein-Braley, C. (1985). A cloze-up on the C-Test. A study in the construct validation of authentic tests. *Language Testing* 2, 76–104.

Klein-Braley, C. (1997). C-Tests in the context of reduced redundancy testing: an appraisal. *Language Testing* 14, 47–84.

Klein-Braley, C. and U. Raatz. (1984). A survey of research on the C-test. *Language Testing* 1, 134–146.

Knight, S. (1994). Dictionary use while reading: the effects on comprehension and vocabulary acquisition for students of different verbal abilities. *Modern Language Journal* 78, 285–299.

Kroll, B. and J. Reid. (1994). Guidelines for writing prompts: clarifications, caveats, and cautions. *Journal of Second Language Writing* 3, 231–255.

Kučera, H. and W. M. Francis. (1967). *A Computational Analysis of Present Day American English*. Providence, RI: Brown University Press.

Lado, R. (1961). *Language Testing*. London: Longman.

Laufer, B. (1990). 'Sequence' and 'order' in the development of L2 lexis: some evidence from lexical confusions. *Applied Linguistics* 11, 281–296.

Laufer, B. (1991). The development of L2 lexis in the expression of the advanced language learner. *Modern Language Journal* 75, 440–448.

Laufer, B. (1992). How much lexis is necessary for reading comprehension? In Arnaud and Béjoint (eds.), (1992), pp. 126–132.

Laufer, B. (1994). The lexical profile of second language writing: does it change over time? *RELC Journal* 25, 21–33.

Laufer, B. (1995). Beyond 2000: a measure of productive lexicon in a second language. In L. Eubank, L. Selinker and M. Sharwood Smith (eds.), *The Current State of Interlanguage* (pp. 265–272). Amsterdam: John Benjamins.

Laufer, B. (1997a). The lexical plight in second language reading: words you don't know, words you think you know, and words you can't guess. In Coady and Huckin (eds.), (1997), pp. 20–34.

Laufer, B. (1997b). What's in a word that makes it hard or easy? Some intralexical factors that affect the learning of words. In Schmitt and McCarthy (eds.), (1997), pp. 140–155.

Laufer, B. (1998). The development of passive and active vocabulary in a second language: same or different? *Applied Linguistics* 19, 255–271.

Laufer, B. and P. Nation. (1995). Vocabulary size and use: lexical richness in L2 written production. *Applied Linguistics* 16, 307–322.

Laufer, B. and P. Nation. (1999). A vocabulary-size test of controlled productive ability. *Language Testing* 16, 33–51.

Laufer, B. and D. D. Sim. (1985a). Measuring and explaining the reading threshold needed for English for Academic Purposes texts. *Foreign Language Annals* 18, 405–411.

Laufer, B. and D. D. Sim. (1985b). Taking the easy way out: non-use and misuse of clues in EFL reading. *English Teaching Forum* 23, 7–10, 20.

Lawson, M. J. and D. Hogden. (1996). The vocabulary-learning strategies of foreign-language students. *Language Learning* 46, 101–135.

Linnarud, M. (1975). *Lexis in Free Production: An Analysis of the Lexical Texture of Swedish Students' Written Work.* Swedish–English Contrastive Studies, Report No. 6. Lund: Department of English, University of Lund.

Linnarud, M. (1986). *Lexis in Composition: A Performance Analysis of Swedish Learners' Written English.* Malmö: CWK Gleerup.

Liu, N. and I. S. P. Nation. (1985). Factors affecting guessing vocabulary in context. *RELC Journal* 16, 33–42.

Longman Dictionary of Contemporary English. (1995). Third edition. London: Longman.

Lorge, I. and J. Chall. (1963). Estimating the size of vocabularies of children and adults: an analysis of methodological issues. *Journal of Experimental Education* 32, 147–157.

Luppescu, S, and R. R. Day. (1993). Reading, dictionaries, and vocabulary learning. *Language Learning* 43, 263–287.

Lynch, B. K. (1996). *Language Program Evaluation: Theory and Practice.* Cambridge: Cambridge University Press.

McCarthy, M. (1990). *Vocabulary.* Oxford: Oxford University Press.

McCarthy, M. and R. Carter. (1997). Written and spoken vocabulary. In Schmitt and McCarthy (eds.), (1997), pp. 20–39.

McDonough, S. (1995). *Strategy and Skill in Learning a Foreign Language.* London: Edward Arnold.

McKeown, M. G. and M. E. Curtis (eds.). (1987). *The Nature of Vocabulary Acquisition.* Hillsdale, NJ: Lawrence Erlbaum.

McNamara, T. F. (1996). *Measuring Second Language Performance.* London: Longman.

McNeill, A. (1996). Vocabulary knowledge profiles: evidence from Chinese-speaking ESL teachers. *Hong Kong Journal of Applied Linguistics* 1, 39–63.

McQueen, J. (1996). Rasch scaling: how valid is it as the basis for content-referenced descriptors of test performance? In G. Wigglesworth and C. Elder (eds.), *The Language Testing Cycle: From Inception to Washback* (pp. 137–187). *Australian Review of Applied Linguistics*, Series S, No. 13.

Madsen, H. S. (1983). *Techniques in Testing.* New York: Oxford University Press.

Meara, P. (1980). Vocabulary acquisition: a neglected aspect of language learning. *Language Teaching and Learning: Abstracts* 13, 221–246.

Meara, P. (1983). Word associations in a foreign language. *Nottingham Linguistics Circular* 11, 29–38.

Meara, P. (1984). The study of lexis in interlanguage. In A. Davies, C. Criper and A. P. R. Howatt (eds.), *Interlanguage* (pp. 225–235). Edinburgh: University of Edinburgh Press.

Meara, P. (1990). Some notes on the Eurocentres Vocabulary Size Tests. In J. Tommola (ed.), *Foreign Language Comprehension and Production.* Turku: AFinLA (Finnish Association of Applied Linguistics).

Meara, P. (1992a). *EFL Vocabulary Tests.* Swansea: Centre for Applied Language Studies, University of Wales.

Meara, P. (1992b). Network structures and vocabulary acquisition in a foreign language. In Arnaud and H. Béjoint (eds.), (1992), pp. 62–70.

Meara, P. (1993). Assumptions about vocabulary acquisition and where they come from. Keynote address at the 10th World Congress of Applied Linguistics, Amsterdam, August (1993).

Meara, P. (1994). Second language acquisition: lexis. In R. E. Asher (ed.), *The Encyclopedia of Language and Linguistics*, Volume 7 (pp. 3726–3728). Oxford: Pergamon.

Meara, P. (1996a). The dimensions of lexical competence. In G. Brown,

K. Malmkjaer and J. Williams (eds.), *Performance and Competence in Second Language Acquisition* (pp. 35–53). Cambridge: Cambridge University Press.

Meara, P. (1996b). The vocabulary knowledge framework, available over the Internet at <www.swan.ac.uk/cals/vlibrary/pm96d>.

Meara, P. and B. Buxton. (1987). An alternative to multiple choice vocabulary tests. *Language Testing* 4, 142–154.

Meara, P. and G. Jones. (1988). Vocabulary size as a placement indicator. In P. Grunwell (ed.), *Applied Linguistics in Society* (pp. 80–87). London: Centre for Information on Language Teaching and Research.

Meara, P. and G. Jones. (1990a). *Eurocentres Vocabulary Size Test, Version E1.1/K10*. Zurich: Eurocentres Learning Service.

Meara, P. and G. Jones. (1990b). *Eurocentres Vocabulary Size Test User's Guide.* Zurich: Eurocentres Learning Service.

Mehnert, U. (1998). The effects of different lengths of time for planning on second language performance. *Studies in Second Language Acquisition* 20, 83–108.

Melka, F. (1997). Receptive vs. productive aspects of vocabulary. In Schmitt and McCarthy (eds.), (1997), pp. 84–102.

Melka Teichroew, F. J. (1982). Receptive vs. productive vocabulary: a survey. *Interlanguage Studies Bulletin* 6, 5–33.

Messick, S. (1989). Validity. In R. L. Linn (ed.), *Educational Measurement.* Third edition. New York: Macmillan.

Mondria, J-A. and M. Wit-De Boer. (1991). The effects of contextual richness on the guessability and the retention of words in a foreign language. *Applied Linguistics*, 12, 249–267.

Moon, R. (1997). Vocabulary connections: multi-word items in English. In Schmitt and McCarthy, (1997), pp. 40–63.

Nagy, W. E. and R. C. Anderson. (1984). How many words are there in printed school English? *Reading Research Quarterly* 19, 304–330.

Nagy, W., R. C. Anderson and P. A. Herman. (1987). Learning word meanings from context during normal reading. *American Educational Research Journal* 24, 237–270.

Nagy, W., P. A. Herman and R. C. Anderson. (1985). Learning words from context. *Reading Research Quarterly* 20, 233–253.

Nation, I. S. P. (1982). Beginning to learn foreign vocabulary: a review of the literature. *RELC Journal* 13, 14–36.

Nation, P. (1983). Testing and teaching vocabulary. *Guidelines* 5, 12–25.

Nation, I. S. P. (1990). *Teaching and Learning Vocabulary.* New York: Heinle and Heinle.

Nation, P. (1993a). Measuring readiness for simplified material: a test of the first 1000 words of English. In M. L. Tickoo (ed.), *Simplification: Theory and Application.* Singapore: SEAMEO Regional Language Centre.

Nation, P. (1993b). Using dictionaries to estimate vocabulary size: essential but rarely followed procedures. *Language Testing* 10, 27–40.

Nation, I. S. P. and J. Coady. (1988). Vocabulary and reading. In Carter and McCarthy, (1988), pp. 97–110.

Nation, P. and R. Waring. (1997). Vocabulary size, text coverage and word lists. In Schmitt and McCarthy (eds.), (1997), pp. 6–19.

Nattinger, J. R. and J. S. DeCarrico. (1992). *Lexical Phrases and Language Teaching*. Oxford: Oxford University Press.

Nihalani, N. K. (1981). The quest for the L2 index of development. *RELC Journal* 12, 50–56.

Nurweni, A. (1995). The English vocabulary knowledge of first-year students at an Indonesian university. Unpublished MA thesis. Victoria University of Wellington, New Zealand.

Nurweni, A. and J. Read. (1999). The English vocabulary knowledge of Indonesian university students. *English for Specific Purposes* 18, 161–175.

O'Loughlin, K. (1995). Lexical density in candidate output on direct and semi-direct versions of an oral proficiency test. *Language Testing* 12, 217–237.

O'Malley, J. M. and A. U. Chamot. (1990). *Learning Strategies in Second Language Acquisition*. Cambridge: Cambridge University Press.

O'Malley, J. M. and L. Valdez Pierce. (1996). *Authentic Assessment for English Language Learners: Practical Approaches for Teachers*. Reading, MA: Addison-Wesley.

Oakes, M. P. (1998). *Statistics for Corpus Linguistics*. Edinburgh: Edinburgh University Press.

Oller, J. W., Jr. (1973). Cloze tests of second language proficiency and what they measure. *Language Learning* 23, 105–118.

Oller, J. W., Jr. (1975). Cloze, discourse and approximations to English. In M. K. Burt and H. C. Dulay (eds.), *New Directions in Second Language Learning, Teaching, and Bilingual Education* (pp. 345–355). Washington, DC: TESOL.

Oller, J. W., Jr. (1979). *Language Tests at School*. London: Longman.

Oller, J. W., Jr. (1986). Communication theory and testing: what and how? In Stansfield (ed.), 1986, pp. 104–155.

Oller, J. W., Jr. and J. Jonz. (1994). *Cloze and Coherence*. Lewisburg, PA: Bucknell University Press.

Oller, J. W., Jr. and B. Spolsky. (1979). The Test of English as a Foreign Language (TOEFL). In B. Spolsky (ed.), *Some Major Tests*. Advances in Language Testing Series, 1. Arlington, VA: Center for Applied Linguistics.

Oxford, R. L. (1993). Research on second language learning strategies. *Annual Review of Applied Linguistics* 13, 175–187.

Ozete, O. (1977). The cloze procedure: a modification. *Foreign Language Annals* 10, 565–568.

Paivio, A. and A. Desrochers. (1981). Mnemonic techniques in second language learning. *Journal of Educational Psychology* 73, 780–795.

Paribakht, T. (1985). Strategic competence and language proficiency. *Applied Linguistics* 6, 132–146.

Paribakht, T. S. and M. B. Wesche. (1993). Reading comprehension and second language development in a comprehension-based ESL program. *TESL Canada Journal* 11, 9–29.

Paribakht, T. S. and M. Wesche. (1997). Vocabulary enhancement activities and reading for meaning in second language vocabulary acquisition. In Coady and Huckin (eds.), (1997), pp. 174–200.

Pawley, A. and F. H. Syder. (1983). Two puzzles for linguistic theory: nativelike selection and nativelike fluency. In J. C. Richards and R. W. Schmidt (eds.), *Language and Communication*. London: Longman.

Pennycook, A. (1996). Borrowing others' words: text, ownership, memory, and plagiarism. *TESOL Quarterly* 30, 201–230.

Perkins, K. and S. E. Linnville. (1987). A construct definition study of a standardized ESL vocabulary test. *Language Testing* 4, 125–141.

Phillipson, R. (1992). *Linguistic Imperialism.* Oxford: Oxford University Press.

Pike, L. W. (1979). *An Evaluation of Alternative Item Formats for Testing English as a Foreign Language.* TOEFL Research Reports, No. 2. Princeton, NJ: Educational Testing Service.

Pitts, M., H. White and S. Krashen. (1989). Acquiring second language vocabulary through reading: a replication of the Clockwork Orange study using second language acquirers. *Reading in a Foreign Language* 5, 271–275.

Porter, D. (1976). Modified cloze procedure: a more valid reading comprehension test. *ELT Journal* 30, 151–155.

Porter, D. (1983). The effect of quantity of context on the ability to make linguistic predictions: a flaw in a measure of general proficiency. In A. Hughes and D. Porter (eds.), *Current Developments in Language Testing* (pp. 63–74). New York: Academic Press.

Postman, L. and G. Keppel. (1970). *Norms of Word Associations.* New York: Academic Press.

Poulisse, N. (1993). A theoretical account of lexical communication strategies. In R. Schreuder and B. Weltens (eds.), *The Bilingual Lexicon* (pp. 157–189). Amsterdam: John Benjamins.

Pressley, M., J. R. Levin and M. A. McDaniel. (1987). Remembering vs. inferring what a word means: mnemonic and contextual approaches. In McKeown and Curtis (eds.), (1987), pp. 107–127.

Quinn, G. (1968). *The English Vocabulary of some Indonesian University Entrants.* Salatiga, Indonesia: IKIP Kristen Satya Watjana.

Read, J. (1988). Measuring the vocabulary knowledge of second language learners. *RELC Journal* 19, 12–25.

Read, J. (1989). Towards a deeper assessment of vocabulary knowledge. *ERIC Document Reproduction Service*, No. ED 301 048. Washington, DC: ERIC Clearinghouse on Languages and Linguistics.

Read, J. (1991). The validity of writing test tasks. In Anivan (ed.), 1991, pp. 77–91.

Read, J. (1993). The development of a new measure of L2 vocabulary knowledge. *Language Testing* 10, 355–371.

Read, J. (1998). Validating a test to measure depth of vocabulary knowledge. In A. Kunnan (ed.), *Validation in Language Assessment* (pp. 41–60). Mahwah, NJ: Lawrence Erlbaum.

Reid, J. (1990). Responding to different topic types: a quantitative analysis from a contractive rhetoric perspective. In B. Kroll (ed.), *Second Language Writing: Research Insights for the Classroom* (pp. 191–210). Cambridge: Cambridge University Press.

Richards, B. J. and D. D. Malvern. (1997). *Quantifying Lexical Diversity in the Study of Language Development*. Reading: Faculty of Education and Community Studies, University of Reading.

Richards, J. C. (1974). Word lists: problems and prospects. *RELC Journal* 5, 69–84.

Richards, J. C. (1976). The role of vocabulary teaching. *TESOL Quarterly* 10, 77–89.

Rodgers, T. S. (1969). On measuring vocabulary difficulty: an analysis of item variables in learning Russian–English vocabulary pairs. *IRAL* 7, 327–343.

Ross, S. and R. Berwick. (1992). The discourse of accommodation in oral proficiency interviews. *Studies in Second Language Acquisition* 14, 159–176.

Ruth, L. and S. Murphy. (1988). *Designing Writing Tasks for the Assessment of Writing*. Norwood, NJ: Ablex.

Sanaoui, R. (1995). Adult learners' approaches to learning vocabulary in second languages. *Modern Language Journal* 79, 15–28.

Saragi, T., I. S. P. Nation and G. F. Meister. (1978). Vocabulary learning and reading. *System* 6, 72–78.

Saville-Troike, M. (1984). What really matters in second language learning for academic achievement? *TESOL Quarterly* 18, 199–219.

Schatz, E. K. and R. S. Baldwin. (1986). Contextual clues are unreliable predictors of word meanings. *Reading Research Quarterly* 21, 439–453.

Schmidt, R. (1990). The role of consciousness in second language learning. *Applied Linguistics* 11, 129–158.

Schmitt, N. (1993). Forms B, C and D of the Vocabulary Levels Test. Unpublished manuscript.

Schmitt, N. (1997). Vocabulary learning strategies. In Schmitt and McCarthy (eds.), (1997), pp. 199–227.

Schmitt, N. (1998a). Measuring collocational knowledge: key issues and an experimental assessment procedure. *ITL: Review of Applied Linguistics* 119–120: 27–47.

Schmitt, N. (1998b). Quantifying word association responses: what is native-like? *System* 26, 389–401.

Schmitt, N. (1998c). Tracking the incremental acquisition of second language vocabulary: a longitudinal study. *Language Learning* 48, 281–317.

Schmitt, N. (1999). The relationship between TOEFL vocabulary items and meaning, association, collocation and word-class knowledge. *Language Testing* 16, 189–216.

Schmitt, N. and M. McCarthy (eds.). (1997). *Vocabulary: Description, Acquisition and Pedagogy* (pp. 84–102). Cambridge: Cambridge University Press.

Schmitt, N. and P. Meara. (1997). Researching vocabulary through a word knowledge framework: word associations and verbal suffixes. *Studies in Second Language Acquisition* 19, 17–36.

Schonell, F., I. Meddleton, B. Shaw, M. Routh, D. Popham, G. Gill, G. Mackrell and C. Stephens. (1956). *A Study of the Oral Vocabulary of Adults*. Brisbane: University of Queensland Press.

Schouten-Van Parreren, C. (1992). Individual differences in vocabulary acquisition: a qualitative experiment in the first phase of secondary education. In Arnaud and Béjoint (eds.), (1992), pp. 94–101.

Schwartz, S. (1984). *Measuring Reading Competence: A Theoretical-Prescriptive Approach*. New York: Plenum.

Scott, M. (1997). *WordSmith Tools*. Version 2.0. Oxford: Oxford University Press.

Seibert, L. C. (1945). A study of the practice of guessing word meanings from a context. *Modern Language Journal* 29, 296–323.

Shanahan, T., M. Kamil and A. Tobin. (1982). Cloze as a measure of intersentential comprehension. *Reading Research Quarterly* 17, 229–255.

Shillaw, J. (1996). The application of Rasch modelling to yes/no vocabulary tests. Vocabulary Acquisition Research Group discussion document No. js96a, available over the Internet at <www.swan.ac.uk/cals/vlibrary/js96a.htm>

Shohamy, E. (1994). The validity of direct vs. semi-direct oral tests. *Language Testing* 11, 99–123.

Shohamy, E. and O. Inbar. (1991). Validation of listening comprehension tests: the effect of text and question type. *Language Testing* 8, 23–40.

Shu, H., R. C. Anderson and H. Zhang. (1995). Incidental learning of word meanings while reading: a Chinese and American cross-cultural study. *Reading Research Quarterly* 30, 76–95.

Sims, V. M. (1929). The reliability and validity of four types of vocabulary test. *Journal of Educational Research* 20, 91–96.

Sinclair, J. (1991). *Corpus, Concordance, Collocation*. Oxford: Oxford University Press.

Sinclair, J. McH. and A. Renouf. (1988). A lexical syllabus for language learning. In Carter and McCarthy, (1998), pp. 140–160.

Singleton, D. (1994). Learning L2 lexis: a matter of form? In G. Bartelt (ed.), *The Dynamics of Language Processes: Essays in Honor of Hans W. Dechert* (pp. 45–57). Tübingen: Gunter Narr.

Singleton, D. and D Little. (1991). The second language lexicon: some evidence from university-level learners of French and German. *Second Language Research* 7, 61–81.

Skehan, P. (1989). *Individual Differences in Second-Language Learning.* London: Edward Arnold.

Skehan, P. (1996). A framework for the implementation of task-based instruction. *Applied Linguistics* 17, 38–62.

Skehan, P. (1998). *A Cognitive Approach to Language Learning.* Oxford: Oxford University Press.

Skehan, P. and P. Foster. (1997). Task type and task processing conditions as influences on foreign language performance. *Language Teaching Research* 1, 185–211.

Smith, H. A. (1996). An individualised vocabulary programme. *TESOLANZ Journal* 4, 41–51.

Spolsky, B. (1995). *Measured Words.* Oxford: Oxford University Press.

Stalnaker, J. M. and W. Kurath. (1935). A comparison of two types of foreign language vocabulary test. *Journal of Educational Psychology* 26, 435–442.

Stansfield, C. W. (1991). A comparative analysis of simulated and direct oral proficiency interviews. In Anivan (ed.), 1991, pp. 199–209.

Stansfield, C. W. (ed.). (1986). *Toward Communicative Competence Testing: Proceedings of the Second TOEFL Invitational Conference.* TOEFL Research Reports, 21. Princeton, NJ: Educational Testing Service.

Stansfield, C. and D. M. Kenyon. (1992). Research on the comparability of the oral proficiency interview and the simulated oral proficiency interview. *System* 20, 347–364.

Sternberg, R. J. and J. S. Powell. (1983). Comprehending verbal comprehension. *American Psychologist* 38, 878–893.

Stubbs, M. (1986). Lexical density: a computational technique and some findings. In M. Coulthard (ed.), *Talking About Text* (pp. 27–48). Birmingham: English Language Research, University of Birmingham.

Sutarsyah, C., P. Nation and G. Kennedy. (1994). How useful is EAP vocabulary for ESP? A corpus based case study. *RELC Journal* 25, 34–50.

Takala, S. (1984). Evaluation of students' knowledge of English vocabulary in the Finnish comprehensive school. Reports from the Institute for Educational Research, 350. Jyväskylä: University of Jyväskylä.

Tannen, D. (ed.). (1982a). *Spoken and Written Language: Exploring Orality and Literacy.* Norwood, NJ: Ablex.

Tannen, D. (1982b). The oral literate continuum of discourse. In Tannen (ed.), 1982a, pp. 1–6.

Tarone, E. (1978). Conscious communication strategies in interlanguage: a progress report. In H. D. Brown, C. A. Yorio and R. Crymes (eds.), *On TESOL '77. Teaching and Learning English as a Second Language* (pp. 194–203). Washington, DC: TESOL.

Tarone, E. (1983). Some thoughts on the notion of 'communication strategy'. In Faerch and Kasper (eds.), 1983a, pp. 61–74.

Tarone, E. (1984). Teaching strategic competence in the foreign language classroom. In S. Savignon and M. Berns (eds.), *Initiatives in Communicative Language Teaching* (pp. 127–136). Reading, MA: Addison-Wesley.

Tarone, E., A. D. Cohen and G. Dumas. (1983). A closer look at some interlanguage terminology: a framework for communication strategies. In C. Faerch and G. Kasper (eds.), *Strategies in Interlanguage Communication*. London: Longman.

Taylor, C. (1994). Assessment for measurement or standards: the peril and promise of large-scale assessment reform. *American Educational Research Journal* 31, 231–262.

Taylor, W. L. (1953). Cloze procedure: a new tool for measuring readability. *Journalism Quarterly* 30, 415–433.

Thorndike, E. L. (1924). The vocabularies of school pupils. In J. Carleton Bell (ed.), *Contributions to education* (pp. 69–76). New York: World Book.

Thorndike, E. L. and I. Lorge. (1944). *The Teacher's Word Book of 30,000 Words*. New York: Teachers College, Columbia University.

Tilley, H. C. (1936). A technique for determining the relative difficulty of word meanings among elementary school children. *Journal of Experimental Education* 5, 61–64.

Tinkham, T. (1993). The effect of semantic clustering on the learning of second language vocabulary. *System* 21, 371–380.

Ure, J. N. (1971). Lexical density and register differentiation. In G. E. Perren and J. L. M. Trim (eds.), *Applications of Linguistics: Selected Papers of the Second International Congress of Applied Linguistics* (pp. 443–452). Cambridge: Cambridge University Press.

Valette, R. M. (1967). *Modern Language Testing*. New York: Harcourt Brace.

van Lier, L. (1989). Reeling, writhing, drawling, stretching, and fainting in coils: oral proficiency interviews as conversation. *TESOL Quarterly* 23, 489–508.

Van Parreren, C. F. and M. C. Schouten-Van Parreren. (1981). Contextual guessing: a trainable reader strategy. *System* 9, 235–241.

Verhallen, M. and R. Schoonen. (1993). Lexical knowledge of monolingual and bilingual children. *Applied Linguistics* 14, 344–363.

Waller, T. (1993). Characteristics of near-native proficiency in writing. In

H. Ringbom (ed.), *Near-Native Proficiency in English* (pp. 183–293). Åbo, Finland: English Department, Åbo Akademi University.

Webster's Third New International Dictionary. (1961). Springfield, MA: Merriman-Webster.

Weir, C. J. (1990). *Communicative Language Testing.* Hemel Hempstead: Prentice Hall.

Wesche, M. and T. S. Paribakht. (1996). Assessing second language vocabulary knowledge: depth vs. breadth. *Canadian Modern Language Review* 53, 13–39.

West, M. (1953). *A General Service List of English Words.* London: Longman.

Willems, G. (1987). Communication strategies and their significance in foreign language teaching. *System* 15, 351–364.

Willis, J. and D. Willis. (1988–89). *Collins COBUILD English Course, Teacher's Books 1–3.* London: Collins.

Xue, G. and I. S. P. Nation. (1984). A university word list. *Language Learning and Communication* 3, 215–229.

Yang, H. (1986). A new technique for identifying scientific/technical terms and describing science texts. *Literary and Linguistic Computing* 1, 3–103.

Young, R. (1995). Conversational styles in language proficiency interviews. *Language Learning* 45, 3–42.

Young, R. and M. Milanovic. (1992). Discourse variation in oral proficiency interviews. *Studies in Second Language Acquisition* 14, 403–424.

Yule, G. and E. Tarone. (1997). Investigating communication strategies in L2 reference: pros and cons. In Kasper and Kellerman (eds.), 1997a, pp. 17–30.

Index